About
COWS

Also by Sara Rath:

The Complete Cow

The Complete Pig

About
COWS

by Sara Rath

Voyageur Press

A TOWN SQUARE BOOK

For Art and Marsha Lindsay,
my brother and sister,
Who both like milk
more than I ever did.

Front cover photo and black-and-white back cover photo courtesy of Minnesota State Fair.

Printed in the United States of America

00   01   02   03   04   5   4   3   2   1

Library of Congress Cataloging-in-Publication Data available

ISBN 0-89658-465-8

Distributed in Canada by Raincoast Books, 8680 Cambie Street, Vancouver, B.C. V6P 6M9

Published by Voyageur Press, Inc.
123 North Second Street, P.O. Box 338, Stillwater, MN 55082 U.S.A.
651-430-2210, fax 651-430-2211
books@voyageurpress.com
www.voyageurpress.com

Educators, fundraisers, premium and gift buyers, publicists, and marketing managers:
Looking for creative products and new sales ideas? Voyageur Press books are available at special discounts when purchased in quantities, and special editions can be created to your specifications. For details contact the marketing department at 800-888-9653.

Contents

viii

Preface

In Defense of the Cow

She is neither slick nor sleek, mean nor lean. She's big, she's awkward, she's ungainly. She moves with studied lack of grace. To see her run is to witness a main-act comedian at work. She is definitely not hi-tech. In a glossy world of computers and microchips gone mad, she is a scandal, a quadrupedal salute to nature's propensity to concentrate on function rather than form. In a word, she is a designer's nightmare. We are referring of course to the milk cow.

Yet if we examine the awesome credentials of the milk cow we must marvel at the singular contributions made by this creature ordained by time & Providence to transmute hay & oats & corn, ordinary things, into a milken harvest, like bees change nectar into honey.

Consider the following: An incredible 20% of the vast agricultural wealth produced each year in America comes from dairy farms—yet only 4.5% of the nation's farm labor force works on these farms, which take up a modest 6.5% of the national farmland.

More than 30% of the actual food value (minerals, vitamins, proteins, fats and carbohydrates) consumed by children, adolescents and adults each year comes from dairy products—and yet Americans spend less than 10% of their food budget on milk and milk products.

Only a million people are directly involved in the production of milk (not to mention the bovines themselves), yet another three million owe their livelihood to the processing, shipping and retailing of dairy products.

And then ponder this: An investment of $1 in skim milk buys a person 270% of their calcium RDA, 225% of their vitamin D, 180% of their protein, 90% of their vitamin A, 75% of their vitamin B, 36% of their vitamin C.

The fact is that dairy products are the dietary sea in which we swim. We star or feature them at breakfast, lunch and supper. They come in sweet and sour form, they are main courses or side dishes—or snacks. And our acceptance and enjoyment of them are reinforced by images of pastoral perfection—golden cornfields, red barns, green pastures, all adrift *"in the blue waters of heaven, the clouds that are spray to its sea."*

And now think about this: These aforementioned wonders are contributions of a mere 11 million milk cows, who report to work 365 days a year, producing five or so gallons of sweet fresh milk daily.

But the impact of the cow is more than economic. This placid, browsing creature has affected our poems, our songs, our images, our language, our values. We speak of the milk of human kindness, we long for the land of milk and honey. The American ideal is the cowboy, a clear and obvious subconscious tribute to the bovine. Cuyp & van Gogh & Rousseau & Mondrian & Cooper & Potter & Dove & Gauguin all caught *"the lowing herd"* on canvas, paying tribute anew to the cow's fecundity and beauty. And when the songwriter wanted to have a fellow tell his girl how crazy he was for her, all he had to do was write, *"You're the cream in my coffee."*

Yet of all the gifts credited to the cow, none is more appealing than that she is the cornerstone of the family farm, the very foundation of American agriculture. It should come as no surprise then that more than 95% of all dairy farms in this huge country are run by single families.

So next time, friend, you see a milk cow browsing in the shade, quietly munching lunch, pause a moment and reflect. Badly designed or not, awkward of gait or not, this placid creature deserves our undying respect and affection.

Acknowledgments

About Cows was not my idea; it was the brainchild of my friend and publisher, Jill Dean. In many ways we have been partners in this project, beginning with that day in January, 1983 when I asked if she'd be interested in publishing a book of my poems and she said sure, if I'd write a fun book on cows. The resulting poetry collection, *Remembering the Wilderness*, was given the Wisconsin Library Association's Banta Award for Literary Achievement in 1984. In the meantime, I began to cast a more than casual glance at the herds of Holsteins that have been an integral part of my Wisconsin landscape all my life. My mother gave me cow potholders. My son gave me a cow butterdish, one of my stepdaughters gave me a wooden cow on wheels and my own daughter began to give me strange looks. When I plunked down $22 for a toy calf that walked and mooed and wagged its tail I told her "It's just because I'm doing this book! I'm not really one of those people who are crazy about cows!"

There are plenty of people around who *do* love cows, however, and they responded to our request for cow anecdotes with a rush of enthusiasm. Clarence Olsen and Robert Neidermeier, professors in the University of Wisconsin Dairy Science Department, gave me scholarly advice and direction. The chairman of that department, David Dickson, added his own doggerel rhymes and humorous stories, and Ed Parmenter at the Wisconsin Department of Agriculture helped me with statistical information. Barry Levinson, self-styled "Bovine Advocate," introduced me to Elm Farm Ollie. My husband, Owen Coyle, introduced me to "Cow Cow Blues."

Now that the manuscript has been delivered I'm left with a roomful of cow paraphernalia, an assortment of cow jewelry, numerous T-shirts featuring cows and the prospect of producing a bovine TV special in the near future. I'm tempted to say this has been a *mooving* experience, or that I've been *udderly* excited by the subject, but that's not fair. The truth is, in writing this book I learned a lot about cows and I've become pretty sentimental about the creatures. In fact, I've grown to love them. In fact, despite my denial, I've become one of those people who are crazy about cows.

About the author: Sara Lindsay Rath— photographed by Brent Nicastro with Holsteins from the herd of Rosalind and Bill Gausman— was born in Manawa, a small town in rural Wisconsin. One of her grandfathers logged the northwoods, the other became an internationally known cheesemaker. Her first two words, according to family records, were "mama" and "dada." Her third word was "cow."

Introduction

The Cow. She has been a part of our lives since we turned away from Mother's breast. And before.

When we learned to talk, we chanted nursery rhymes about the cow that jumped over the moon or the cows in the corn. And is there a child alive who has not sung of Old Mac Donald's cow, "With a moo-moo here, and a moo-moo there . . . "?

Cows are a part of the countryside idyll, painted by artists, pictured in our minds, and taken for granted when we drive along rural roads. The cluster of black and white Holsteins lying in the shade chewing their cud has become a symbol of placid contentment.

The more practical among us might scoff at such a romantic point of view. They are the sort that cleverly create doggerel like this:

Though eulogies are penned perforce
In honor of the dog and horse,
The cow excells them definitely
In matters of fidelity.
In winter wind or summer breeze
She labors for our milk and cheese,
And scientific tests have shown
She puts the ice cream in the cone.
When in Elysian fields she rests,
She leaves us numerous bequests—
Wallets, gelatins, and shoes,
Soaps and pocketbooks and glues;
Bequeaths her very bones, indeed,
To pulverize for poultry feed.
The briefcases she leaves behind
Protect the plans of humankind,
And belts—her halo and her crown—
She keeps our pants from falling down.

—Nat Curran
The Chicago Tribune
1945

Truthful as that may be, the influence of cows in our lives goes much deeper than mere measurement of material goods. Once cattle were wild animals. They were hunted, just as all wild animals were hunted. Then they became domesticated. No one really knows how that happened, but one hypothesis is that in that transitional period of prehistory, when man was changing from hunter to pastoralist, from time to time the hunter brought home the offspring of the species he slew. He might have thought a calf was too small and useless for meat and hide, or he might have had pity on the poor trusting creature and brought it back to the cave for his own family to play with and raise.

Whatever the case, in the early days of our existence, we became a cattle culture. As proof, much of our vocabulary has been derived from words that once related to cattle. The word "daughter," which corresponds to the Greek "thaughter" and the Sanskrit "duhitar," means the *milker*. In Sanskrit, "soldier" meant *one who fights about cows*. The "morning" was *the calling of the cattle*; the "evening" was *the milking-time*. The Latin word for money, "pecunia," (from which "pecuniary" and "impecunious" derive) and the word "fee" both come from the old word *pecus*, meaning *cattle*. "Stock" (as in "stocks and bonds") refers to the use of cattle as currency. In old Anglo-Saxon, movable property is called "cwichfeoh," or *living cattle*, whereas immovable property, such as buildings and land, has a name that translates as *dead cattle*. *Chattel*, meaning non living personal property, comes from the word "catel," which was used in the sense of "wealth." And the words for prince, king, lord, and the like, all meant *herdsman*, or *head of pastoral family*.

Thus, virtually from the beginning, livestock became man's chief interest, his main source of wealth, and his principal means of exchange. Cows led men from a state of savagery to higher planes of existence, pulling plows, drawing carts, assuaging hunger and thirst. The influence of cattle upon the mental development and material advancement of humanity is immeasurable. This was recorded in Biblical times (Abraham was "very rich in cattle, in silver, and in gold"), exemplified in mythology (where cattle were fleecy clouds pasturing "in the infinite meadows of heaven," whose full udders dropped down "rain and fatness" upon the land), and stamped into the coinage of ancient Greece, where the image of an ox was imprinted on new money.

So, what it comes down to is this. Your grandparents may have had a farm and raised cows. You may have been born on a farm. You may have milked twenty-five cows a day for thirty years, and that's how you learned to love these gentle animals. But even if you've never had any "hands-on" experience, cows have had an important role in your life . . . even before you eagerly reached for your bottle of baby formula.

Cows have rarely inspired patriotic fervor, but this one graced the cover of the Midway section of the *New York Daily News* and was made into a poster. It is the work of artist Charles F. Wickler, who often includes cows in his compositions. For posters, write to Wickler, 1170 Downing Drive, Waukesha, Wisconsin 53186.

THE GREAT AMERICAN COW

All About Cows

"The cow is the original vending machine, yet is not looked upon with the excitement and mystery it deserves."
Spokesman at World Dairy Expo,
Madison, Wisconsin

This afternoon I came over a hill on a winding country road and saw a dozen black and white Holsteins lying in the shade, chewing their cud. But I didn't think "cows" when I saw them. Instead, the phrase "placid contentment" flashed through my brain.

I have a suspicion that cows are currently a fascinating subject because of that very association. The image of the cow represents a simple way of life. A California artist who paints life-size plywood cutouts of cows says, "I wanted them in my backyard because they remind me that I can be like that. They are so unstressful."

But even though a rose may be perhaps a rose, a rose; a cow is not necessarily a cow, a cow. To begin with, there are many colors of cows, different sizes, backgrounds and temperaments. And then there are different versions of the whole cow-family (usually known as "cattle"). Take a *heifer*, for instance. A heifer is kind of like a cow but it's not a cow yet and won't actually be a cow, won't begin to have its birthdays recorded or even be taken seriously as a cow, until it has given birth to its first calf. And don't go around pointing at a bull and calling it a cow, or you can get into real trouble. Bulls are rather macho creatures and they're not "cows" any more than men are women. A *bull* is (according to my dictionary) "an adult male bovine animal." A *steer* is "a young ox, especially one castrated before maturity and raised for beef." An *ox* is "an adult castrated bull of the genus *Bos*."

Indeed, that's what we're here to celebrate: the Cow, in general, and (to be more specific) the genus *Bos*.

Ever wonder why you call, "Come, Boss; Come, Boss . . ." when you call the cows? Or why so many cows are named "Bossy"? The Latin word for cow is *Bos*. The cattle of Europe descended from two original types: *Bos Longifrons* (which some call *Bos Sondacious*); and *Bos Primigenius.*

The *Bos Longifrons* cattle were small, short-bodied, with small horns. Our Brown Swiss, Jersey, and Guernsey breeds are descendents of this strain.

The *Bos Primigenius* cattle were much larger and had long curving horns. They ran wild until the thirteenth century, and are the ancestors of cattle in northern Europe, and the Longhorns and Scotch Highland breeds in England.

Cattle moved around Europe with the conquests of successive invaders who brought along their favorites. For instance, the Simmenthaler breed in Switzerland has the same characteristics of a skull found among the original cattle of Sweden.

There are many more breeds of cattle than we in the United States are familiar with. Europe is the home of between forty and fifty breeds, and although we have imported many of our breeds from England, eleven breeds were established in that country.

In the United States we have six major breeds of dairy cattle: Ayrshire, Brown Swiss, Guernsey, Holstein, Jersey, and Milking Shorthorn.

The Ayrshire

The *Ayrshire* originated in the County of Ayr, Scotland, which is also known as a "shire." It is pronounced "air-shear." The climate of Ayr is not favorable to livestock raising because it is cold and damp for most of the year. In the early development of this breed there was scant forage as the soil of this part of Scotland is not fertile. The extreme hardiness of the Ayrshire is undoubtedly due to the character of the country where she was developed, as only those individuals with unusual ruggedness could have survived to reproduce. Originally the Ayrshires were known as Dunlap, later they were known as the Cunningham breed and not until 1803 were they generally known as Ayrshire.

The Ayrshire is notable for being the only true dairy breed developed in the British Isles.

The Ayrshire is an alert appearing animal, of a bright cherry red and white, or, nearly all white, with small patches of red. She has wide, arching horns that must possess the right curves. To encourage the horns to turn upward the growth is directed by means of weights hung on cords that have been attached to the horns and then run over pulleys.

The Ayrshire cow will weigh, on the average, around 1,150 pounds. Her calf will weigh 75 pounds at birth and is very active when only a few hours old. She has a well-formed udder and is easy to milk, but Ayrshire cows are quite nervous and are sometimes hard to manage. Because of their nervous disposition and well developed horns, considerable damage may be done to members of the herd from horn injuries. The bulls are frequently vicious.

The Ayrshire was first imported in 1822, by the first Scottish settlers of Canada. It is the youngest of the dairy

DAIRY BREEDS
in the
Western Hemisphere

Jersey

Holstein Friesian

Guernsey

Ayrshire

Milking Shorthorn

Brown Swiss

Artist Eugene Hoy devoted nearly two years to painting America's six major dairy breeds. His work is reproduced courtesy of Purina Mills, Incorporated, St. Louis, Missouri.

19

breeds; the chief development took place following 1750 when the other dairy breeds were already well established. In fact, in 1750 the Ayrshire cattle were described as being small, ill-fed, ill-shaped and producing little milk, but there was a great improvement in the breed during the latter half of the 1800's.

Brown Swiss

There are two distinct breeds of cattle in Switzerland, the Simmenthaler and the *Brown Swiss*. A Brown Swiss cow is dark brown in color, with black horn tips. She resembles the Jersey in many respects, except that she is larger and darker.

The Brown Swiss is the largest and most hardy of the dairy breeds. Originally the Brown Swiss was regarded as a triple-purpose cow: in her native country, she is used as a draft animal on the small valley farms, and is the source of practically all the meat used. She matures rather slowly, weighing around 1,400 pounds when she is five years of age. Her calf is very rugged.

The Brown Swiss are docile and not easily excited. Frequently, however, they can be stubborn and resist attempts to alter their regular routine, such as changing them to another stall or training them for showing.

The Brown Swiss are the slowest of the breeds to mature; normally, heifers are not sufficiently developed to come into milk until they are 34 to 36 months of age. However, compensating for their lateness in maturing, the Brown Swiss live and produce and re-produce longer than other breeds. Brown Swiss authorities claim a higher proportion of old cows for their breed than those found in other dairy breeds.

The first importation of Brown Swiss to this country was made in 1869, and it is now a widely distributed breed throughout our dairy sections. From research into literature it seems that the cattle of Switzerland at the time of Caesar have the description of being Brown Swiss. Bones found in the ruins of the Swiss Lake Dwellers date back to 4000 B.C. and resemble the skeleton of the modern Brown Swiss cow.

In Switzerland, Brown Swiss are found from the shores of Lake Constantine (1,400 feet above sea level) to the snow line in the Alps. The cattle are usually pastured on the mountain slopes, beginning at the foot in the spring and going up the mountain side as the snow recedes. In the fall they are brought down the mountain side and housed in barns located in the valleys.

The Holstein

The *Holstein* is also known as the Holstein-Friesian. Some pronounce this "hole-steen," while others call it "hole-stine."

This well-known black-and-white cow has been raised in Holland for over 2,000 years. The breed was originally developed in two provinces, North Holland and West Friesland. Since the fertile soil and abundant rainfall in that region produces luxuriant pastures, the Holstein-Friesians of Holland have always lived almost entirely upon grass during the summer months. Poor grazers were at no particular disadvantage and were therefore not eliminated in the development of the breed. Because the winters were cold, the cows were frequently stabled under the same roof as the family home and therefore contributed to the selection of docile animals. The low fat content of Holstein milk can also be explained by environmental factors— the chief dairy product of Holland, probably even before the beginning of the Holstein breed, has been cheese. Large quantities of milk are of more importance than high fat content for cheese making and since the selection for one of these characters has a tendency to reduce the other, the Holsteins were selected for large quantities of milk production without regard to fat content and that is a characteristic of the breed today.

The Holstein breed is also one of the oldest breeds in the United States, brought in by the Dutch when they settled New Amsterdam, now New York, around 1630.

It is the largest of the dairy breeds, with cows averaging around 1,500 pounds apiece. It is also a leader in total milk production, and is preferable for veal production because of the size of the calf at birth and the light color of the body fat.

In color, the Holstein is usually a mixture of black and white, but the relative amounts of either black or white vary from white with only a small black spot to an almost total black, except for the switch, which must always be white. In Holland red and white Holsteins are common and they are growing in popularity in the United States.

The Holstein is very rugged and a good feeder. For this reason she is an easy keeper, and will consume all kinds of grain and roughage with equal enjoyment. The Holstein bull can frequently be difficult to handle.

The Guernsey

The *Guernsey* comes from the Isle of Guernsey, in the English Channel. It was first known in this country as the "Alderney," from an island nearby.

The Guernsey is thought to be a cross between the large, brindle-colored cattle of Normandy, and the small, red cattle of Brittany, both in

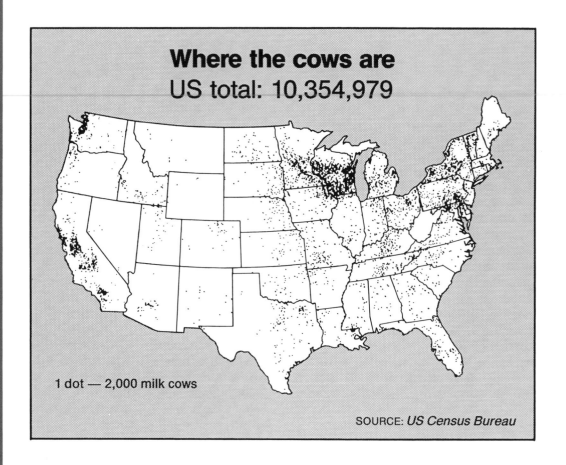

Where the cows are
US total: 10,354,979

1 dot — 2,000 milk cows

SOURCE: *US Census Bureau*

France. Early accounts indicate that in the year 960 an order of monks settled on the Island and brought a small group of cattle from Brittany. About 1061 another monastery was established there and these monks introduced the larger brindle cattle of Normandy—the crossing of these two breeds is believed to have laid the foundation for the current Guernsey breed.

In color, the Guernsey may range from a light fawn and white, to a deep yellow, with white patches. She has well-arched horns and a cream-colored nose. Her average weight runs around

1,100 pounds, being a little larger than the Jersey. Her calves will run from 60 to 75 pounds at birth.

The Guernsey is one of our leading dairy breeds, producing milk with a high butterfat content. Records of butterfat production have reached 1,200 pounds a year during one period of lactation. The average cow produces only a third of this amount.

One of the outstanding characteristics of Guernsey milk is its yellow color; the Guernsey possesses the ability to secrete a large proportion of the carotene pigment of her feed into her milk. The American Guernsey Cattle Club has copyrighted the trademark "Golden Guernsey" for Guernsey milk.

The first Guernseys brought to this country were imported in 1830 by a Mr. Prince of Massachusetts, but the real start began about 1870. Since then, the Guernsey has become a very popular milk cow all over the United States.

The Jersey

The Channel Islands (Jersey, Guernsey, Alderney and Sark) are in the entrance to the English Channel about nine miles from the coast of France and about seventy miles from England. The *Jersey* cow was first developed on the Isle of Jersey. The story of her ancestry is much the same as that of the Guernsey, and these two breeds are sometimes called the Channel Island breeds.

In color, she is usually cream, fawn, or a light brown with or without white patches. Of all breeds, the Jersey is the most variable in color. She possesses wide, arching horns and has a beautiful, alert appearance. She is the smallest of the dairy breeds, weighing around 1,000 pounds at maturity. Her calf will weigh between 50 and 60 pounds at birth.

Her milk is very rich, and many Jersey cows will produce a pound of butter a day, in addition to the milk consumed by the family. For this reason, she is ideal for a small family. About 60 percent of our "family cows" are Jerseys.

She is inclined to be a dainty eater and has her decided likes and dislikes. Her skin is very tender, and she should be given adequate shelter from the flies of summer or the cold of winter.

The Jersey cattle probably have the most highly developed nervous system of all the dairy breeds; they are very sensitive and react quickly to stimuli. When Jersey cows are treated well they are quick to respond favorably. The Jersey bull is more likely to be vicious than are bulls from other breeds.

Jerseys are the earliest of all breeds to mature. Heifers are usually sufficiently mature to calve when 24 to 26 months of age. The calves, however, are small at birth and also represent a

Old Times

Cows, if left alone, can be expected to live to be about eighteen years of age. There are exceptions, however—old timers who make it to 25 or 30.

smaller percent of the weight of the dam.

Jerseys have been raised in this country since 1850, when the first importations were made in Hartford, Connecticut.

A law has been in force on the Jersey Island since 1789 which forbids the importation of cattle except for slaughter.

The Shorthorn

The present *Milking Shorthorn* breed was developed by selecting Shorthorn cows that gave an extra large quantity of milk. In England they are termed "Dairy Shorthorns."

The common name of the Shorthorn is "the Durham cow," because of the breed's origination in the County of Durham, England. Hence, when an owner explains that his animal is "part Durham," it means that she has Shorthorn ancestry.

The cow is relatively large, weighing from 1,200 to 1,600 pounds, with excellently formed calves, suitable for veal in case they are males and not subject to registry.

In color, the most common is a beautiful strawberry roan, or red and white. They have short, strong horns.

They have become very popular in this country due to their dual-purpose excellence—they are bred to be between the beef and dairy types. They were first brought to this country in 1783.

Judging Cows

The earliest score card for a modern dairy breed was published on the Isle of Guernsey in 1828. It reflected the islanders' ideas concerning the ideal type for their breed, plus the pressure of English buyers for a more refined animal:

1. Pedigree of bull and (or) cow, yellow ears, tail, and good udder 7
2. General appearance, handsome color, cream, light red, or both mixed with white 3
3. Handsome head, well-horned, and bright and prominent eye 4
4. Deep barrel-shaped body 3
5. Good hind-quarter and straight back 2
6. Handsome legs and small bone ... 1

Total Points 20

The first *Guernsey* score card was adopted in the U.S. in 1877 and included a total of 100 points. The score card allocated 20 points for evidence of color in the milk and 10 points for escutcheon.

The first American *Jersey* score card was adopted in 1875. It also included a total of 100 points and allowed 32 points for udder and only 9 points for head.

Score cards were adopted by the American *Holstein-Friesian* Association in 1885; the *Ayrshire* Association in 1889; and the *Brown Swiss* Association in 1930. The score cards for the several breeds varied in minor details. In 1941 all breed associations adopted the Unified Dairy Cattle Score Card as developed by the Purebred Dairy Cattle Association.

Some Fascinating Facts

- A cow grazes by curling her tongue around the grass, rather than by nibbling it like a horse. She will probably eat about 100 pounds of grass in a day.
- In winter, a cow kept inside a barn will spend equal time standing up and lying down. Cows get up and down an average of 14 times in 24 hours.
- Heavy producing cows may drink as much as 300 pounds of water daily. Milk contains 87 percent water. Moisture in feed (e.g. silage contains 65 percent water and lush pasture as much as 90 percent) serves as another form of water in addition to the 300 additional pounds. All of this, of course, results in the fact that the average cow produces 30 pounds of urine and 65 pounds of feces daily. This varies with the amount of feed consumed and bedding used, but at least 15 tons of waste are produced per cow per year.
- Dry cows average 6.1 urinations per day.
- Milking cows average 7.9 urinations per day.
- Dry cows defecate 13.7 times per day as compared with 15.7 for cows in milk.
- An average cow will spend six hours a day eating and an additional eight hours ruminating or chewing her cud. She chews at a rate of 50 times per minute.
- Total daily jaw movements average 41,630, divided in the following manner:
  Eating grain and silage 4,700
  Eating hay 10,530
  Ruminating 26,400
- The average cow's temperature is 101.5 degrees Fahrenheit.
- Breeds differ in pulse and respiration rates per minute:

	Pulse	Respiration
Ayrshire	69.6	28.6
Guernsey	59.8	18.6
Holstein	68.6	28.6
Jersey	62.7	21.7

- The average cow in the United States produced 12,316 pounds of milk and 455 pounds of butterfat in 1982.

- Cattle communicate in various ways: in sounds of hunger (bawling) by young; distress calls like the bellowing of a bull; sexual behavior and related fighting; mother-young interrelations to establish contact and evoke care behavior; and maintaining the group in its movements and assembly.
- Cattle have a very acute sense of hearing, perceiving higher and fainter noises than the human ear.
- Cattle can smell at a greater distance than people. On a day with a 5-mile wind and a humidity of 75%, a cow can smell up to 6 miles away; as wind and humidity increase, she can smell even further.
- In cattle, females in estrus secrete a substance that attracts males. Hence, bulls locate cows that are in heat by the sense of smell.
- When several strange cows are brought together, there is much threat posturing, as well as butting, in order to establish a dominance hierarchy. Also, bulls will strike a hostile stance prior to fighting.
- The age of a cow is always based on her age when she calved, which is when her record begins. It is estimated, on a rule-of-thumb basis, that at two years of age a cow produces approximately 70 to 80 percent of her mature milk production; at three years, 80 to 91 percent; at four years, 91 to 96 percent; five years, 97 to 100 percent; and at six years her mature record.

Teeth and Bones

A calf has twenty "baby" or milk teeth soon after it is born. There are eight lower front teeth, or nippers, and six back teeth or grinders in the upper jaws, and the same in the lower jaws. There are no upper front teeth.

The cow has 32 permanent teeth; eight lower front teeth or incisors; no upper front teeth; but instead, a tough, dental pad. There are twelve back teeth or grinders in the lower jaws, and the same number in the upper jaws.

The yearling has two big, white, central teeth, which are the permanent ones and they have pushed out the temporary teeth in the lower front jaw.

The two-year-old has two more big white teeth, one on each side of the new centrals.

The three-year old has six permanent teeth in the lower front jaw.

The four-year old has all eight permanent teeth in the lower front jaw and is now termed a "full-mouth."

There are about 207 bones in the cow's body, with many strong muscles, tendons and ligaments, all held together by genuine cow hide.

It Takes a Lot of Gall

Q. *What comes from a cow and costs $169 per ounce?*
A. Gallstones. Specifically, a cow gallstone, a solid mass that forms inside the cow's gallbladder and is sold by the Packerland Packing Company, Green Bay, Wisconsin, to buyers in eastern Asia who believe it to be an aphrodisiac.

Digestion—All Those Stomachs?

The cow has four stomachs, with a capacity of about 35 gallons in all:

1. *Rumen* (ROO-men), or paunch, holding about 30 gallons.
2. *Reticulum* (ree-TICK-u-lum), containing one gallon.
3. *Omasum* (oh-MAY-sum), or "manyplies," holding two gallons
4. *Abomasum* (AB-o-MAY-sum), or true stomach, holding two gallons.

The rumen or paunch is merely a reservoir for food, much like the crop in a chicken. When the food is first taken in without chewing, it goes to this organ, where it is softened by various juices. Among these is hydrochloric acid, which is formed from salt, and prevents excessive fermentation. This is why salt is so vital to cud-chewing animals, such as the cow, sheep, goat or deer. It is also the stomach "tapped" for bloat in the left flank. The reaction of the stomach contents is alkaline.

The reticulum or second stomach is the smallest, and is located near the heart. It secretes an alkaline solution essential to digestion. The interior structure of the reticulum resembles a honeycomb, and this acts as a collection compartment for foreign objects. Sometimes permanent magnets about three inches long and a half inch to one inch in diameter are placed in the reticulum as a precautionary measure to pick up iron objects and prevent them from puncturing the stomach lining.

The third stomach or omasum, commonly called the "manyplies," is shaped like a cabbage head, with a number of membrane-like leaves.

The fourth or true stomach, the abomasum, is where rennin and pepsin are secreted and where digestion begins.

These stomachs may be compared to a four-cylindered motor, and all must work in unison to keep the cow in normal condition.

In a cow, the bowels are often 170 feet in length. This is why it takes so long for food to pass through her digestive tract. The liver will weigh from ten to twelve pounds in the average-sized cow. The heart weighs about five pounds, and must pump 400 pints of blood through the udder to produce one pint of milk. That means it takes nearly 10,000 pints of blood pumping through a cow's udder every day to produce three gallons of milk.

The kidneys weigh abound twenty pounds each.

Digestion is very complex in the cow, due to her four stomachs and long, tortuous intestinal tract. For these

Heavy Metal

When a calf is born, its liver contains about a four-months' supply of iron and copper, useful in preventing anemia and in the manufacture of red blood corpuscles. This is why calves' liver is so beneficial in human anemia.

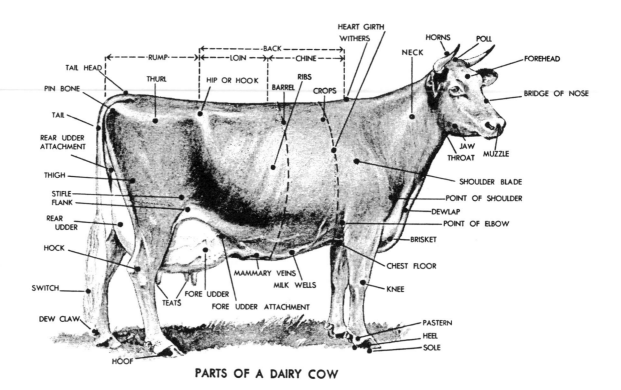

PARTS OF A DAIRY COW

An ideal dairy cow is depicted on the Dairy Cow Unified Score Card, copyright 1943, 1957, 1971 by The Purebred Dairy Cattle Association.

reasons, it usually takes from three to five days for food to pass through her body, and its progress may be traced as follows:

The cow "gulps down" her food without chewing it, and it goes into the first stomach or paunch, where it remains for some time, until softened by various juices.

Later on, when the cow lies down to rest, she raises up a "cud" to be thoroughly masticated by her powerful molars or grinders.

When she swallows this food for a second time, a curious thing happens. Instead of going back to her first stomach, where it came from, it now goes to the third stomach (omasum or many-plies). It has been switched from the first stomach to this organ by means of a little groove in her gullet that runs from the mouth to the stomachs. This diverts the "cud" to its new destination much like a switchman working at a railroad yard. It requires no special effort on her part; it's just an act of nature, like the beating of her heart.

When this masticated "cud" enters the third stomach, the membrane-like leaves begin rubbing against each other, and reduce the food to a fine paste. This passes into the fourth stomach (abomasum or true stomach), where rennin and pepsin mix with it. The food is now ready for the first part of the bowel, where absorption and assimilation of nutriment takes place.

Other juices, such as the bile and pancreatin, now mix with the food, and, as it passes slowly through the bowel, small, nipple-like projections in the lining of the intestine, called lacteals, absorb the nourishment.

Because of this complicated digestive system, true vomiting is impossible in the cow.

About one-eighth to one-tenth of the cow's body weight is in blood. Thus, a 1,000 pound cow will have from 100 to 125 pints or pounds of blood, or from 12 to 15 gallons. It takes approximately a minute for blood to circulate through the body. This is the reason intravenous injections into the neck vein act so quickly in milk fever. A cow can lose several quarts of blood without much harm. This accounts for her being able to withstand hemorrhages following dehorning or from barbed-wire cuts.

Bovine Behavior

Most cattle exhibit eight general functions or behavioral systems as defined by M. E. Ensminger in his book *Dairy Cattle Science*:

Agonistic behavior (combat): This type of behavior includes fighting, flight (distance between animals), and other related reactions associated with conflict. Among all species of farm mammals, males are more likely to fight than females. Castrated males are usually quite passive, which indicates that hormones (especially testosterone) are involved in this type of behavior.

High-yielding cows generally have excellent temperaments; and high-producing herds have tame cows, with zero flight distances.

Allelomimetic behavior (mutual mimicking): When one member of a group does something, another tends to do the same thing; and because others are doing it, the original individual continues.

In the wild state, this trait was ad-

The Bovine Pecking Order

Cows set up a rigid social hierarchy; it is not democratic. Every cow is superior to all the cows below her, and the fawning subject of all the stronger cows in the herd.

There is always one cow that becomes the Boss of the Herd, has unlimited access to the best shade, the best grass, the choicest spot in the milking line-up. She chooses her privileges and the other cows bow to her. And then there's the cow at the bottom of the ladder. She gets the rawest end of the deal, has no privileges and simply takes what is left behind.

A cow's rank is established when she joins the herd, and once it is established it isn't likely to be challenged until another newcomer arrives on the scene. Status seems to depend mostly on the ability to push and shove.

vantageous in detecting the enemy, and in providing protection.

Cows moving across a pasture toward a milking barn often display allelomimetic behavior. One cow starts toward the barn, and the others follow. Since the rest of the herd is following, the first cow proceeds on.

Because of stimulating and competing with each other, there is usually a higher per animal feed consumption among a group of calves than by one calf alone.

Care-giving and care-seeking: Nature ordained that cows seek isolation at calving time. So, where possible, they'll hide out.

Following birth, the care-giving behavior of the new mother becomes evident almost immediately. She gets up and begins to dry her newborn calf by licking it. Simultaneously, some cows "talk" to their newborn. They may become quite concerned and nervous as their "baby" first attempts to stand, takes a few footsteps—falters. Aided by its mother's licking and encouraged by her "talking," eventually the calf makes it to its unsteady feet and commences to search for a teat.

A newborn calf cannot see too well, but it can smell, touch, and taste. It associates everything that is good and that cares for it with its mother. This is the beginning of herd instinct.

If on pasture, the new mother usually hides her calf. During the first day or two, the calf sleeps a great deal, while the mother grazes nearby. But a mother takes great pains not to disclose

TONS OF MANURE (Free of bedding) PRODUCED PER YEAR PER *1,000* POUNDS WEIGHT

12 TONS

8.5 TONS

6 TONS

16 TONS

8 TONS

4.5 TONS

Drawing by R. F. Johnson, used with permission from *Dairy Cattle Science*, by Dr. M. E. Ensminger, copyright 1980 by The Interstate Printers & Publishers, Incorporated.

the hiding place of her calf. At intervals, she returns to feed it. If it is necessary for her to leave her calf in order to get water or supplemental feed, she does not tarry much along the way. Frequently, where there are a number of newborn calves, the cows "baby-sit" for each other. Part of the cows will leave for feed or water, but one or two will remain behind and guard all the calves. Then, when the first cows to leave have returned, the "baby-sitters" will take their turn and depart. In this manner, there are older cows with the calves at all times.

When a calf in hiding is approached by a human, it will usually lie as close to the ground as possible, without any movement except for its eyes. If picked up, and if scared, it may bawl (cry) for its mother. If the mother hears the call, she will come running—often ready to fight. Frequently, other cows in the vicinity, especially if they have calves of their own, may join in the response. If the disturbed calf runs away, it will return to the area after the danger has passed.

Dairy calves are normally removed from their mothers when they are from one to four days of age, with the result that the tie between the mothers and offspring is soon severed.

After weaning, the calf looks for care and shelter from the herd. Thus, if an animal is separated from the herd, it is stressed. It may even jump fences because of its strong instinct to rejoin the herd.

Ingestive behavior: The first ingestive behavior trait, common to all young mammals, is suckling.

Each species has its own particular method of ingesting food. The natural feeding (grazing) position of cattle is heads down. In this position, they produce more saliva; and saliva aids digestion. When grazing, cattle wrap their tongues around grass, then jerk their heads forward so that the vegetation is cut off by the lower incisor teeth. (There are no upper incisor teeth, only the thick, hard dental pad). When grazing, cattle also move their heads from side to side. This movement, aided by protuberant eyes and thin legs, gives them a continuous view of their entire surroundings, an essential for wild cattle in an environment containing dangerous predators.

Eliminative behavior: Nature ordained that if animals eat, they must eliminate.

The eliminative behavior in farm animals tends to follow the general pattern of their wild ancestors; but it can be influenced by the method of management.

Cattle deposit their feces in a random fashion. Although cows can defe-

Hair-Raising Cows

The *London Sunday Telegraph reported on March 4, 1984 that "Mr John Coombs, a Wiltshire farmer, bald for twenty years, found hairs sprouting again after one of his cows licked the top of his head."*

cate while walking, with the result that their feces are scattered, generally they deposit their "chips" in neat piles. Most cows hump up to urinate, whereas bulls are inclined to stand squarely on all fours.

Investigative behavior: All animals are curious and have a tendency to explore their environment . . . If they are not afraid, cattle investigate a strange object at close range. They proceed toward it with their ears pointed forward and their eyes focused directly upon it. As they approach the object, they sniff and their nostrils quiver. When they reach the object, sniffing is replaced by licking; and if the object is small and pliable, they may chew it or even swallow it.

Cattle exhibit investigative behavior when placed in a new pasture or in a new barn. As a result, if there is an open gate in a pasture or a hole in the fence, they usually find it, then proceed to explore the new area.

Calves are generally more curious than older cattle. Perhaps this is due to the fact that older animals have seen more objects, with the result that fewer things are new or strange to them.

Sexual behavior: Reproduction is the first and most important requisite of dairy breeding.

Sexual behavior involves courtship and mating. It is largely controlled by hormones, although males that are cas-

trated after reaching sexual maturity (which, among farm animals, are known as stags) usually retain considerable sex drive and exhibit sexual behavior. This suggests that psychological, or learned, as well as hormonal factors may be involved in sexual behavior.

Males in most species of farm animals detect females in heat by sight or smell. Also, it is noteworthy that courtship is more intense on pasture than under confinement, and that captivity has the effect of producing many distortions of sexual behavior compared to wild animals.

A bull can often detect a cow that's coming in heat 24 to 48 hours before she will mate, at which time he will remain in her company. Courtship of the bull consists of following the in heat cow, licking and smelling the external genitalia, with the head extended horizontally and the lip upcurled, and chin-resting, with the chin and throat resting on the cow's rump.

Shelter-seeking behavior: All species of animals seek shelter—protection from the sun, wind, rain and snow, insects, and predators.

Cattle seem to be able to sense the coming of a storm, at which time they may race about and "act up." During a severe rain or snowstorm, they turn their rear ends to the storm and tend to drift away from the direction of the wind. By contrast, bison (buffalo) face a storm head on.

Ensminger also points out several factors which influence social rank; among them, age—both young animals and those that are senile rank toward the bottom; early experience—once a subordinate in a particular herd, usually always a subordinate; weight and size; and aggressiveness or timidity.

According to Ensminger, in dairy confinement operations, social facilitation is of great practical importance. Dominants should be sorted out, and, if possible, grouped together. Of course, they will fight it out until a new social order is established. In the meantime, both feed efficiency and milk will suffer. But, as a result of removing the dominants, the feed intake of the rest of the animals will be improved, followed by greater feed efficiency, production, and profit. Among the more settled animals, social facilitation will become more evident. After the dominants have been removed, the rest of the animals will settle down into a new hierarchy, but within the limits of their dominance. Their interaction or social facilitation will be far more likely to have a calming effect on this group, to both the economic and practical advantages of the operator.

Ensminger observes that dominance and subordination are not inherited as such, for these relations are developed by experience. Rather, the capacity to fight (agonistic behavior) is inherited, and, in turn, this determines dominance and subordination. When combat has been bred into the herd, such herds never have the same settled appearance and docility that is desired of high production and intensive animals.

The leader, he adds, is the cow that is usually at the head of a moving column and often seems to initiate a new activity. It is important to distinguish leader-follower relationships from dominance. In the latter, Ensminger notes, the herd is driven, rather than led. After the dominants have been removed from the herd, the leader-follower phenomenon usually becomes more evident. It is well known that the dominant animal is not necessarily the leader; in fact, it is very rarely the leader. When a string of cows moves from the pasture into the milking parlor, the dominant animals are generally in the middle of the procession; with the leader in front, and the subordinate ones bringing up the rear.

Kindness & Cows

There's an old joke about the country girl and the city girl: the former says, "If you treat a cow with affection, it'll give more milk," and the city girl says, "Big deal, so will the milkman." But Jack Albright, a Purdue University ethologist (one who scientifically studies

A Cow in Spring

Betsy Bossy, fair of form,
Ventured forth one April morn,
Out onto fresh, vernal pasture,
Scarce could she contain her rapture.
Dainty hoofs danced o'er the green
Right to the sparkling, spring-fed stream.
There her roving, bovine eye
Some water-cress was quick to spy.
It looked so tender and so luscious,
Verdant green among the rushes.

animal behavior), says someone with a quiet personality can induce more milk production from his or her cows than someone who is a noisy extrovert. And a pat on the head of the cow can be just as important as pitching a bucket of feed.

The success of Swedish dairy farms is due to their soft-voiced milkmaids, Albright says, and Israel, with the world's highest per-cow production, emphasizes women milkers. One of Albright's former students wrote from a kibbutz that "the reaction of the cows depends on the mood of the handlers. We try to have quiet people."

According to Albright, when a cow moos, the novice thinks the cow is just making a noise. But the bellow could mean she is thirsty, or discomforted by a harness or a milking machine, or that she needs milking. She may even be disturbed by something seemingly as unimportant as slats in her stall walls.

Studies at Purdue showed a Holstein would sleep an hour longer each night and produce an extra three pounds of milk every day after being switched from artificial bedding to natural bedding.

Albright says the best approach to dairying is to realize a contented cow needs plenty of space, respect for the herd's social order, and handlers who are as sweet as cream.

She Does?

Bumper sticker: *"Lena likes butter better than Ole."*

Motherhood

A Perspective by Jackie Jackson. You are a cow. Rather, you are about to begin to become one. One half that will be you is an egg in one of your mother's ovaries. The other half is a sperm in one of your father's testicles. Perhaps that half has been removed from your sire by stimulating him with an artificial cow, or a nympho-cow, and now Amos, the artificial inseminator, has you and a couple million of your siblings in a chilly test tube.

The moment arrives. Your mother is in heat. Either the bull's penis, or Amos's syringe, shoots the sperm part of you into your dam's vagina. That sperm swims vigorously, a little more vigorously than all the others, and meets the egg (called at this point an ovum) up above the uterus in one of your dam's fallopian tubes. They join. You are now you, a fertilized egg.

Your cells immediately begin to divide. They divide all the time you travel down the tube and into the two-horned uterus. You implant yourself in one of the horns. The side of it is a thick, juicy wall, ready with nutrients for you. You grow in a sac called a placenta. You grow for about nine months. Then labor begins; your mother is calving. The contractions force you down the birth canal and you are dropped—onto the ground, or barnyard, or stall floor.

Your mother turns around and licks you. She licks you dry, for you came out wet from the fluid in the birth sac. The rough tongue invigorates you, tottering, to her udder. You nose around, find a tit, and start to suck. You are born knowing how. You stay with your mother several days, then you are taken from her. She bellows her grief; you bawl like a banshee. You're put in a box stall in the small barn that opens off the cowbarn, along with other newborn calves. You all smell like milk. You all cry and cry.

A barn hand brings a pail with a rubber tit sticking off the bottom rim. He holds it up so that you still suck as from an udder. The milk is warm and foamy, fresh from the cows in the cowbarn, maybe even from your mother. If someone wanders by to see you and offers you a finger, you will suck the skin right off.

One day the barn hand brings you a pail without a tit. He gives you his fingers to suck. You suck vigorously for you are ravenous. He gently guides your head down to the pail and, along with his fingers, you find you are sucking milk. He removes his fingers—you are sucking from a pail! But perhaps you don't catch on quickly. You can't follow his fingers down to the pail; to

you, drinking is done with your neck arched upward. Finally, he straddles you and holds you firmly between his legs. With his fingers he grasps your wide, wet nostrils like a bowling ball, and plunges your nose into the pail of warm milk. You try to buck, to jerk your head out. You can't. You get a nose-full. You also get a mouthful. MILK! You recognize it, you start to suck. You suck up the milk with your tongue curved like a straw. The fingers let go of your nostrils, and you can breathe. Your breath is mixed with milk until you get the hang of it. You drain the bucket and bunt it around the stall with your head. You want more.

You are lucky to be a girl calf, a heifer calf. You will grow up. Had you been a bull calf you'd have been shipped to market to make veal.

The vet comes and gives you your shots. A metal tab is stapled to your ear which is your identification as well as your inoculation information. You grow. You are moved to the older calf barn. You grow some more until you are no longer a calf but a heifer, not a baby but a girl. You are put out to pasture with the other heifers. You frisk like a lamb, and do a lot of running. In between, you graze on sweet grass and chew your cud.

You grow some more. Your body

Smart Farmer

To protect his herd from hunters a farmer painted "COW" in huge letters on the side of each animal. "Why didn't you paint a different sign on your bull?" a neighbor asked. The farmer shrugged. "Why confuse a city slicker with details."

Myron Stephenson proudly shows off his calf at the Weber dairy farm (the family raised Ayrshires) in Door County, Wisconsin, in 1918. The picture was taken by Arthur Leo Weber, fulltime dairyman and sometime photographer.

matures. At about fifteen months, you come into heat. You've become a young lady. If you are bred, you can have a calf. Sometimes a young bull is allowed to run with the heifers when they're old enough: eighteen months is a good age for a first calf. The bull is attracted to you by your special odor. Because you are in heat, you accept him. He mounts on your back and impregnates you. The mating is successful. You are going to have a calf.

The calf grows inside you. You are out in the pasture when your labor begins. The other cows cluster around you in a circle, watching you give birth. Your calf drops onto the grass. You have "freshened." You lick and lick your calf. The other cows crowd around and try to lick your calf, too. The afterbirth comes out, and you eat it. This will keep the wolves from knowing you've given birth. Perhaps the afterbirth has not all come out, for the placenta is buttoned to the uterus lining and sometimes the labor action is not enough to loosen it. Then in a day or two, the farmer or the herdsman will reach down your vagina to your uterus, unbutton the placenta, and draw it carefully out. In a hard case, the vet will come. But usually the placenta comes out naturally.

Your calf is on its feet now, and sucking. You lead it to a far corner of the pasture and hide it in a clump of bushes. But the hired man finds it, and

takes you both to the barn. You nurse your calf for a few days. Then it is taken from you. You bellow and cry in loneliness. Off in the side barn, it bawls and bawls.

You join the herd of milking cows and learn the rhythms of the cowbarn. You have a pleasant life there. You are fed hay and silage and a balanced grain ration. You drink from your drinking cup, or the cow tank, or the creek. You are protected from cow diseases. No wild animals threaten you, only a feisty little dog who runs into the barnyard and yaps at your heels. Twice a day a milking machine is hung under you. The tit cups are snapped on, and you are milked. You listen to music on the radio. You are cleaned and curried. Your manure is scooped up. The farmer or the herdsman checks you in the evening, "puts you to bed." When you lie down your bed is straw or sawdust. In the summer, you sleep out under the stars.

Two or three months after you calve you come back into heat. Now is the time to inseminate you again, so that you will have a calf about once a year. But this is ideal spacing; no cow achieves it regularly. This keeps your milk flowing; 305 days of lactation, the rest of the year a dry period before the birth of your next calf. Amos comes this time and inseminates you artificially. The sire of your calf is a famous bull at a bull stud farm that gives your

Rent-A-Cow

*D*on't want to buy a cow? Then rent one. There are several firms in Wisconsin that offer this service; one of them is Darcy Rent-a-Cow in Watertown, organized in 1962 with 125 to 150 Holstein 2 year olds. Today they rent about a thousand. The heifers from Rent-a-Cow are spring and fresh or first-calf heifers purchased from farmers. Their biggest customer, up in Door County, rents 70 cows, while the smallest leases only two. The average renter takes about 15 cows, the values of which vary from $900 to $1,050 apiece. Per-month rental is from $30 to $35 per cow. Why lease a cow? To begin with, you get to keep the milkchecks and all the calves that are born from your rented cow. Besides, your cash flow is improved and you can use your funds for farm equipment or whatever. And there are tax advantages.*

Why lease a cow? Well, why buy a cow when you can rent 3½ for the price of one?

owner hundreds of bulls to choose from for you.

You grow old in service. You may live and milk for as long as ten or twelve years. At the end of a noble life, when your milk is waning for the final time and you have had seven or eight calves, you will be patted on the flank, put in a truck, and driven to the slaughterhouse. You will be killed painlessly. You will not make USDA Prime, for you weren't bred to be a beef cow. You are also too old. You are an old and faithful dairy cow. You will end up as hamburger.

Cows in Heat

When not pregnant, the cow usually comes in "heat" or estrum every 18 to 24 days. The duration of this period is from several hours to a day.

The duration of pregnancy in a cow is nine months, or about 283 days. After pregnancy takes place, there are no further periods of heat, and the cow is said to be "settled."

Usually, a heifer may be able to breed when six months or older, depending on the breed and climate. The smaller the breed and the warmer the climate the earlier the age of puberty. The heifer should not be bred the first time until around fifteen to eighteen months of age.

You will notice that a cow is in heat if you have other cattle around her. She will jump on them, and they will jump on her. But when two cows are involved in this activity, it is not the cow doing the mounting that is in heat—rather, the cow that tolerates the mounting. This is true even if the other cow seems to be more excited. When a cow does not object to holding another like this it is called "standing heat," and means she is definitely ready to be bred.

Heifers can come into heat as young as six months and it is not unknown for a heifer to try to mount a familiar human being. If she is big enough she will knock you flat on the ground. It is a good practice to never turn your back on a bulling heifer.

There is a belief that a cow is more likely to give you a heifer if she was aligned with her head to the north and tail to the south when bred.

During the process of birth:

- The cervix and vagina relax, uterine contractions start, and you will probably see a clear mucus. This stage usually takes about six hours, though in a heifer it might be as much as twenty-four hours.
- The delivery. The cow now strains in earnest, either lying or standing. The first waterbag bursts to release clear straw-coloured liquid. The sec-

ond water bag holds the calf in the uterus and is filled with a clear or greyish mucus. The bags might be visible before bursting, or they may burst before they protrude. Normal delivery of the calf is completed within one-and-a-half hours of the appearance of the first waterbag. The calf should arrive front feet first, followed by the muzzle at about knee level. After delivery the cow starts to wash the calf.

The placenta is ejected, normally within six to twelve hours of the birth.

The womb is very peculiar in the cow because it is provided with from 60 to 80 cotyledons or "buttons," to which the afterbirth is attached. When a few of these buttons become congested at calving time, they prevent the afterbirth from being expelled in a normal manner. This is commonly known as "the cow not cleaning."

Calves

In his book *Keeping a Cow*, Val Spreckley suggests that the calf be left with the cow for at least a couple of days to take full advantage of the colostrum and additional antibodies acquired from close contact with its mother. He also recommends that unless you intend to leave the calf on the cow until it is weaned, take it away after the first two or three days, because the longer you leave them together the more cruel the parting. Remove the calf to a warm calf box, tying up the mother while you do so to frustrate her protective instincts.

The cow will bawl furiously for a couple of days. Make sure the calf is out of earshot because hearing her own calf will make matters ten times worse and she will make strenuous efforts to reach it. She may be reluctant to let her milk down for you but be patient and persist. She will settle down in due course, Spreckley concludes.

Twinning is not a desirable trait in cattle, and no one has ever bred specifically for it although it is inherited. Twins represent about one percent of the total number of calves, and twins are seldom identical.

A *freemartin* occurs when a heifer is a twin to a bull. Ninety-two percent of all freemartins are sterile because of the inhibitory effect the embryonic male hormones have upon the development of the female reproductive organs. The term "free-martin" originated in England, where it meant a cow free for fattening. "Mart" is an old provincial English and Scottish abbreviation of "Martinmas," and it meant a cow or any other animal slaughtered at Martinmas-time, a festival in honor of St.

Martin of France, on the eleventh of November.

Milking

The milk yield from a freshened cow (one who has recently given birth to a calf) naturally increases rapidly from calving to a peak at between three and six weeks (depending on the breed and the individual). After that, the yield gradually drops at two and one-half percent per week (one and one-half percent for a first-calf heifer) towards the drying-off period about six or eight weeks before calving again.

In an ideal situation, a cow is milked at twelve-hour intervals. Cows appreciate routine.

Extra teats do not mean a better cow.

The most generally accepted standard length of lactation records is 305 days. When a cow is milked longer than 305 days, her yield for the first 305 days is used as the standard lactation yield.

The udder is a highly developed gland in the dairy cow. Its conformation often determines the value of the cow as a milk producer. The ability of the milk-producing cells to extract milk from the ingredients furnished by the blood as it passes through the udder determines not only the quantity, but also the quality of the milk. There are four quarters in the udder, and they

are separated. That is the reason why one quarter may be "caked" and the others remain normal. The blood is pumped into each quarter by a single artery, which branches into a network of capillaries, or fine, thread-like blood vessels. The latter surround the milk-making bulbs, called "alveoli," which resemble a bunch of grapes. These produce the milk, drop by drop, from the lymph which carries the milk-producing ingredients from the blood.

The milk cisterns are little reservoirs or storage chambers in each quarter. They contain the milk secreted before actual milking time. It has been estimated that 85 per cent of the milk is thus secreted, and this is why regular milking is so important. Each cistern may hold up to a quart of milk when full.

The teats should be large and well-formed to make milking easier. When the teat canal is too small, or the walls too thick, the condition may result in the cow being a "hard milker."

Milking is the act of removing milk from the udder. It is routinely carried out through three methods described by M. E. Ensminger:

Suckling. The fastest means of removing milk from the udder is through the use of the calf. The calf grasps the teat with its tongue and presses it against the soft palate on the roof of the mouth. Milk ejection is accomplished through the creation of a negative pressure in the mouth by the widening of the jaws and the retraction of the tongue. This action causes the streak canal to open, thereupon releasing milk from the udder. When the calf swallows, a positive pressure is created, which acts as a resting and a massage phase for the teat.

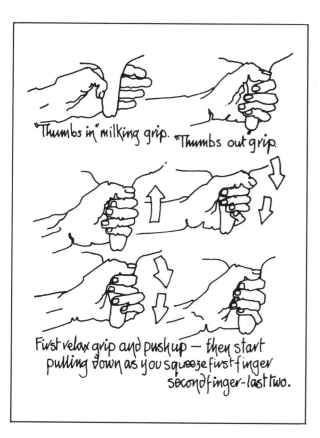

"Thumbs in" milking grip. "Thumbs out" grip.

First relax grip and push up — then start pulling down as you squeeze first finger second finger-last two.

Hand-Milking. Hand-milking is still widely used in the lesser developed countries where labor is cheaper than automation and in modern operations to milk out quarters which are infected or have been injured.

In hand-milking, the teat is grasped between the thumb and fore-finger; then, by applying pressure with the other fingers, milk is forced from the teat cistern through the streak canal. Through this method, more milk can be obtained than by the use of a milking machine.

Machine Milking. The history of machine milking in the United States goes back over 100 years. The first vacuum-type milking machine was patented by L.O. Colvin in 1865. It was a rather crude apparatus. In 1878, Mrs. Anne Baldwin came out with her Hygienic Glove Milker, an apparatus that used a hand pump to provide milking action. In 1884, J. P. Martin devised a milking machine that had individual teat cups, connecting tubes, and vacuum pump. The pulsator was patented by Modestus Cushman in 1885. In 1892, the Mehring milker, powered by a hand pump and later by foot power, began to gain acceptance as a practical aid in milking. In 1902, an Australian, Alexander Gillies, developed the first prototype for what was eventually to develop into the modern milking machine. This machine had a source of

To milk, squeeze downward from index to little finger, as shown in this drawing from *Butter, Milk & Cheese from your Back Yard*, reproduced courtesy of Prism Press, 2 South St., Bridport, Dorset, England DT6 3NQ. This feels wrong at first—the natural tendency is to start squeezing with the little finger—but is fairly easy to master.

vacuum, a collection receptacle, pulsator, hoses, and individual teat cups and liners.

The Old-Fashioned Way

No one can teach you how to milk a cow. You have to acquire the knack by practice. If you have no experience, visit a friendly farmer and practice every day on a quiet old cow that gives about one and one-half gallons of milk a day. At first you'll find muscles in your arms and hands that you didn't know you had (that's why you should practice on a cow that can, if necessary, be finished off by someone else or by a machine). If you get frustrated, the cow will sense it and get upset herself and can shut off her supply. If you alarm her or lose your temper, she may react by urinating, which is not good for the milk in the bucket between your knees.

Use a three-legged stool; it is more maneuverable in case you have to move quickly. Sit right next to the cow and at right angles to her; the closer you are the more control you have. It is traditional to sit at her right side. Press your head firmly into her body so you can feel any imminent movement. Do not let your hair tickle her: a cow has a sensitive hide; she feels every fly and every hair, and she reacts with a swish of her tail.

Grip the bucket between your knees

so you have complete control over it—you can then swing it out of range if necessary. Make sure that everything you use is scoured clean—the bucket and your hands, and the udder. Washing the udder with a warm cloth will stimulate the cow to let down her milk (that doesn't mean it comes pouring out of its own accord—it means it drops into the bag and starts to fill the teats).

Grasp the first teat (try the ones in front first) firmly, with the four fingers wrapped around and the thumb coming around to close off the top of the teat (the base of it, as viewed from the udder) with the thumb and index finger. Then squeeze with the other three fingers to shoot the milk into the bucket.

Nothing? Try again. Relax your grip and take hold once more. Squeeze at the top, then squeeze down. Release at the top, then repeat. Don't give up if it takes ten or fifteen minutes before she lets down—she may be trying to beat you.

It's a good idea to send the first squirt of milk from each teat onto the ground, to remove any dirt that might be left on the teat orifice.

It is generally believed that a cow only lets down her milk for eight minutes and that milking should be completed within that time. Once you have stimulated let-down, allow nothing to distract you until you have finished the job. But do not panic about how long it is taking. If you've chosen a reasonable cow she'll be lenient with you, although she might not think much of it.

Get as close to all of the milk as you can—the last milk contains a high percentage of butterfat. Besides, the cow is encouraged to produce more milk if she is milked out completely.

A cow should be milked clean. Not a drop, if it can be avoided, should be left in the udder . . . The cares created by the cow are amply compensated for by the education that these cares will give to the children. They will learn to set a just value upon dumb animals, and will grow up in the habit of treating them with gentleness . . . It may be the best way to sell the calf as soon as calved; if you cannot sell it, knock it on the head as soon as calved.

—William Cobbet
Cottage Economy, 1822

Cows and UFO's—Yes or No?

In the early 1970's, mutilated cattle were found on Wisconsin hillsides, down in Crawford County. Frequently their udders had been removed in what seemed to be a clean and bloodless operation. A number of spectacular rumors circulated. Subsequent similar mutilations occurred in Utah, Washington, Colorado and South Dakota.

The Fortean Times, a journal of strange phenomena published in England, recently published an article on the subject, in which they asked four psychics to give their impressions of these mutilations: All four psychics were unified in their belief that the mutilations stemmed from a massive, covert operation led by what is described as the 'military-industrial complex.'

"That not so much as even the slightest support was given to the popular predator, cult, and alien theories, comes as an extraordinary surprise . . .

"All the more surprising is the fact that two of the psychics were inclined to accept the possibility of 'close encounters' with occult and alien forces, but failed to establish any such connections during their readings. Each psychic was firmly committed to the view that the mutilations were terrestrial in origin, though practically all sensed that phenomena suggestive of extraterrestrial involvement had been introduced as a means of creating confusion and uncertainty."

The Wisconsin mutilations were investigated at the time of discovery by a state veterinarian who is certain that some of the mutilations were the result of pranks involving animals who were dying from natural causes, like blackleg. In conclusion, the veterinarian could find no evidence of a "cult" or UFO involvement.

Bovine Bras

The Franksville Specialty Company in Franksville, Wisconsin, makes brassieres for U.S. and Canadian dairy cows. The bovine bras were invented by William Tamm in 1945. A full udder can weigh from 75 to 80 pounds, and the bras (in basic "barnyard brown" only), come in four sizes, including extra-large. Dorothy Rice, who manufactures the bras in her small factory with four other women, is the daughter of the bra inventor. She says the bras, known officially as Tamm Udder Supports, keep the udder warm and also prevent damage to the udder which often occurs if a cow steps on it."

The Great Kansas Cownapping.

One of the great classics of UFOlogy, this story first appeared in the *Yates Center Farmer's Advocate*, a small weekly newspaper in Yates Center, Kansas, on April 23, 1897. It was reported by Alexander Hamilton, a prosperous Kansas farmer:

Last Monday night aboaut 10:30 we were awakened by a noise among the cattle. I arose thinking that perhaps my bulldog was performing pranks, but upon going to the door saw to my utter astonishment that an airship was slowly descending upon my cow lot, about forty rods [600 feet] from the house.

Calling my tenant, Gid Heslip, and my son Wall, we seized some axes and ran to the corral. Meanwhile the ship had been gently descending until it was not more than thirty feet above the ground and we came within fifty yards of it.

It consisted of a great cigar-shaped portion, possibly three hundred feet long, with a carriage underneath. The carriage was made of glass or some other transparent substance alternating with a narrow strip of some material. It was brightly lighted within and everything was plainly visible— it was occupied by six of the strangest beings I ever saw. They were jabbering together but we could not understand a word they said.

We stood mute with wonder and fright. Then some noise attracted their attention and they turned a light directly upon us. Immediately on catching sight of us they turned on some unknown power, and a great turbine wheel, about thirty feet in diameter, which was revolving slowly below the craft, began to buzz and the vessel rose lightly as a bird. When about three hundred feet above us it seemed to pause and to hover directly above a two-year-old heifer which was bawling and jumping, apparently fast in the fence. Going to her, we found some material fastened in a slip knot around her neck and going up to the vessel from the heifer tangled in the wire fence. We tried to get it off but could not, so we cut the wire loose to see the ship, heifer and all, rise slowly, disappearing in the northwest...

The story was told and re-told through the years, and never doubted, for Hamilton's reputation was quite solid. However, *Fate* magazine finally gave the matter a thorough investigation in 1977 and published an article in their February issue entitled "The Great Airship Hoax," in which they exposed the hoax. Even Hamilton's granddaughter admitted that Alexander Hamilton had a "darned good imagination."

Cow Myths & Superstitions

Almost since the beginning of time, the cow has been the object of superstition and myth. The Roman Poet Tibullus (c. 48–19 B.C.), spoke of the magical use of milk: "Now with magic howlings

Spaced Out Cows

N ASA sent some cows up in a rocket a few years ago, to orbit the earth and test their reactions to outer space. It was the herd shot round the world.

she keeps the swarms of the grave before her: now she sprinkles them with milk and bids them retreat."

A medieval inducement to rain was to kill a white rooster. After it was torn apart, the entrails were extracted and the carcass was filled with myrrh, white pepper, frankincense, milk and wine. The rooster was then held toward the sun and an incantation given, while everyone stood around and waited for the rain to fall.

Albertus Magnus (1206–1280) was the Bishop of Ratisbon and he was interested in the occult arts. He experimented with alchemy and magic and wrote *Book of the Marvels of the World*, in which he said:

And Aristotle said in the Booke of Beastes: *If any man put wrought ware upon the hornes of a cow's calf, it will goe with him wheresoever he will without labor. And if any man anoint the hornes of kine with ware and oyle or pitch, the paine of their feet goeth away. And if any shall anoint the tungs of oxen with any tallow, they neither taste nor eat meat, but they shall die for hunger, except it be willed away with salt and vinegar.*

- It is bad luck to milk a cow on the ground, she will go dry.
- If you kill a toad, your best cow will give bloody milk.
- Kill a toad and your cows will go dry.
- If you pull a tooth and throw it away and a cow walks over it, you will get a cow's tooth, if a dog walks over it, a dog's tooth, and so on.
- Two cowlicks are a sign of riches.
- If it thunders heavily, it will sour the milk.
- If a cow bawls at night, there will be a death or some very bad luck.
- In Ireland when a calf is born the farmer says, "God bless" three times, "and three spits for luck."
- The first time a heifer has a calf, the owner should take the first milking and throw it into running water. If this is done, the heifer will always give milk until her next calf is born.
- Lanterns must never be placed on tables inside barns, or cows will lose their calves.
- It is ill luck for twin calves to be born.
- To touch a calf on the back will cause it to fall ill; to step over one, while it is lying on the ground, will kill it.
- Farm animals must never be gelded under a waning moon.
- If a calf has a white streak down the middle of its back it will never thrive.
- When a calf is taken from the barn to grass for the first time it must be taken with the tail foremost.
- When a man's cow gets into his

DO NOT ADJUST YOUR BOOK! WE CONTROL TRANSMISSION! WE NOW TAKE YOU ONE STEP BEHIND...

NOW, ONE STEP IN FRONT!

UNDERNEATH!

AND INSIDE...

WE NOW RETURN YOU TO THE BOOK...

Wisconsin cartoonist Jay Rath—creator of this strip—features cows in his comics and lobbies to change the state mascot from Bucky Badger to Bucky Guernsey. One of his characters is a bovine-of-steel named Supermoo.

45

Cow Riddles

F*our stiff-standers*
Four dilly-danders,
Two lookers, two crookers,
And a wig-wag.
It has been said that this is
a "world riddle," which can
be traced for thousands of
years through the traditions
of every people, but seems
to have first appeared in
print, in English, in 1820.
Compare the above version
with one that is more
current:
Two hookers, two snookers,
Two lookers,
Four dilly-danders,
Four stiff-standers
Two flip-flops,
One fling-by.
What is it? a COW—with
horns, nostrils, eyes, teats,
legs, ears and a tail.

Q. What has 4 legs and
flies?
A. A cow in the summer.

Q. What do you call a cow
that's just had a calf?
A. A de-calfinated cow.

neighbor's pasture she is said to be unlucky.

- To make an offer for a cow that is not up for sale is unlucky, and one may bring on the cow's death by doing so.
- When a farmer is about to sell a cow he must not milk her on the morning of the sale or he will have no luck in selling her.
- When cattle are sold, the seller must return a coin or a small sum for luck.
- When beastings are taken to a neighbor he should not wash the pitcher out, or the cow and her calf will die. He should return the pitcher unwashed.

- *Come, butter, come,*
  Come, butter, come;
  Peter stands at the gate
  Waiting for a butter cake.
  Come, butter, come.

When pixies get into the churn and prevent the cream from clotting, English farmwives repeat this charm, preferably three times, to make the butter come. The charm has also been recorded in North Carolina, where it is said that "The ugliest face peering into a cream jar will help clot the cream so that churning is possible."

- Another method of removing a spell from cream is to pass a dead man's hand widdershins (withershins means counterclockwise) three times around your churn. If you cannot find a dead man's hand you can use a sprig of rowan.
- Or, to remove witches from your cream you may put a hot horseshoe in the cream and burn the witches. After this process is carried out, the cream will turn to butter with ease.
- When you are churning and butter will not come, take a red-hot poker and touch each corner of your house with it, thereby driving the witch away.
- Another way to get rid of the witches in your cream: set the churn in a chimney corner and whip the milk with a switch, or drop a dime in the churn.
- A charm once used by the dairy-maids of Clydesdale, Scotland, to induce bewitched cows to give them milk:

Bonnie ladye, let down your milk
And I'll gie you a goun of silk,
A goun o' silk and a ball o' twine,
Bonnie ladye—your milk's no mine.

- In Dumfries and Galloway, Ireland, they dealt with bewitched cows in the following manner: The tainted milk was boiled in a brass pan, pins were added, and the mixture was stirred with a wand of a rowan tree. When the brew came to a boil, rusty nails were dropped in and then the witch immediately felt the power of the medicine. She would announce her arrival by knocking at the window. The gudewife would negotiate with her for the "hale loan o' kye" (the whole herd of cows), the pan was cooled, and the cow's udder would swell with good milk.

- At Willington, Warwickshire, in the 1800's, a servant lifted a spell on the cows by taking a cow's heart, sticking it with pins and roasting it in the oven so the witch should be drawn there. A small animal, the like of which none of them had ever seen, came and "scratted" at the door, trying to reach the heart. When the creature died, the spell was broken.

- Scottish witches were said to be able to procure a supply of milk by obtaining a small quantity of hair from the tail of a cow, tying a knot in the hair and tugging it while reciting these lines:

  Meer's milk, and deer's milk
  And every beast that bears milk
  Between St. Johnston and Dundee
  Come a' to me, come a' to me.

- To dream of milk is a lucky omen, unless the milk spills!
- To find bubbles on your milk is a sign you will get rich.

- If you put milk or cream in your coffee, it will poison you.
- If you put cream into your tea before you put the sugar in you will cross your love.
- Cut a potato in two, rub the parts over the warts, feed the potato to the cow and the warts will leave.
- Hot milk and pepper mixed and used as a drink is a remedy for a cold.
- To cure a boil, place some sour cream that has been stirred until it is real thick on the sore place.
- Take a pint of cream, place it in a cloth sack, bury it in the ground until the cream is decayed, dig it up and use it as an ointment to cure skin eruptions.
- To cure ringworm, use a salve made by placing a two-cent copper piece to soak in cream. The soaking process develops a thick green salve.
- For whoopingcough, drink mare's milk, or milk from a dish at which a fox has previously drunk (because witches were believed often to assume the shapes of foxes in Europe—that is, when they were not changing into cats, toads or spiders).
- For tuberculosis, eat the butter made from the milk of cows that have been grazing in churchyards or cemeteries.
- Once a popular superstition in the southern states, a country girl who

Q. What is the most important use for cowhide? A. It holds the cow together.

Q. What 2 animals do you always take to bed with you? A. Your calves.

Q. When did beef go the highest? A. When the old cow jumped over the moon.

Q. Four bottles of milk are uncorked and upside down, and not a drop leaks out. What is it? A. A cow's udder.

Q. While I did live, I food did give Which many one did daily eat. Now being dead, you see they tread Me under feet about the street. A. A cow.

47

had gone to the woods after dark would say:

If I am to marry near
Let me hear a bird cry.
If I am to marry far
Let me hear a cow low.
If I am to single die
Let me hear a knocking by.

- Death is said to be approaching if you hear a ringing in your ears, if you see a star fall, or if a cow lows three times in your face.
- Omens of death in the family include hearing a cow low at midnight; or cattle breaking into the garden.
- In many rural areas, some member of the family must formally tell the cattle of their owner's death, or the animals will pine and die.
- It is a good omen if cattle lie down on Christmas Day. And in parts of Europe, it is still thought that cattle kneel at midnight on Christmas Eve, honouring the memory of the stable at Bethlehem.
- During Hogmanay (New Year's Eve) in the Highlands of Scotland, a curious custom prevailed. The people of the area assembled and the stoutest of the party was presented with a dried cow hide which he dragged behind him while the rest followed, beating the hide with sticks and singing:

Hug man a!
Yellow bag,
Beat the skin;
Carlin in neuk,
Carlin in Kirk,
Carlin ben at the fire;
Spit in her two eyes,
Spit in her stomach,
Hug man a!

After going around the house three times, each person uttered another rhyme extolling the hospitality of the master and mistress, and the visitors were regaled with bread, butter, cheese and whiskey. Before leaving, one of the group burned the breast part of a sheepskin and put it to the nose of everyone present as a charm against witchcraft and infection.

When a cow tries to scratch her ear,
It means a shower is very near.
When she thumps her ribs with her tail,
Look out for thunder, lightning, and hail.

- Cows may be able to forecast the weather. Scientists attribute changes in cows' behavior to the lowering pressure preceding a storm system. Cows may refuse to graze if they sense an impending storm, and will lie down. They may also bunch together before a storm hits and move down from the crests of hills into sheltered valleys. They have also been observed to huddle under

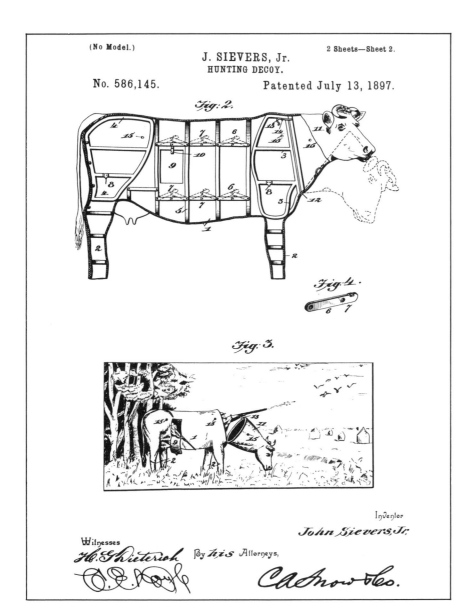

A party who wishes to remain anonymous mentioned the adolescent prank of "**Cow tipping**." He grew up in Iowa, and reported, "You go out at night while the cows are asleep and they're standing up and their legs are locked. And then you give them a nudge and tip them over." When asked what kind of response the cows have to this rude awakening he replied, "They're real surprised."

trees if they sense the storm to be a short one and as a result have sometimes been struck by lightning.

- If cows lie down early in the morning, it will rain before night.
- When cattle stand with their backs to the wind, rain is coming.
- When cows refuse to go into the pasture in the morning, it will rain before night.
- If a bull leads the cows going to pasture, expect rain.
- The best known sign of an imminent earthquake is extreme restlessness on the part of domestic animals, especially cattle.
- In Britain, rain is predicted by a cuckoo's persistent call, or by cattle lying on low ground.
- In Yorkshire, England, children sing cow-charms about the weather. At the first snow of the year they chant:

  Snow, snow faster,
  The cow's in the pasture.

  And when they've had enough of the snow, they sing:

  Snow, snow, give over,
  The cow's in clover!

- This Finnish charm, also used at one time in Minnesota, encouraged the cows to come home from the wild pastures when they were first let out in the spring. Salt was fed to the lead cow from the inside of a cow bell, then the bell was fastened to the cow's neck and the *loihtija* [wise woman] chanted:

  I lash the bell to the neck
  The well-known bell for my cow.
  Sound, bell, echo, bell,
  Echo from the farthest meadows
  Echo even to the home farmyard.
  You are the largest of my cattle
  The strongest of my calves.
  Bring ye home the herd
  Clanking to the farmyard,
  Lead it to the evening smudges
  While yet the sun is shining
  In the glow of midevening.
  Bring in a row the cattle of God,
  The herd of the generous mistress.

- In Norwegian folklore, some of the mythological characters dwell in the underground and are called *huldrefolk*, or the hidden people. They resemble ordinary people, but are often described as being somewhat smaller in size, and the huldre women usually have a cow's tail and a hollow back.

  Human beings and huldrefolk live invisibly side by side. But the dividing line between the two worlds is no wall—if anything, it is a mist or a veil. Now and then the veil is lifted to one side, and representatives of the two parallel worlds confront one another.

A huldre woman once showed herself to a man who was standing in a forest, splitting a big trunk of a pine tree. She tried to make him fall in love with her—she spoke to him kindly and seated herself on the trunk right in front of him, so he could see how beautiful she was. All the same, he noticed that she had a long tail, which she concealed in the crack in the trunk. Then it occurred to him to loosen a big wedge that stood in the middle of the trunk. Now when he knocked this wedge loose, the cleft snapped together so the huldre's tail was caught fast. Then she became frightened and ran away. And she was so strong that she dragged the trunk with her, and tore down a lot of the forest before she was able to free herself.

Holsteins are a departure for Minnesota wildlife artist Dan Metz. Commissioned for publication in *Down Wisconsin Sideroads*, they are reproduced courtesy of the artist and Tamarack Press, a division of Wisconsin Trails, Incorporated.

A cow in front of a house in Jodhpur, Rajasthan, India. Stray cows often stop at Indian homes, seeking to be fed. Because cows are sacred to Hindus, most people regard the chance to feed a cow as a blessing. Original photo by Arvind Garg.

Famous Cows

"The Cow is the foster mother of the human race."

William Dempster Hoard,
Governor of Wisconsin

Audumla

One of the first Holy Cows, Audumla was mentioned in the Edda, an ancient Icelandic literary work that was assembled in the early 13th Century. Audumla was born from drops of the melting primeval ice and by licking a mass of the salty ice she exposed the first god, Buri. But her most important mission was suckling the giant Ymir with four rivers of milk. Ymir was the earliest being and the progenitor of the giants—the earth was made from his flesh; the water was made from his blood and the heavens were created from his skull:

Then said Gangleri: "Where dwelt Ymir, or wherein did he find sustenance?" Harr answered: "Straightway after the rime dripped, there sprang from it the cow called Audumla; four streams of milk ran from her udders, and she nourished Ymir." Then asked Gangleri: "Wherewithal was the cow nourished?" And Harr made answer: "She licked the ice-blocks, which were salty; and the first day that she licked the blocks, there came forth from the blocks in the evening a man's hair; the second day, a man's head; the third day the whole man was there."

The Celestial Cow

For the Hindus, the cow has been the most useful of animals from time immemorial.

According to one part of the Hindu religion, "a radiance first came out of the Creator's face and later it was split into four parts—the Vedas, the Fire, the Cow and the Brahmin." Hindus perform "Yagas" as a part of their belief: a Yaga is the offering of Ghee (a kind of butter), curd, and milk to the deities invoked by the chant of Vedic mantras as recited by the Brahmins.

The cow occupies a prominent place in ancient Sanskrit literature, and there are many hymns relating to the cow. The cow world is considered the highest and greatest of all worlds. Cows are spoken of as "mothers to all beings."

Not only the ancient Hindu seers, but even the intellectuals of the modern age such as Gandhi and Satishchandra Das Gupta, believed that a nation which approved of the slaughter of cows would not progress economically. In fact, it is said that Gandhi laid more stress on the issue of cow-protection than on the removal of foreign rule from India.

The Dun Cow

Sir Guy of Warwick had an international reputation. In 1562 he was listed (along with Caesar, King Arthur, Charlemagne and Alexander) as "one of the nine worthies of the world." He is reputed to have lived in Saxon times, during the reign of King Athelstan, who died in 939. Sir Guy set out from Warwick to slay dragons and giants and other treacherous enemies in Greece and Persia, but his combat with the Dun Cow in Warwickshire, at Dunsmore Heath, gave him equal billing (with Lady Godiva) as the greatest of figures in Warwickshire folklore.

Of Guy Earl of Warwick
  our country can boast
Who in fighting and thumping
  ruled lord of the roast;
He with courage resistless
  his foes did assail,
For he strengthened his sinews
  with Birmingham ale.
  —Birmingham street ballad

The Dun Cow belonged to a giant and was kept on Mitchell Fold, Shropshire. She was a large and benign creature, generous with her inexaustible

supply of milk. One day an old woman who had already filled her pail with milk wanted her sieve filled as well. This so enraged the cow that she broke loose from the fold and wandered to Dunsmore Heath in a wild fury.

On Dunsmore heath I alsoe slewe
A monstrous wyld and cruell beast,
Calld the Dun-cow of Dunsmore heath;
Which many people had opprest.
Some of her bones in Warwicke yett
Still for a monument doe lye.
  —Percy
  Reliques

Indeed, a huge tusk (perhaps that of a mammoth?) is still kept at Warwick Castle as one of the horns of the Dun Cow.

When he was an old man, Sir Guy returned to Warwick and lived, unknown, in a cave. Every day he begged at the castle gate and was given food by his wife, who did not recognize her husband. As he lay dying he sent her a ring, which identified him, and she rushed to his death-bed. Two weeks later she dove to her own death into the River Avon from a spot eventually known as "Guy's Leap."

The first mention in print of the Dun Cow appeared in 1579, in a Latin text. There Dr. Caius described what he took to be a huge cow's head, and vertebrae seven and one-half inches in circumference at Warwick Castle; and a rib over six feet long and nine inches around which he saw at Guy's Chapel at Guy's Cliffe. In 1661 a play, said to have been written by Ben Jonson, was performed about the Dun Cow.

The Dun Cow Inn opened in Dunchurch, Warwickshire, in 1655. It is still there, and still open for business on The Green, CV22 6NJ. The inn has 26 rooms, priced at eighteen pounds to 38.50 pounds per day (breakfast included).

The nickname, "The Old Dun Cow" may or may not be related to The Dun Cow Inn: this was a derisive epithet given by the troops to the steamer, River Clyde, which was beached at Gallipoli in 1915 during World War I. The name was taken from a song, popular at that time, which contained the words, "The Old Dun Cow, she's done for now," and described a public house that had run dry.

The Book of the Dun Cow has nothing to do with Sir Guy or the monstrous bovine. Rather, it is an early manuscript account of an even earlier Irish romance, and derived its name from the fact that it was a copy of one of several stories originally written on the hide of a cow, by St. Kieran of Clonmacnoise.

The Cow of Forfar

A proverbial phrase from Scotland, "Do as the cow o' Forfar did, tak' a standing drink," came about because of a tub of beer.

One day a woman in the village of Forfar set a tub of beer in her doorway to cool. A passing cow paused, realized she was thirsty, and drank the contents dry. The owner of the beer sued the cow's master for damages, but the wise Balies of Forfar found for the defense. In the Highlands, the farewell drink, called a "doch-an-doris," or a stirrup cup, is customarily taken by the guest while standing. And the guest is never charged. So, the Balies said, because the cow had taken a standing drink she was not to blame, and her owner was not liable for the cost of her refreshment.

Halkerston's Cow

Halkerston was a Scottish lawyer and a landed proprietor, who gave one of his tenants permission to graze a sickly ox on one of Halkerston's pastures along with a heifer that belonged to the lawyer. The heifer apparently didn't enjoy the company of the ox and she gored it to death. The tenant went to Halkerston and for some reason told the reverse of what had actually happened. "Why then," said the lawyer, "your ox must go for my heifer, the law provides that." "No," said the man, "your heifer killed my ox." "Oh," said Halkerston, "the case alters there," and then changed his tactics.

Holy Cow

They violate the Sacred Cow
And lace her hide around a ball
Profaning her with spittle now,
Then flailing her against the wall
Each time she's pounded, thousands cheer,
but that is not what has her vexed.
Poor thing! She lives in mortal fear
They'll loft her to the bull pen next.

The Equitable poet

The Mehring milker was introduced in the 1890's. The popular milking machine was originally powered by a hand pump, but later models—like the one shown here in use on a Maryland farm—were foot powered. Photo reproduced courtesy *Hoard's Dairyman* and Hoard Historical Museum.

"That's Halkerston's cow, a' the ither way," is an old Scottish phrase spoken when a person alters his opinion about something that is now seen at a closer range.

The Aroostook Cow

During one of the minor wars of the nineteenth century, the Aroostook War over the Maine-New Brunswick boundary claimed a strange casualty that was frequently referred to at the time: an unfortunate cow was shot by a guard near the St. John's River boundary.

The Canadian Cow in the War of 1812

Although her name has not gone down in history, this cow played an heroic role in the war between the United States and Canada. The cow belonged to Laura Secord, a Canadian heroine. Laura's husband, James, was a soldier in the British militia, but he had been badly wounded and although most of their neighbors had been driven out, they were allowed to continue to reside behind what were then American lines. One day in 1813 James and Laura learned of a surprise attack being planned by the Americans against a British outpost known as the Beaver Dam. Laura vowed to take word to the men at the post and warn them of the proposed attack. But how to get past the American sentries?

Laura Secord awoke at 3 a.m. on the morning of June 23, fixed breakfast for her children and left her house at daybreak. She told the American sentry she was going out to milk her cow and he could watch. She took her milkpail and did proceed to milk the cow, who seemed somewhat contrary and kept moving to the edge of the nearby bushes. Before very long, both Laura and the cow disappeared into the greenery and Laura was on her way—past infestations of rattlesnakes, through the Black Swamp and right smack into an Indian camp. The woman was terrified, but she told one of the chiefs of her mission and he guided her to the Beaver Dam. As a result of her heroic act, 542 American soldiers who attacked the post the next morning were captured, and the British provisions and ammunitions were saved.

There is a monument to Laura Secord near Niagara Falls. Poems have been written in her memory and a candy was named after her. But no one has recognized the bravery and courage of her cow. Until now.

Mrs. O'Leary's Cow

At 8:30 on Sunday evening, October 8, 1871, the fire that became the holocaust of the century started in the barn of Patrick and Catherine O'Leary at 137 De Koven Street, and spread out of control to turn Chicago, the largest city west of Pittsburgh into a sea of glowing ashes.

The O'Learys had company Sunday evening, their neighbors Daniel Sullivan and Dennis Rogers. When their guests left, the O'Learys retired early, about 8 o'clock. Sullivan didn't go straight home, but sat down across the street in front of Thomas White's place. It was balmy and the bit of breeze was pleasantly cool.

From where Sullivan sat, the O'Leary barn was in his line of vision. At 8:30 he saw flames coming from the barn. Immediately he rushed across the street, yelling "Fire!" Already the flames were licking at the stored hay and trapped animals. Sullivan had to work slowly because of his wooden leg, but he managed to loose the tethered cows before the fire got too hot.

The sun came up Tuesday morning, October 10, on the blackened ashes of a once great city. On 73 miles of her streets, 17,500 buildings were gone. So were the lumber mills, bridges, and the million-dollar courthouse. The Chicago Fire will live in memory as long as Mrs. O'Leary's legendary cow, said to have started the holocaust by kicking over a lantern.

The *Chicago Fire Academy* at 558 West DeKoven Street occupies the site where the 1871 fire was kicked off by Mrs. O'Leary's cow. Firefighters train here. Tours are offered Monday through Friday, 9 and 10 AM; 2 and 3 PM, and reservations are needed two weeks in advance. Call 312-744-4728.

Governor Schofield's Jersey

A Jersey cow played a starring role in the birth of Wisconsin's Progressive Party, and helped defeat an incumbent governor's reelection bid.

Edward Schofield of Oconto was elected Republican governor in 1896. He was elected on a platform that, among other things, criticized the common practice of public officials accepting passes and franks from railroads and express companies. Schofield was against this plank, and upon moving into the governor's mansion, had the railroad ship the Jersey on down to Madison along with a sewing machine and other boxes and barrels, free of charge. The "one cow (crated)", as it was listed on the shipment, proved to be political dynamite. A faction in Schofield's party protested loudly. Photos of Schofield's Jersey appeared everywhere. Schofield barely won renomination over Robert M. La Follette, Sr. in 1898, and in 1899 Schofield asked the legislature to draw up an anti-pass statute.

The memory of that Jersey's free ride, however, was deeply etched. La Follette was elected governor of Wis-

In 1899, using a process patented by Swiss inventor John Meyenberg, Carnation Company founder E. A. Stuart began manufacturing evaporated milk in an abandoned hotel at Kent, Washington. This cartoon from the 1920's spoofed the firm's motto, "The Milk from Contented Cows," by showing the discovery of a discontented cow.

consin in 1900 and the protesting GOP faction he'd organized evolved into the Progressive Party, a part of the state and national political scene well into the twentieth century.

May Echo Sylvia & Son

E. A. Stuart, the founding father of the Carnation Company, thought that May Echo Sylvia was "the greatest Holstein living." Indeed, by 1918 the cow had achieved world-wide fame as the only cow ever known to have produced 152.1 pounds of milk in one day, 1,005.8 in seven days and 12,899 in one hundred days. A former University of Wisconsin dairy professor, A. C. (Oostie) Oosterhuis, had his doubts about this astonishing feat and said "No cow can carry 152 pounds of milk between two legs day after day and keep up." But the young Canadian fellow who milked her said her udders hung so low to the ground she had to be milked with a dishpan instead of a pail.

Some months earlier the parsimonious Stuart had passed up a chance to buy a particular six-month-old bull calf of May Echo Sylvia's for $35,000. By June 8, 1918, Stuart was prepared to bid as much as $25,000 for him at auction, and opened the bidding with an offer of $10,000. However the price on the baby bull grew by leaps and bounds until it reached $75,000, at which point two of the five bidders dropped out and left only E. A. and an agent for the president of the Morton Salt Company who balked when E. A. made an offer of $101,000. E. A. then upped the ante $5,000 to $106,000 and the calf was his. It was the most money spent on a calf, ever.

Sadly, the $106,000 bull failed to live up to the expectations of Carnation, and he died at the age of three. The actual star of the Carnation Stock Farms turned out to be King Segis Tenth. His blood still flows through the veins of some of the greatest (and most contented) milk cows on earth. He cost $5.

Amazing Circus Cows

There were a lot of circuses born in the state of Wisconsin, but none was more unusual than an early Wisconsin truck show originated by John M. Kelley in the early 1920's.

Actually, the Fun on the Farm Circus wasn't really a circus at all, it just looked like one. Kelley, and Johnny Agee, who had been a horse trainer for Ringling Brothers, had talked a group of country bankers into advancing them $25,000 to put together a show to promote Wisconsin's dairy and beef interests. The circus, which played before grandstands at county fairs, was also designed as a vehicle to get farmers riled up enough to hold out for bet-

John M. Kelley, dairyman and former attorney for Wisconsin's Ringling brothers, operated a circus of his own in the 1920's. The Fun on the Farm Circus—featuring acrobatics on the back of a bull—promoted dairy interests. State Historical Society of Wisconsin photo.

ter money for their cattle. At some point during the performance, Kelley, who owned a cattle farm north of Baraboo, would step into the ring and provoke farmers by telling them city slickers were taking advantage of them and explaining why it was important for them to band together and demand higher prices for their products.

The Fun on the Farm Circus featured such unconventional attractions as horses that leaped into and out of silos, and bulls that were trained to do everything from playing possum to swaying on swings. The sensation of the show was Kelley's emerald green bull with golden horns.

Kelley told farmers, many of whom traveled great distances to see the bull, that the animal had been born two years earlier in a remote part of Ireland. So far as he knew, Kelley lectured, both the mother and father of the green bovine were normal, contented cattle who never attracted any attention in the pasture. However, the mother of the bull had been feeding on shamrocks for some time before parturition because of a shortage of hay on the Emerald Isle. "When the owners of the mother went to the stable and saw the new calf," Kelley insisted, "they were astounded to find that it was of green color. The prenatal influence, it seems, was manifested in the pigmentation of the calf."

Kelley said that he'd arranged to have it shipped to America, along with several tons of baled shamrocks. "So long as they feed the animal the shamrocks, there has been no indication that the color will fade or change," Kelley reported.

Kelley's Fun on the Farm Circus was disbanded after the 1924 season. But forty years later the Wisconsin delegation of the American Dairy Association voted unanimously to have a plaque inscribed in Kelley's memory, honoring him as founder of Wisconsin's first milk and beef cow promotion program.

Bootlegging Bovine

During the days of Prohibition, residents of Waupaca County, Wisconsin, frequently observed a particular Holstein cow riding around in the back of a cattle truck. Down rural sideroads and along village streets, wherever the truck wandered, the Holstein placidly gazed at the landscape and watched the miles go by. No one, it seems, questioned the cow's vagaries.

But the cow was the property of a certain stock buyer in the county, who also had another business: he was a traveling salesman . . . of bootleg whiskey. The cattle truck had a false bottom, and the Holstein was hauled around on top of the hooch as the dealer made deliveries to his thirsty customers.

Elm Farm Ollie

Elm Farm Ollie was the first flying cow; the first cow to be flown in an airplane, that is. The event took place on February 18, 1930, and Ollie was accompanied by a group of reporters who duly recorded the details of the unique occasion. During the flight, she was fed and milked, and her milk was sealed in paper containers that were then parachuted over the city of St. Louis, Missouri.

Intrepid Ollie was a 1,000 pound Guernsey, and the flight was part of the celebration of the St. Louis International Air Exposition. Because of her historic feat she made the front page of the *St. Louis Times* where she was referred to as "The first air queen." The newspaper said the flight was meant "to blaze a trail for the transportation of live stock by air," and to gather scientific data "by observations of her behavior and tests."

Another account of the ascent of this lofty bovine is contained in the *St. Louis Globe-Democrat*, February 19, 1930, where it was reported that the cow "journeyed here by way of trimotored airship from her pasture at Bismarck, Mo, a point seventy-two miles distant." There was a last-minute change in plans regarding the flight's grand finale, however. According to the paper, "Originally it had been intended to land the large ship at the Forest Park field; however the plan was abandoned in face of the fact that many spectators dotted the area," presumably to catch the milk that was raining down upon them.

The anniversary of Elm Farm Ollie's dairy-aeronautical achievement is celebrated each year by the official Elm Farm Ollie Fan Club, located in Madison, Wisconsin.

Enola Gay

This Iowa cow belonged to Mrs. Tibbets. Her son, Paul W., piloted the Boeing B-29 that dropped the atomic bomb on Hiroshima, Japan, at 9:15 a.m. on August 6, 1945. Ironically, Paul Tibbets named his airplane for his mother's gentle bovine. The bomb wiped out the entire Japanese Second Army and razed four square miles of the city, killing more than 60,000 people.

Julieann, the Free Spirit

In March of 1983, Julieann, a pregnant, 700-pound Brahman heifer, decided she was homesick. She'd been sold by Sidney Kraftsow to Read Hayes, a rancher who lived 35 miles away from her former home near Geneva, Florida. But Julieann, who had a reputation for her freedom-loving ways, was experienced in jumping five-foot cattle guards

Watcher's Digest

J osie the Cow retired from the Wisconsin State Fair in 1985. She was the cow with a hole in one of her stomachs. Actually, the hole was a window, and she would stand at the State Fair placidly eating and chewing her cud, while thousands of fairgoers could watch the process of digestion take place inside. Usually a veterinarian stood nearby to explain cow nutrition and cow anatomy to the cityfolk.

and had often wandered in and out of her own rural community, eating oranges and grapefruit as she browsed through the citrus groves.

During the night, Julieann leaped over a pair of four-foot barbed wire fences surrounding Hayes' pasture and hit the road. In her cross-country tramp she forded the Econlockhatchee River and several small creeks, crossed highways, and ignored the driving rain. Twenty hours later she was home.

Her old pal Sidney, said "I've heard of dogs and cats doing that, but a cow? Never. All the cattle people around here are flabbergasted."

Sidney's wife confessed that they'd considered selling Julieann for hamburger because of her wandering habits but decided against it because she was a purebred and was carrying a calf.

Later that week Julieann went back to her new home in Orange County, to a pen with higher fences. Once she had her calf, it was felt, she'd settle down to more matronly behavior. But it's hard to keep 'em down on the farm, after they've seen . . . etc, etc.

Chatty Belle, the World's Largest Talking Cow

Located in Neillsville, Wisconsin, "Chatty Belle" stands near *The Largest Cheese in the History of Mankind.*" If you push a button, Chatty Belle will tell you about Wisconsin dairy products. The 17-ton World's Largest Cheese is a cheddar, made for the Wisconsin Pavilion of the New York World's Fair in 1965, and is displayed in a semitrailer with one glass side. The cheese has grown somewhat old by now and was recently described by a visitor as looking like "a block of compressed burlap."

The Giant Holstein of North Dakota

In the October 1983 issue of *Outside* magazine, writer Tim Cahill described his encounter with this bovine behemoth:

"Recently, I drove through North Dakota on the way to Wisconsin to visit my parents. I hadn't been in the state for more than ten years and was delighted to discover that there is now a genuine tourist attraction along I-94. Just outside the National Grasslands, I was amazed to see, in the distance, a huge cow standing on a ridge. This cow was at least five miles away, and it dwarfed all the other cows that were standing around in little groups talking about the best way to get out of North Dakota.

"At 80 miles an hour, which is the only way to drive through North Dakota, you stare at that big cow for quite some time before you get to the sign saying that you have been looking at

Nostalgia

M OO, a National Milk Bottle Collectors Club is located at Box 5456, Newport News, Virginia 23605. The club has members all over the United States, and provides a monthly newsletter.

the world's largest Holstein cow. There is a turnoff and an arrow. You can drive right up to the world's largest Holstein cow. My guess, having missed the turnoff, is that the cow was fashioned from ferro-concrete. Clustered about its hoofs were a cafe, a gas station, and perhaps a motel. All else was utter desolation.

"I doubt if the businesses under the cow prosper. By the time you get to the sign showing you where to turn off to see the world's largest Holstein cow, you've pretty much already seen it."

Jessica and the Lovesick Moose

For about three months during the winter of 1986-87, Jessica, a Hereford cow, was courted by an ardent Shrewsbury, Vermont, moose who was searching for a meaningful relationship. The odd couple never actually coupled, and Jessica was unmooved. Eventually (as is wont to happen even in the best moose circles), the moose's antlers fell off and he, as a consequence, lost his libido and went back to the woods. Jessica seemed unconcerned, although the ill-fated affair had brought her cold-hearted snub of her unlikely suitor to worldwide attention.

Famous Cows in Advertising

Alka-Seltzer Cows.   In autumn of 1984 the Alka-Seltzer people were looking for a new way to promote their product. Realizing that dairy farming in the 1980s was certainly a source for a lot of headaches, the people from the New York advertising agency of Wells, Rich, Green, went to America's Dairyland and hired a student from the University of Wisconsin-LaCrosse to drive them around southwestern Wisconsin in search of credibility.

At least fifty dairy farmers were interviewed before the ad folks decided on Wayne Selbrede, of rural Sparta. The commercial was shot in the milking parlor of the barn, and in the barnyard, with a crew of fifty and their own electrical generators to provide the necessary lighting. Selbrede was paid actor's scale—$360 per day.

Appropriately enough, the young farmer says he was sick as a dog when the Alka-Seltzer Plus (a cold remedy) crew showed up for the shoot. So he reached for some of the actual product right in his own medicine cabinet. "The director said it was the first time he actually saw an actor—or whatever you want to call me—actually use the product," Selbrede reported.

Elsie the Cow.   Elsie was born in the 1930's. She began life as a cartoon character in medical journal ads. She was initially known as "Flossie the Cow," and then "Bessie the Cow." The Borden Company tried everything before ending up with "Elsie." At the 1939 New York World's Fair, the first live Elsie—a docile Jersey named "You'll Do's Lobelia," from Elm Hill Farm in Brookfield, Massachusetts—made an appearance. She was subsequently killed in a truck accident, but since then succeeding Elsies have traveled over 500,000 miles throughout the United States and eastern Canada, starred in a movie, ("Little Men," 1940—see *Cows in Hollywood*), appeared in wartime bond sales, at charity events, on television, at countless state and county fairs, and at hundreds of civic and public celebrations. Elsie was awarded a college degree (Doctor of Bovinity), and welcomed into an Indian tribe. She has modeled hats made especially for her by famous designers. She has been seen by more than 250,000,000 people, and her image is recognized by people in 107 countries of the world. During World War II she was a pin-up girl, and her picture appeared on planes named for her. She once appeared on network television as a "mystery guest" on "What's My Line." In 1971 she opened up the Ice Cream Parlor in Walt Disney World's "Magic Kingdom." She was guest of honor in the 1972 Rose Bowl Parade and rode on her own float, "Please Don't Eat the Daisies," sponsored by the community of Montebello.

In 1947, Elsie took on Beulah, a new family member; and shortly thereafter Beauregard was born. A contest to name the baby brought a million entries.

At Elsie's tenth birthday party (held at New York's Roosevelt Hotel), Jack Benny gave her a pocketbook with a pricetag reading 39¢; Lana Turner gave her bath salts; Ray Milland sent a jar of pickled beets; Frank Sinatra presented her with a barrel of molasses; and Bette Davis sent a telegram addressed to the "First Lady of Cowdom." Guy Lombardo said she was the "sweetest cow this side of Heaven."

Whenever Elsie tours a community, her first visits are to children's hospitals in the area. She brings ice cream and other party goodies. In many instances, she is the only cow the children have an opportunity to see and touch.

Easter. Ladies and gentlemen, meet Easter, Wisconsin's newest celebrity, the black-and-white star on your color TV hawking America's Dairyland for the Division of Tourism.

Her ads have given her status in her hometown of Delavan, where Easter has replaced the alligator on tourist shirts as Walworth County's most recognizable animal.

For all her celebrity status, though, Easter has been an enigma, as reclusive as Cagney, mysterious as Garbo, silent as Coolidge.

Until today, that is. In an exclusive interview with this column, Easter has

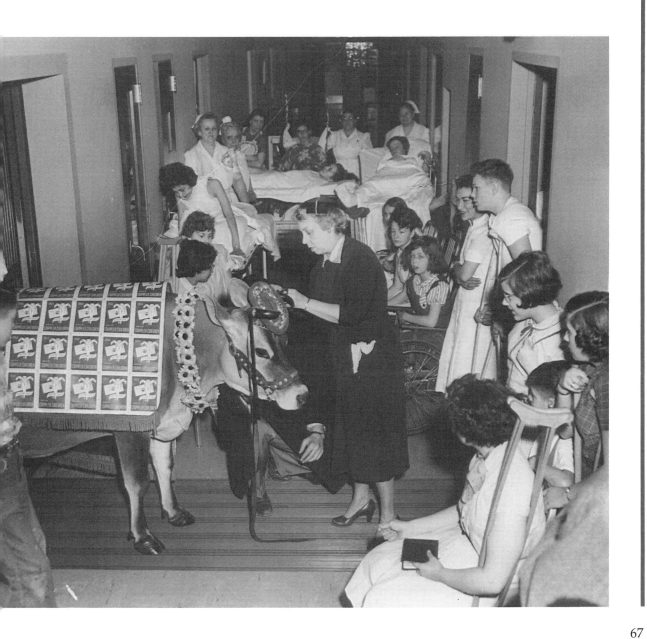

Elsie, the Borden company's mascot, visited the Children's Home and Hospital in Utica, New York, during an Easter Seal campaign in 1954. The gentle Jersey models a chapeau presented by Ruth Cole, head of the Boston Store's millinery department. State Historical Society of Wisconsin photo.

Ralston Purina Company—whose "Chex" brand cereals are popular as snacks—gave consumers a humorous reminder that "Chex" cereals are good for breakfast, too. The firm's recent advertising campaign features cows marching into an unemployment office and interviewing for jobs. "Don't put a cow out of work," the ads plead. "Eat 'Chex' with milk." Photo courtesy Ralston Purina Company.

revealed a little of the bovine behind the sunglasses, the shady side, as it were, of a small-town cow gone Hollywood, a cow even her owner says has stars in her eyes.

"To a point, yes," said Art Dibble. "She got out the other day and I thought she was quite arrogant."

Indeed, in our interview, Easter sounded more like the cow who jumped over the moon than your everyday milker.

"It's because I'm a star," she said pointedly. "Did you think I was born in a barn?"

"Well, er, let's talk about something else, if we could. Your full name is Dibble Citamatt Easter but you've decided to use just your last name professionally. Can you tell us why?"

She rolled her big eyes.

"Have you ever heard of an actress named Dibble? Come on, they'd laugh me out of Beverly Hills. My agent said if it was good enough for Cher and Madonna, it was good enough for me."

"How did you get your start in show business, anyway?"

"It was easy. They wanted a cow to add cheesecake to the tourism campaign and they wanted the best. I am the cream of the crop."

"Did your parents groom you for this, like Brooke Shields' mom, maybe?"

"Parents, who needs them," she snorted. "My mother was bossy and my father was a bully. They didn't know anything about show business. But I don't want to talk about that now," she said as she tossed her head away. "You can read that in my book."

"You're writing a book?"

"Sure, a tail-all book like that Joan Crawford story. I'm going to call it 'Moomy Dearest' and it'll blow the lid off the barn. It'll make a great screenplay."

"A screenplay? You mean you're going from commercials to movies already?"

"Moovies, if you please. I think I'm ready to step up. If Farmer Brown out there would just let me go, I'd be in Tinsel Town tonight. I tell you, I've got what it takes. I've got nice hips, calves that won't quit. . . ."

"You'd leave your kids for show business?"

"No, no. Calves, you nincompoop. Gams, drumsticks, pins. Mr. Ed never had legs like these, and he had his own show."

—Dennis McCann
The Milwaukee Journal
May 20, 1985

La Vache Qui Rit; The Laughing Cow. This cow is a trademark of the cheese manufacturer Fromageries Bel, Inc.,

A red cow enjoying a hearty laugh has been the trademark of the French cheese manufacturer Fromageries Bel since the 1920's. The cow's earings are miniature cheese containers.

The farmer's best friend. Minnesota State Fair photo.

with U. S. offices at Leitchfield, Kentucky 42754. The jubilant bovine has been advertising cheese and chuckling ever since 1920, although the initial artist's rendering was far from satisfactory, according to company spokesmen, because the cow looked too happy.

They called it a "vache hilare," or hilarious cow. Company officials asked several illustrators to present them with a "vache qui rit" (laughing cow) which, while having a laughing expression, became no less a cow. Reported the officials, "We examined many drawings representing a veritable beast of the Apocalypse. In contrast, Benjamin Rabier sent us an illustration which corresponded with our viewpoint. This drawing remained in our office on the rue des Quarts for more than a year before the decision was made to use it."

With the success of La Vache Qui Rit came a herd of imitators with similar names, including La Vache Qui Lit (The Reading Cow), La Vache Qui Frise (The Grazing Cow) and La Vache Qui Fume (The Smoking Cow).

La Vache Qui Rit was an advertising innovation in 1920. Prior to this time the name on the cheese label was usually just the name of the manufacturer.

Although the symbol has been somewhat modernized over the years it still retains the three original elements: a red cow; the use of a human expression—the laugh; and human attributes, usually feminine—earrings.

Stew Leonard's—World's Largest Dairy Store

It's in Norwalk, Connecticut, and covers 10 acres. But it didn't start out that way—actually, when he was a little boy, Stew Leonard's aspiration was to become a milkman. "My family was in the dairy business—that's what I knew best and it's all I wanted." Now he sells 10 million quarts of milk a year, a million pints of cream, 500,000 pounds of butter, a million cartons of yogurt and 100 tons of cottage cheese. One hundred thousand customers shop at his milk plant/grocery store every week.

The store opened in 1969, shortly after the state of Connecticut condemned Leonard's farm for a highway. "Milk was all I knew," he says. "So I went around my milk route and asked customers what they thought." They told him to open a retail dairy store with low prices. Now his original store has been expanded 22 times. His shopping bags have become a status symbol, known not only in Connecticut but all over the world.

The veterinarian paid a call in this engraving from the June 1875 edition of *The American Agriculturist*. State Historical Society of Wisconsin photo.

THE COW-DOCTOR. — *Drawn and Engraved for the American Agriculturist.*

Milking History

While the date and manner of the domestication of cattle is an enigma, the precise nature of their wild progenitors is an even greater mystery. The most plausible theory suggests that a hunter may have brought home to his cave or his encampment the young of the species he slew.

In his book *Make Mine Milk*, Fred Rawlinson reminds us that Bible writers mention milk 44 times in the Old Testament and that Sanskrit writings 6,000 years old refer to milk as one of the most essential foods.

According to Rawlinson, the oldest record picturing a milking scene is in the form of a stone panel four feet long showing cows and their calves, with men milking into tall jars. This pane was found in the ruins of a temple in Ur, near Babylon, variously estimated to be from 5,000 to more than 6,000 years old.

Egyptian civilization dating from about 4000 B.C. left records of three kinds of cattle—longhorned, hornless and humped (Zebu)—and gave information on dairy products at that time. The Vedic hymns of India, dating from about 2000–3000 B.C., indicate the use of milk and butter, Rawlinson adds.

Greek records going back to about 1550 B.C. and Roman records to about 750 B.C. show that milk, butter and cheese were all important items in the diet of the people, he says. Greek writers even described the composition of milk.

The people of Rome used dairy products and cheese became an important article of commerce. From Rome a knowledge of the use of milk and its products spread over Europe. Milk cows were found all over Europe from the beginning of the Christian era. So important was the cow to these early peoples that barter transactions and wealth were measured in terms of cattle. Coins were stamped with a cow or an ox. The Roman word for money was "pecunia," from pecus, cattle.

Rawlinson reports that during the Dark Ages the art of cheese-making was best known and largely developed in monasteries. The monks for several centuries were the leaders in carrying on the business and in teaching it to others. By the year 1000 A.D., cheese had become an important article of

A Roman coin and a Persian procession, reproduced from *The Complete Encyclopedia of Illustration*, which was originally published in 1851 under the title *Iconographic Encyclopaedia of Science, Literature, and Art*.

trade in the cities of Europe, and by the fifteenth century some important cheese markets were in existence in Switzerland.

In the Colonial days in America, he says, the cow was seldom expected to give milk in winter time. She calved in the spring, milked fairly well on grass, dried up in the fall, and sometimes died of starvation in the winter. Children's health suffered for lack of milk. Utensils and methods were crude and the products inferior. Dairying was strictly a home or domestic activity.

These conditions changed slowly up to 1850. Since that date more progress has been made in the dairy industry than had been made from the dawn of history up to that time.

The Chronology

9000 B.C.   First records kept regarding the milking of cattle.

6000 B.C. The domestication of cattle was first documented when the ancestors of the Lake Dwellers of Switzerland migrated from Asia, taking their cattle with them.

4000 B.C. Egyptian civilization made note of three kinds of cattle: long-horned, hornless and humped (Zebu), and the dairy products at that time.

4000 B.C. Cheese was being made in Switzerland.

1000 A.D. Cheese had become an important article of trade in the cities of Europe.

1322 Arabs bred horses with a primitive kind of artificial insemination.

1611 Cows arrived at Jamestown, Virginia in May.

1624 Cows reached the Plymouth Colony, imported in March from Devon, England by Edward Winslow, governor. By 1632 "no farmer was satisfied to do without a cow; and there was in New England not only a domestic, but an export, demand from the West Indies, which led to breeding for sale. But the market was soon overstocked, and the price of cattle went down from fifteen pounds and twenty pounds to five pounds; and milk was a penny a quart."

1630 The Massachusetts Bay Colony received its first shipment of cattle.

1647 Cattle arrived at the Delaware Colony.

1707 Cattle were brought to Detroit and soon thereafter appeared at most of the French outposts from Sault Ste. Marie and Mackinac to Vincennes and Kaskaskia. These were small black and brilled cattle, known as French Canadians, and accompanied the *voyageurs* as they moved across the country.

1760 Robert Bakewell of England expressed an interest in the improvement of the quality of cattle through selective breeding, liberal feeding and general good management. The Collings brothers began improving the Shorthorn breed around 1780; the movement begun by these men spread over Great Britain and influenced the whole world.

1780 First experiments with artificial insemination by Italian scientist Spallanzani.

1783 Early Wisconsin travelers, Peter Pond and Robert Dickson, referred to cattle being brought in from the Illinois country, where they had been taken in the early part of the century as part of the missionaries' efforts to interest the "savages" in the civilizing pursuit of animal husbandry.

1810 Nicholas Appert first successfully preserved milk by sterilizing it in sealed bottles.

1813 Edward Howard invented the vacuum pan in England, a principal development in the eventual success of

THE AYRSHIRE COW.

The Wisconsin Farmer and Northwestern Cultivator published its first issue in January of 1849. One of the articles extolled the virtues of dairying in New York and asked, "Shall we not have dairy farms in Wisconsin?" Another reported on the qualities of the Ayrshire cow— "hardiness, a sound constitution, and a moderate degree of life and spirits."

canned milk, although no commercially significant quantities were initially produced.

1831 The first Guernsey cattle were imported, one bull and two heifers. They were shipped to Boston and taken to the farm of General Moody Adams Pillsbury at Guernsey Island, Lake Winnepesaukee, N. H.

1834 Purebred shorthorns were imported by the Ohio Company; seven bulls and twelve cows arrived at the farm of Felix Renick in Chillicothe, Ohio, in June. In October of that year the first public auction sale of cattle took place on Renick's farm and 43 head sold for $34,540, an average of $803.25 apiece.

1837 Charles Rockwell began making cheese at Koshkonong, near Fort Atkinson, Wisconsin.

1838 Morgan L. Martin, a prominent

Green Bay politician and promoter, introduced the first full-blood Durham shorthorn bull.

1840 The first "tin canisters" began to appear; fish, vegetables and meats were experimentally canned and the tin "canister" became known as the "tin can."

1841 First shipment of milk by train by Thaddeus Shelleck, from Orange County to New York City.

1848 U. S. patent granted on an ice cream freezer.

1850 New York produced more than a quarter of the nation's butter and almost half the cheese supply. New York's place in the dairy business was being recognized in farm journals and agricultural meetings. The product of a good cow in a single season was estimated "at more than thirty dollars," but in small dairies of ten to twelve cows the livestock was worth around $15 to $20 per cow.

1851 First commercial cheese factory opened by Jesse Williams in Rome, New York.

1851 Mechanical refrigeration patented by John Gorrie.

1854 F. S. Eldred, Esquire, read an essay on dairy cows before the Rock County Agricultural Society and Mechanics' Institute on March 6, 1854, in which he reported:

Among our native cows are many superior milkers, and many individual cases have been found which were equal in yield of milk and butter, to any registered in the herd books. For instance, the Cream-pot breed, built up by Col. Jacques, of Charlestown, Mass., whose calves were be-spoken at $100 each. The celebrated Oaks cow, of Danvers, that gave, on evidence satisfactory to the Massachusetts Agricultural Society, 484 lbs. of butter from the 5th of April to the 25th of September. And the wonderful prize cow, Kaatskill, property of Mr. Danielson, of Blithwood, N. Y., which received the prize of the New York State Agricultural Society, at Poughkeepsie, in 1854, on satisfactory evidence that she yielded, when kept on grass only, 38½ qts. of milk per day; and that from the milk given by her in two days, 6 1/2 lbs. of butter were made—being at the rate of 22¾ lbs. per week. When such cases turn up, almost by chance, why may not a breed of superior milkers be established, and confidently relied upon, as it is known that like produces like?

1856 Condensed milk patented by *Gail Borden*, in both U.S. and England. Borden was returning home from the Great Council Exhibition in London in the fall of 1851, the sailing ship was slow, the voyage was rough, and the cows in the hold became so seasick that they could not be milked—with the result that the cries of the immigrant babies on board were very upsetting to him. Borden spoke to the ship's captain who laughed in his face. Other passengers were unconcerned. Borden decided that he would find a way to preserve milk in such a fashion that it would maintain its normal purity and freshness for weeks or longer, while at the same time it would lose none of its life-sustaining qualities.

Borden struggled with this problem for years. The addition of sugar finally enabled him to can the product—he could not overcome the problem of canning the unsweetened variety. However, the sweetened canned milk was quickly commandeered by the Union Army in 1861 and its future success was assured. The word of "Borden's Milk" spread across the country as returning soldiers and sailors described the pleasure and nourishment it had brought to the sick and wounded when no other safe milk was available.

1857 A French scientist, *Louis Pasteur* announced that he'd discovered that milk will not sour as quickly if it has been heated. In Great Britain it was commonly said that "Typhoid follows the milk-man." When proper care was taken in the disposal of sewage, and water systems were safeguarded, a great advance was made in the protection of public health. But almost no attention was given to the sanitary production of milk.

Pasteurization, the process of heating a foodstuff, usually a liquid, for a definite time at a definite temperature and thereafter cooling it immediately, had been noted by Pasteur when he'd heated beer or wine for a few moments at a temperature between 50 and 60 degrees Centigrade (122 and 140 degrees Fahrenheit) and had witnessed no subsequent abnormal fermentation and souring.

In France, Nicolas Appert, the founder of the modern canning industry, discovered in 1810 that he could preserve milk and cream, besides other foods, by the application of heat to the food in a closed container. He sterilized milk in sealed, glass containers with such success that the product was used by the French navy.

1857 Refrigerated freight cars were developed, making broader distribution of dairy products possible.

1857 The first successful condensary was built by Gail Borden at Burrville, Connecticut.

1859 More than 3,500,000 pounds of butter were made on Wisconsin farms by Wisconsin farmwives, and 400,000 pounds of cheese were manufactured.

1859 First creamery established in the United States.

1865 The first Cattle Importation Law was passed on December 18, "to prevent the spread of foreign diseases among the cattle of the United States."

William D. Hoard, founder of *Hoard's Dairyman* and a Wisconsin governor, addressed a turn-of-the-century G.A.R. meeting in this postcard view reproduced courtesy of Hoard Historical Museum. The following notice was posted in his barn: "Remember that this is the Home of Mothers. Treat each cow as a Mother should be treated."

This act was first applied on July 31, 1875, when meat, cattle and hides from Spain were excluded because of foot-and-mouth disease in that country.

1867 Wisconsin's dairy cow population reached 245,000. It would grow to 1,500,000 by 1912.

1868 The first export of cattle to Great Britain, by Nelson Morris who shipped a few cattle from Chicago to London and Glasgow.

1871 *W. D. Hoard* founded the first dairymen's association in Jefferson County, Wisconsin. One year later, he led the "seven wise men" (Stephen Faville, A. D. Faville, H. C. Drake, W. S. Greene, H. C. Dousman and Chester Hazen) in founding the Wisconsin Dairymen's Association.

William Dempster Hoard, known as the Father of American Dairying, was born in Madison County, New York, on October 10, 1836. He moved to Wisconsin in 1857, where he lived and worked on a cousin's farm.

He began a weekly newspaper, *The Jefferson County Union* and attempted to inspire his rural audience to the virtues of their calling by noting that the gentle cow had been worshipped by the ancient Hindu. After he'd made a hit with the farmers he moved on to politics.

Hoard was the "cow candidate" for governor of Wisconsin in 1888 on the Republican ticket. Despite the fact that cowbells were rung before he spoke at rallies, he won the election by 20,000 votes. He was a strong supporter of the dairy industry and urged the state legislature to organize the Dairy and Food Commission to ensure that Wisconsin butter and cheese were top-grade. He was also a champion of the "Bennett Law," which required that English be taught in public and private schools. This cause led to his overwhelming defeat in a reelection bid, but Hoard returned to the newspaper business and began *Hoard's Dairyman*, to promote Wisconsin's dairy industry. The magazine celebrated its 100th year of publication in 1985 and is currently read in every state of the U.S. and over 80 foreign countries.

1871 Production of factory-made butter was begun.

1871 The major board of trade for the dairy industry was established in Little Falls, New York.

1873 Four Aberdeen-Angus bulls were imported from Scotland by George Grant of Victoria, Kansas, and crossed with native longhorn Texas cattle.

1874 The Ice Cream Soda was created by Robert M. Green for the semi-centennial celebration of the Franklin Institute in Philadelphia.

1878 *Dr. Carl De Laval* invented the first continuous discharge centrifugal cream separator, which was superior to

Double Diptych   10/12   May '77   Colleen Michel

"Double Diptych," an original collagraph by Colleen Michel, celebrates Wisconsin's dairy confections. The ice cream sundae was originated by Ed Berners in Two Rivers, although the name "sundae" was coined by George Giffy of nearby Manitowoc. William Horlick, of Racine, supplied the Amundsen, Peary, Byrd, and Scott polar expeditions with his invention—malted milk. The ice cream cone itself was introduced at the St. Louis World's Fair in 1904.

any other method of skimming, for it saved labor, made possible the separation of milk while still fresh, separated the butterfat more thoroughly, and required less space. The first De Laval Separator had a separating capacity of 300 lbs. of milk per hour.

Among his other dairy inventions were the lactocrite, for testing the percentage of butterfat in milk, which led to the development by Dr. Stephen Babcock of the simpler butterfat test that did so much for dairying; the centrifugal churn for continuously churning the cream as delivered from the separator; and the centrifugal emulsor.

In 1894 he took out his first patent on a mechanical cow milker and continued to work on such a machine at various later periods.

Milk Snakes?

An old yellowed clipping, probably from Hoard's Dairyman, answers the age-old question, DO SNAKES SUCK COWS?

"In reply to a query as to whether or not snakes suck cows, letters have come from five states saying that they do. At the same time, the July issue of 'North Dakota Outdoors' carries an article on snakes that says: 'The milk snake has the reputation of stealing milk from cows. Of course this is not true. Any person who has milked cows knows the pressure or suction required to obtain milk.'"

Yet Olga Knapp, of Clintonville, Wisconsin, says "We pastured the cows in our woodland pasture and one time I went to bring the cows home but I could not find them. Finally I heard one cow mooing as if she'd had a calf but I knew she was not due to calve yet. Emery had been wondering if a cow had been sucking her as it was apparent she had been milked, but instead I saw a big Pine Snake coiled around her, sucking her. I called to the dog who was off a ways, and then the snake let go of the cow's teat and came toward me. I'll admit I was scared stiff.

1880 First commercial pasteurizer employed in Germany.

1880 The average yearly milk production per cow was 2,003 lbs. The Franklin Co. Creamery, St. Albans, Vermont, was built, and developed into the first centralized butter-making plant.

The Brown Swiss Breeders Association was organized.

1881 The Ice Cream Sundae was created in Two Rivers, Wisconsin, by Ed C. Berners, who operated an ice cream shop at 1404 Fifteenth Street.

A customer, George Hallauer, asked Mr. Berner to put some chocolate sauce on his ice cream. Prior to this golden moment in time, chocolate sauce had been used only in ice cream sodas. But Berners complied and the resulting concoction cost 5 cents. It was served only on Sunday.

1883 *William Horlick* of Racine, Wisconsin, perfected the method of making malted milk from milk, malted barley and wheat flour. Malted milk was the first dry milk product to be commercially produced in the United States. It was invented by Horlick at the request of physicians who desired a baby food prepared from milk and cereals, and it appeared on the market in 1887. Today all of the malted milk in the United States is made in Wisconsin.

1883 Cream cheese was first made.

1884 Invention of the glass milk bottle by *Hervey D. Thatcher* in Potsdam, New York.

Prior to this time, milk had been kept in jars, pails, and pottery containers. Early dairymen kept milk cool and fresh by suspending the milk in some type of container in the cold, clear water of a springhouse, in a spring, or in a cool cellar.

The first actual "milk" bottle may have been a Swiss bottle dated 1866. This bottle was very roughly engraved with a picture of a cow wearing a huge bell suspended from a chain.

Round, quart, wide-mouth jars with a heavy wire clip to hold a glass top on the jar (made by or for A.V. Whiteman of New York) are thought to have been introduced to the market in about 1880.

Dr. Hervey D. Thatcher, Potsdam, N.Y., is considered the "father of the milk bottle," because of his patent of 1884. Dr. Thatcher's first milk bottle weighed 40 ounces. An early Thatcher manufactured bottle, the 24-sided Borden bottle, made in 1889 was a tin closure held by a wire snap and weighed 28 ounces. The round bottle with the short neck of 1914 had a disc cap and weighed 28 ounces. In 1925 the round bottle had a long neck (disc cap) to show a better cream line. The first milk bottle with Pyroglaze or colored lettering, was made in 1931.

1884 The square box churn was patented by David Curtis, Fort Atkinson, Wisconsin, and was an improvement over the dash churn. The De Laval Company introduced the centrifugal emulsor, which was the first device for reconstructing milk or cream from the component parts of milk.

1885   Steam turbine separator invented by Dr. De Laval. The rapidly increasing importance of the dairy industry was recognized by the Federal Government by the creation of the Dairy Division of the Bureau of Animal Industry of the U.S. Department of Agriculture.

At this time skimming stations were being established in communities which did not produce enough milk to support a creamery. Farmers brought their milk to the station, where it was separated by a factory-size centrifugal separator. The oil test churn proved a means of paying each producer according to the richness in butterfat of his milk or cream. A certain amount of milk or cream from each patron was placed in a glass tube and agitated in a specially devised churn. Then the tube was placed in warm water to melt the butter, which would float as oil and could be measured by a graduated chart. This method was put into use at this time and extensively used until the Babcock test replaced it.

1885   The first evaporated milk factory began operating in Highland, Illinois.

1885   *Hoard's Dairyman*, a journal devoted to dairy farming, began publishing in 1885. It was founded and published as a supplement to the 15 year-old weekly, *The Jefferson County Union*, and was edited and published by W. D. Hoard.

1886   One of the first cooperative creameries was organized at Maynard, Iowa. The automatic bottle filler and capper was patented.

1890   *Dr. Stephen Moulton Babcock* of the University of Wisconsin devised his famous test which enabled the fat content of milk and cream to be determined quickly and in a simple manner.

This butterfat test permitted milk to be bought and sold on the basis of its butterfat content, thereby eliminating the possibility of water adulteration and the removal of cream prior to marketing. This soon provided the foundation for the rapid development of the cheese and milk-based industry throughout the United States.

1891   The first dairy school in the United States was organized at the University of Wisconsin. Classroom instruction in livestock judging was begun by John A. Craig, the first Professor of Animal Husbandry in the United States.

1891   *Hoard's Dairyman* published first article on alfalfa.

1892   The first cattle tuberculosis test was made on March 3 on a herd of

Swimming Cows

A herd of cows near Glens Falls, N.Y. was isolated from their usual pasture in 1915 when the state dug a canal across their owner's farm. The cows were not pleased, and work on the sixteen foot channel was barely completed when one grass-hungry cow waded in and "cowpaddled" across. Since then, except when the water was too cold, the entire herd has swum the canal twice daily.

cattle belonging to Dr. J. E. Gillingham, Claremont Farms, Villa Nova, Pennsylvania, with tuberculin brought from Europe by Dr. Leonard Pearson, Dean of the Veterinary Department of the University of Pennsylvania.

1893 Certified milk was developed. The rules concerning certified milk set a high standard for the dairy industry.

1893 The round barn was designed by Professor F. H. King of the Wisconsin Agricultural Experimental Station for a dairy farmer near Whitewater. The concept of the round barn came about with the realization that cows and horses are wedge shaped, requiring less space in front than at the rear. In round barns, the silo is usually constructed at the center, with the barn built around it. The University of Illinois promoted round barns in the early 1900's.

1893 M. F. Ivanov, a Russian scientist, successfully accomplished the first artificial insemination with cattle and sheep.

1894 The dairy industry recognized the need for a mechanical milker if the industry was to grow and be an economic success. Dr. De Laval's first patent on a milker, issued in 1894, had mechanically operated members that imitated the pressure of human hands.

1895 *Hoard's Dairyman* began a promotion of tuberculosis eradication, a bitter campaign which was to last 45 years. The struggle would cost the magazine thousands of subscriptions and lost revenue as it battled almost alone in the early years to free dairy herds from heavy health losses and to protect consumers from milk-borne tuberculosis.

1896 Patents were applied for in 1896 and issued in 1898 to Klein and Wright, employees of the De Laval Company, on a mechanical milker. This machine operated under constant vacuum with manipulation. It was not commercially practical. Casein was first used during this year for coating paper. A starter can for preparing butter culture was invented by Sam Haugdahl, a famous creamery buttermaker.

1899 Process of homogenization patented by August Gaulin.

1900 Official testing for purebred dairy cows in Advanced Registry and Register of Merit Classes was adopted by the breed associations as follows: Holstein, 1900; Guernsey, 1901; Ayrshire, 1902; Jersey, 1903; and Brown Swiss, 1911.

1901 A small quantity of dry or powdered milk was produced in this year, but not until the Merrell-Gere Spray Process was perfected in 1906 did the manufacture of powdered milk begin in a big way.

1903 Patents were applied for in 1903

and 1904 and experiments continued on a milker known as the "Ljunbgstrom" milker by the De Laval Company. This machine imitated hand milking by means of a teat press consisting of a stationary member and three movable members actuated by hydraulic pistons. Again, it was too complicated to be of practical value.

1904 The Ice Cream Cone was introduced at the St. Louis World's Fair, Louisiana Purchase Exposition. An ice cream vendor ran out of dishes and a Syrian vendor seized the moment to roll a "zalabia"—a sugar waffle—into a cone and come to his rescue. It was an instant success.

1905 The National Dairy Show was organized. The first show was held in Chicago, Illinois, in 1906.

1906 First cow testing association organized in Michigan. This movement was one of the most important ever begun for raising the level of productiveness and profit of dairy cows.

1906 The paper single-service milk container was patented.

1907 Patent applied for in 1907 and patents issued in 1910 on the "Dalen" milker. This machine imitated the action of human hands by means of teat presses consisting of a stationary and movable member, which was operated by pneumatic pressure.

1908 First bull association organized by the Michigan Agricultural College.

1908 The first compulsory pasteurization law went into effect in Chicago, applying to all milk except that from tuberculin tested cows.

1911 Perfection of the first rotary-type milk bottle filler.

1912 The U.S. government established different grades of milk.

1913 First transportation of milk by motor truck from processing plants to wholesalers in New York City. National Dairy Council organized.

1914 The California Central Creameries were among the first to transport milk in a tank mounted on a motor truck.

1915 First cooperative cheese factory organized in the Southern mountain section at Cove Creek, North Carolina.

1915 The National Dairy Council was founded.

1917 National Cooperative Milk Producers Federation organized.

1917 The federal government finally launched a program of tuberculosis eradication which led to the "cattle testing wars." Farmers fought condemnation of tubercular cattle and bootlegged them into untested areas.

1917 A Madison, Wisconsin, newspaper reported that oleo was a dime cheaper than butter at the stores. There was also something on the market called *troco*, made from coconut oil;

Number One

ALASKA *is the Number one ice-cream eating state; Alaskans consume about six gallons per person per year. The national average is four gallons, or fifteen quarts apiece, or about fifty three billion scoops . . . enough to serve everyone in the world twelve ice cream cones.*

Joining a midwestern movement protesting dismal milk prices, dairymen halted a Soo Line freight train near Burlington, Wisconsin, on January 10, 1934, and dumped the train's load of milk. Photo by *The Milwaukee Journal*, reproduced courtesy of the State Historical Society of Wisconsin.

and *nutolo*, manufactured from vegetable oils churned in milk. In 1950 Congress lifted the tax on oleomargarine, but in Wisconsin it was banned completely. When a Wisconsin housewife managed to purchase oleomargarine she bought a white lard-appearing product with a little capsule of yellow coloring, and she had to stir the product with a wooden spoon to break the capsule and distribute the artificial color.

During the 1960's State Senator Gordon Roseleip doomed the case for outlawing oleomargarine when he failed a blindfolded taste test at the State Capitol, choosing margarine over butter. In 1972 Wisconsin lifted its ban.

1918 The first De Laval Milker introduced as a result of patents, research and experiments by Stoddard, Leitch, Hulvbert, Hall, Daysh, Forsyth, Hapgood, Beckman and others. It embodied the best principles of mechanical milking discovered during 24 years of continuous research.

1919 Chocolate Milk was introduced. Homogenized milk was first sold successfully in Torrington, Connecticut.

1924 *Adda Howie* was the first woman to have her portrait hung in the Wisconsin Agricultural Hall of Fame.

Wisconsin citizens called Adda Howie ''our beloved farm woman,'' for her lifetime efforts at improving the care of dairy cattle. She began dairy farming with two cows in 1894. Each week her stables in Waukesha County were cleaned with soapsuds and boiling water; her barn windows had screens and curtains. Water was piped into her barn, milkers washed their hands and put on white uniforms and washed each time they moved to a different cow.

Adda Howie developed one of the largest and finest herds of purebred Jersey cattle in Wisconsin; they were displayed at state, national and international shows. She was the first woman to be appointed to the Wisconsin State Board of Agriculture.

1925 The stop-and-go horse driven milk wagons were replaced by stop-and-drive milk trucks.

1929 The De Laval Magnetic Milker was introduced. The same principal of controlled and uniform pulsations as used in previous De Laval Milkers was maintained in the Magnetic except that it was accomplished by magnetic force instead of a second vacuum pipe line.

1929 First paper container for milk was used.

1932 Milk with vitamin D added was commercially available to Detroit customers from the Borden Company.

1933 Fluid milk was included in army rations.

1933 On May 19, nearly 5,000 farmers held a demonstration on the grounds of the State Capitol in Madison, Wisconsin, as a part of a state-wide Milk Strike. Over 400 farmers had been arrested for strike violence throughout the state and many gallons of milk had been dumped to protest twelve years of falling farm prices. Violence had occurred throughout the Midwest.

1937 June Dairy Month was initiated.

1938 Farm bulk tanks for milk began to replace milk cans.

1940 The entire United States was declared free from tuberculosis in cattle, the successful culmination of a campaign begun by W. D. Hoard 45 years earlier.

1942 Every-other-day milk delivery was begun, initially as a war conservation measure.

1945 "Window pane cows," with permanent openings in their stomachs through which observations are made of bacteriological processes in the digestive tract were now commonplace in many of the agricultural experiment stations across the U.S.

1946 The vacuum pasteurization method was perfected.

1948 *Hoard's Dairyman* published the first article on the subject of artificial breeding of dairy cattle.

1948 Ultra-high temperature pasteurization was introduced.

1948 Plastic coated paper milk cartons were manufactured for commercial use.

1948 Wisconsin inaugurated the "Alice in Dairyland" program at the month-long Centennial Exposition in August. The following year "Alice" toured the United States representing Wisconsin's dairy industry. In 1949 the Wisconsin Department of Agriculture began sponsoring the "Alice" program, and in 1952 the woman yearly granted that title was made a full-time employee.

1949 A small group of leaders in the dairy industry organized the formation of America's Dairy Shrine in Fort Atkinson, Wisconsin, with the specific objective of acquiring and assembling pictures, histories, books and other records and mementoes of those who have made notable contributions to the development of outstanding breeding herds and the advancement of dairying.

1950 Milk vending machines were put in distribution.

1951 First cow/embryo transplant at University of Wisconsin.

1952 Bulk milk dispensers for restaurants and institutions introduced.

1955 Flavor control equipment for milk was introduced.

1964 Plastic milk containers were commercially available.

1968 Official acceptance of electronic testing for milkfat content.

1969 Dairy Research Inc. was created.

1971 United Dairy Industry Association formed.

1972 The ban on oleomargarine was lifted in Wisconsin.

1974 Nutrition labeling of fluid milk products was begun.

1976 First non-surgical embryo transplant perfected by Dr. Robert M. Rowe, Middleton, Wisconsin.

1981 UHT (ultra high temperature) milk gained national recognition.

1981 First cloning of cattle, sheep and horses performed in Cambridge, England.

1983 Milk Diversion Program legislation signed into law.

1984 National Dairy Promotion Board appointed.

1985 United States dairy farmers faced severe losses in light of the 1985 farm bill which proposed a dairy herd buy-out. Because of a surplus of dairy products, 14,000 farmers across the country were getting rid of 1.5 million cows. Branding each of his doomed cows with an "X" on her cheek caused pain for the cow and farmer alike.

1986 Research was progressing on the bovine growth hormone (BGH) which would improve the efficiency of the dairy cow. Injection of the hormone into the cow could boost her milk output from 10% to 40%. Better feeding and management had already resulted in an increase in the average cow's milk production from 4,100 pounds of milk in 1924 to 13,000 pounds in 1985. At the same time the number of cows actually decreased from 21 million to 11 million.

1987 The Milwaukee County Zoo opened its million-dollar Dairy Complex featuring an actual (rebuilt) dairy barn and herd of real cows, from which one was selected each half hour to be milked as a demonstration for visitors.

Historical Tidbits

The Milkmaid. If any of my little readers wish to be as healthy and merry as Betty the milkmaid, they must work hard, and rise early in the morning, instead of lying in bed while every body else is about his business, and idling their time till they go to bed again. Betty is obliged to get up as soon as it is light; and then takes a walk into the fields to fetch her cows. When she has milked their full udders into her clean pails, she sets off again, and carries it from door to door, time enough for her customers to have it for breakfast. As every one knows the business of a milkmaid, I shall say no more about it; but advise those to remember her example, who wish to make themselves happy or useful.

—*Select Rhymes for the Nursery*
London, 1808

Milk Cakes.   A Mr. Louis, of South-wark, England, has lately taken out a patent in England, for preserving cow's milk, goat's milk, etc., by converting it into solid cakes, which are soluble in warm water, and which may be kept for a long time without losing their original sweetness. The process consists in using some loaf sugar, agitating the milk, evaporating it by heat and then pressing it into cakes while soft and evaporating them to dryness after being moulded.

—*Wisconsin Farmer*, 1849

The Weight of Live Beef Cattle. This may be ascertained by the follow-ing rule. Take the girth of the animal just behind the shoulderblade and the length from a point on the tail-bone, whence a perpendicular line will just clear the thigh, then along the back-bone to the foreside of the top of the shoulder-blade. Reduce the girth and length to inches. Multiply the square of the girth by the length, and that prod-uct by the decimal .002, which will give the weight in pounds and decimal parts.

Suppose an ox to measure 7 feet or 84 inches in girth, and $5\frac{1}{2}$ feet or 66 inches in length; then, the girth $84^2 = 7056$, multiplied by the length, $66 = 465696$. This product, multiplied by the decimal, .002, gives 931.392 pounds, the weight of the ox.

The above rule gives the weight of the meat, hide, and tallow of oxen hav-ing from forty to eighty pounds of rough tallow, cows from thirty to sixty pounds, and two year olds having from fifteen to thirty pounds.

—*New England Farmer*, 1848

About Cows.   Every one has felt the inconvenience of having his cows calve during the night. In all seasons, but especially in winter, this is exceed-ingly annoying, and not only demands continual, useless watching, on the part of the cow's keeper, but very often in-directly causes the death of the calf and its mother. Now, it has been ascer-tained by a person living in the neigh-borhood of Utrecht, that a cow with calf, milked for the last time at night instead of the morning, calves in the day and not at night. Out of 30 cows on which the experiment was tried, only three or four are mentioned by Mr. Numon, Professor of Agriculture at Utrecht, as being exceptions. As con-firming the above statement we may mention the fact, that a large farmer in the campine has also tried the same plan with success.

—*Eastern Gazette*, 1853

Running a Dairy.   Every dairy-farm has a dairy barn of greater or less ex-cellence. This barn is not only the win-ter habitation of the cow, but as the

In 1847, *Maine Farmer* magazine carried a recipe for making cheese: "Boil good white potatoes and maarsh them till not a lump remains. To five pounds thus prepared, add a pint and a half of sour milk and enough salt to season the mass. Work well and let stand for two to four days. Work again, then shape cheeses and dry them in the shade." Small wonder most people left cheesemaking to the professionals.

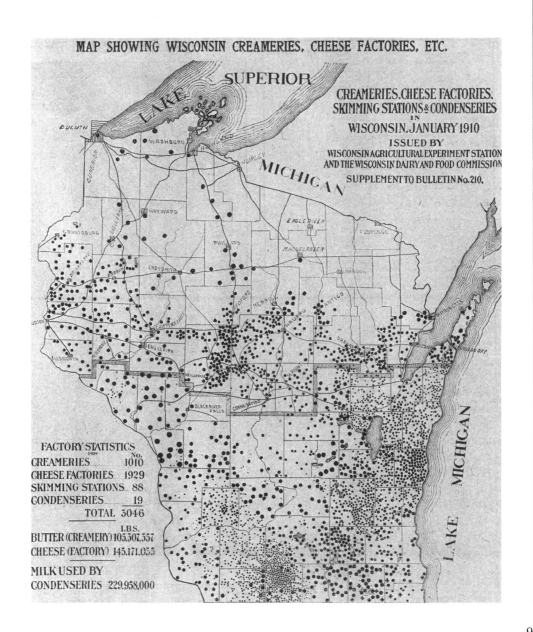

MAP SHOWING WISCONSIN CREAMERIES, CHEESE FACTORIES, ETC.

CREAMERIES, CHEESE FACTORIES,
SKIMMING STATIONS & CONDENSERIES
IN
WISCONSIN, JANUARY 1910
ISSUED BY
WISCONSIN AGRICULTURAL EXPERIMENT STATION
AND THE WISCONSIN DAIRY AND FOOD COMMISSION
SUPPLEMENT TO BULLETIN No. 210.

FACTORY STATISTICS
	1909 No.
CREAMERIES	1010
CHEESE FACTORIES	1929
SKIMMING STATIONS	88
CONDENSERIES	19
TOTAL	3046

	LBS.
BUTTER (CREAMERY)	105,507,557
CHEESE (FACTORY)	145,171,055

MILK USED BY
CONDENSERIES 229,958,000

system of soiling is gaining wider introduction, becomes her summer residence as well. The dairy barn in its best estate is a large handsome building, oblong, two stories high, smoothly finished and painted, and surmounted by a cupola. It generally has a basement extending its whole length and breadth, and here the cows are kept, standing side by side in a long row, fastened by stanchions which close about each side of the neck, and allow up-and-down, but very little lateral motion of the head. As one enters a dairy barn he sees a long row of horned heads, which calls to mind pictures of pillories. In this position the animals pass nearly all the time in winter, half an hour or so being allowed for a run in the yard in mild weather. The milking is done while the cows are in the stanchions.

The dairy-maid going singing to the pasture with milk-stool and pail is either a myth or a tradition in the dairy regions. The milking is done chiefly by men, and amidst surroundings which suggest no poetry. As each man fills his pail he carries it to the can and pours it through a strainer suspended two feet above the mouth of the can. The airing which the milk obtains by falling in thin streams from the high strainer has been found very effective in ridding it of a part of its animal heat and odor, which hasten its decay if not removed. When the herd is milked, the cans are started off for the factory at once, where the system of single delivery is practiced. Here we may find, perhaps, the traditional dairy-maid transmuted into the Jehu of the milk wagon, for very often we find the pride of the dairy-man's family at the receiving door of the cheese factory. A more systematic milk delivery is in vogue in many factory neighborhoods. One man is employed to draw all the milk of patrons residing upon a single highway. Then each farm is furnished with a rude platform by the wayside, upon which the cans are placed to wait for the wagon of the man who "runs the milk route." The man of the milk route is often a creature of peculiar mould, and his horses are remarkable neither for speed nor beauty. Of necessity he must be a creeping animal, for the milk is not better for much shaking. His wagon is covered with a wide platform instead of a box, and the large cans are held by an encompassing rope. And yet the man of the route is a character in the neighborhood, and children run out to see him pass, as our grandfathers watched the old-time stagecoach. Sometimes he gathers milk at a distance of three or four miles from the factory, and then he is on the road at two o'clock in the morning on his first outward trip.

At the receiving window of the

cheese factory there arise questions which end sometimes in ill temper, sometimes in the courts of law. All is not milk which comes in cans, and all milk is not good milk. In this State there is a stringent law against watering milk or otherwise interfering with its natural quality. Sometimes the proof is easy, as when small fish are found in the can. . . .

—*Harper's Monthly Magazine*, 1854

Typographical Error. There has been tremendous confusion at Ganong's last week, all growing out of a little misprint in the *Union*. In the business notices appeared a notice advising people to go to Ganong's for most everything, and among other things "Diaries" for 1876 were mentioned, or should have been, but the compositor got the first two vowels transposed and it read "Dairies." Ganong has always been rather skeptical about the benefits of advertising, but he is convinced now. As soon as Walt Prosser got his paper, he saw that Dairy announcement, and so posted for the town and told Ganong he would take two or three cows . . . then Milo Morrison sauntered in and said he thought of keeping a few more cows next season, and he would like to buy some good ones, and hinted he would like to buy from a man who has some experience, and knew a Berkshire steer, from a

Cochin China milker. Dolp Damuth called to compare last year's results in dairying, and offered to propose Ganong's name for membership in the Grange. Dave Curtis sent him word to be sure to be on hand at the next dairy convention, and report how he got along as a milkist. Milo Jones merely stopped to enquire whether he found the Alderny or the South Down churn the most successful, and whether he packed his butter in saw-dust or tanbark. Dave Whitaker offered to hire out as a dairy maid, and Lyme Goodhue merely wanted to know whether he considered it more profitable to climb a seven rail fence or a six inch burr oak when a mad bull is in the rear. Ganong is getting wild as a hawk, and says there will be a funeral or two if this thing doesn't stop pretty soon.

—*Jefferson County Union*
December 24, 1875
W. D. Hoard, publisher

Cheap Cheese? In the 1870's, a cheese dairy of 30 cows would have involved the following items at the following expense:

1 120 gallon self-heating vat with hot water tank	$82.00
2 cheese hoops, 15 inch, with followers $4.50 ea.	9.00
2 cheese press screws, $4.00 each	8.00
1 curd knife, 7 x 20 inches	4.25
1 curd scoop	.75

Mandy

We have a cow. Her name is Mandy.
She sure thinks that she's a dandy.
She doesn't pay her food or rent,
Cause all she gives is two percent!

—Carolyn Lumsden

93

1 curd pail	1.25
1 dipper	3.00
2 thermometers, 50 cents each	1.00
1 rubber mop	.50
Total	$119.75

—*Dairy Industry in Wisconsin*

Milk Bottles. On a sultry day in August, 1886, the first delivered milk in bottles were sitting on doorsteps in the city of Ogdensburg, New York.

The late William C. Wilcox had been persuaded by Hervey D. Thatcher to purchase a supply of these new sanitary milk bottles.

On the sultry morning referred to, Wilcox loaded his Thatcher bottles full of milk into the bottom of his wagon. They rested on a bed of straw without benefit of crates and as there were no caps — only glass stoppers held in place by small gaskets and wire bails, the milk spilled all over the bottom of the wagon as it jogged along the dusty roads. Upon arriving at his first customer's home, Wilcox discovered that the milk bottles were partly empty and Wilcox had to return to his farm, refill the bottles and start again.

An indignant Wilcox penned a letter to Thatcher: "My dear Doctor: You must think a man is a fool to be driving around the streets with milk in glass bottles. It is a failure and will never amount to anything."

Nevertheless, Wilcox continued to

George Barham, founder of the Express Dairy group, marketed goats' milk in bottles with wired-on closures in England in 1884. At about the same time in the United States, Hervey Thatcher and Harvey Barnhart were experimenting with sanitary methods for distributing milk. They pioneered the manufacture of glass milk bottles.

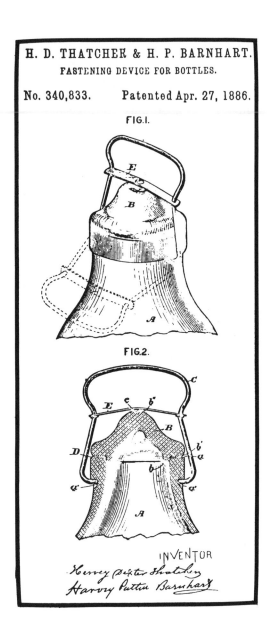

H. D. THATCHER & H. P. BARNHART.
FASTENING DEVICE FOR BOTTLES.

No. 340,833.   Patented Apr. 27, 1886.

FIG.1.

FIG.2.

INVENTOR

deliver bottled cream and milk after his first aggravating experience. This meant the beginning of added security for milk against germs.

In 1889, Dr. Thatcher produced further protection for bottled milk by the replacement of the loose-fitting glass covers with tight-fitting caps. . . .

A newspaper article in a New York newspaper of April 25, 1945 states: "Dr. Thatcher like many another genius, died a poor man and some of his staunch friends at Potsdam recall seeing him as an old man, his head still full of dreams, walking absent-mindedly along the street; his slight ascetic figure all too certain an indication that he was not taking the best of care of himself. Sometimes such a friend would invite him to one of the hotels on some pretense and while engaging him in conversation, unobtrusively guide the aged doctor toward the dining room and a substantial dinner."
—*Make Mine Milk*

Sanitary Milk. Milk from healthy cows. Stables as clean as a house and always open for inspection. 6 cents a quart or 3 cents a pint. Milk from Jersey cows 8 cents a quart or 4 cents a pint in glass bottles. Delivered anywhere in the city. J. E. Langslow.
—ad from *Daily Press*
Newport News, Virginia
January 14, 1898

My Life at the Jones Grocery. Most cheese [in 1922] came in large wheels and was sold in bulk. These wheels were placed on a counter under glass covers suspended from the ceiling by a system of weights and pulleys. But even with the care given to cheese, it spoiled occasionally and in such cases I thought that the whole wheel would have to be thrown out. Not a bit of it! Mr. Jones carved and whittled and scraped away at what I thought was completely spoiled until in due time the bad parts were cut out and the remainder put on sale at a higher price to compensate for what had been lost in the process. At first, this shocked me until I learned that it is quite a common practice—that even after a cheese has started to spoil, it can be trimmed and that the remainder is as good as ever, maybe better. Once, I saw Mr. Jones cut away a section of cheese that was teeming with maggots and thought that here is a cheese that cannot be saved. But it was! It was carefully trimmed and eventually sold. As there were no complaints, I assume that it must have been satisfactory.
—Gerald M. Van Pool

The Good Old Days. Notes from a magazine called *Milk Plant*, in 1941 contained an extensive list of milk prices at the time from all of the States.

Here are the figures from lowest to highest:

MILK QUART (Home Delivery) 10 cents to 15 cents
CREAM PINT 24–29 cents. ½ pint 12½ to 25 cents
WHIPPING CREAM PINT 41 to 48 cents; ½ pint 22–24 cents.

Chiropractic for Dairy Cow. Upon close observation of the cow's spine you will see the vertebrae out of line if she is going to be sick. What to do is the next step to learn. Naturally, the vertebrae must be re-set to avoid the ailment. Take the thumb and forefinger and rub them over the spine firmly two or three times. Next take the middle finger and let it rest on the side of the dislocated vertebra in which direction it is to be moved. With the other hand pound gently, but firmly, and attempt to reset the vertebra. Several adjustments may be required to get it in perfect place. It is better to give several adjustments than to attempt to reset the vertebra in one adjustment. Which vertebra is out of place will depend on what is ailing the animal . . . The results are noticeable much quicker on Guernseys and Jerseys because their nervous systems are much more delicate than those of the larger breeds of dairy cattle.

—*Hoard's Dairyman*, 1945

Make Mine Milk. Edna Ferber, the noted authoress, has recently been visiting the American forces in Europe . . . "American boys," writes Miss Ferber, "all want two things above all else. It may sound sissy, but, it most definitely isn't. From the generals living in chateaus or villas to privates billeted in tents or Nissen huts, they long to come back home, and they crave a long, cool glass of fresh milk . . ."
—*Hoard's Dairyman*, 1945

The Milkmaid. As far back as history takes us, the dairy-maid has been an important factor in the dairy world. Songs are sung and poetry written about the queen whose gentle hand and caresses have always been so acceptable to the bovine mother. There is something in the hand of woman that appeals to the maternal instincts of this dumb mother and makes her respond more bountifully to it than to the hand of man. It is motherhood responding to motherly instincts; like sympathies in touch with other; a maternal instinct in each, which no man can understand; these make the milkmaid and the cow so thoroughly in harmony with each other.

The milkmaid not only exists in song and poetry, but she is found in the actual walks of life, and always successful with dairy cows. We have been per-

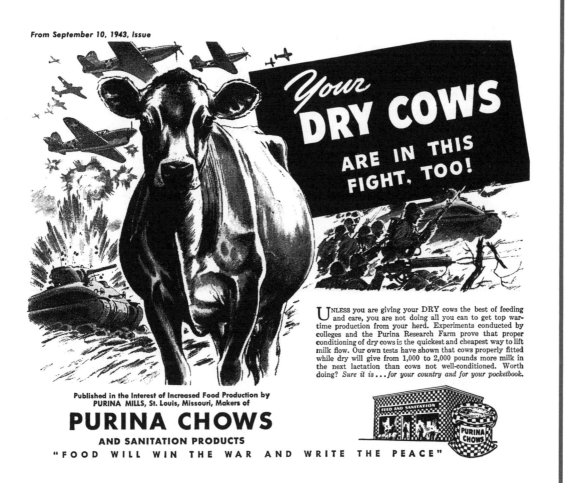

World War II created heightened demand for milk, perhaps because Germany was stripping Europe of cattle and commandeering cheese and butter for its own consumption. In America, dairymen on the West Coast were shown how to black out their barns, and the National Selective Service told farm boys: "It is more important for you to stay on the farm and do a good job than to volunteer or be drafted into the armed services." Ad reproduced compliments of *Hoard's Dairyman* magazine.

sonally acquainted with women whose husbands have died leaving them a legacy of debt, but with their natural adaptability to this industry, they have lifted the mortgage from the farm, improved the buildings and livestock, and accumulated bank accounts.

Women not only know how to appeal to the maternal instincts of the cow, but they look after the many little things that too many men consider unimportant and, consequently, think these trifling matters do not pay.
—*Hoard's Dairyman*, 1945

P. H. Kasper, World's Greatest Cheesemaker. I was born in the Town of Rhine, Sheboygan County, October 11, 1866. From early childhood I was greatly interested in cows and young stock, so I had full charge of them as long as I remained at home. Work on the farm was done almost entirely without aid of machinery, and the days were long. There were meager returns for our milk hauled to the cheese factory—about fifty or sixty cents per hundred.

While waiting for a job as a country store clerk, an incident occurred which changed the entire trend of my thinking and doing. I was aroused from sleep one midnight by the son of our local cheesemaker who had driven over the two miles of rough, hilly road to urge me to come to work in the cheese factory, as he was going away. The father operated the farm and the mother made cheese. She had instructed him that he must get Phillip Kasper to come and help her.

The factory had been sadly neglected, but the work there appealed to me. I thought I had the finest position in the world. I knew how to scrub—I had helped with the housework at home, and my mother had impressed upon me the importance of cleanliness and order. So I washed and scoured the inside of that factory and the utensils until everything was shining. I still remember the man who patted me on the back and said, "My boy, if you keep this up you will be a real cheesemaker some day and you will never be without a job." And I never was.

After that I worked for several years making cheese in Sheboygan County, but the farmers there wanted quantity, while my ambition was to make *quality* cheese. But it requires more milk to make *high quality cheese* than it does to make just cheese. I also made cheese in Cobb for a few years, and then I went to Raymond, Minnesota, for fifty dollars a month with board, room, and work for the entire year.

I found the cheese factory still under construction. No machinery had arrived. I then said that I would go to Sioux falls, South Dakota, for a visit with my brother and that when the machinery arrived they might wire me at my expense.

In a few days a telegram to return arrived. But to my confusion, there was an eight-horsepower boiler instead of the self-heating kind to which I was accustomed. All I know about a boiler I learned that first day. Working by lantern light we finished the job late that night. The milk was strained into the vat after we were done, and cooled. The next day we added the morning's milk and we were all set to make cheese.

As I made cheese that day, the

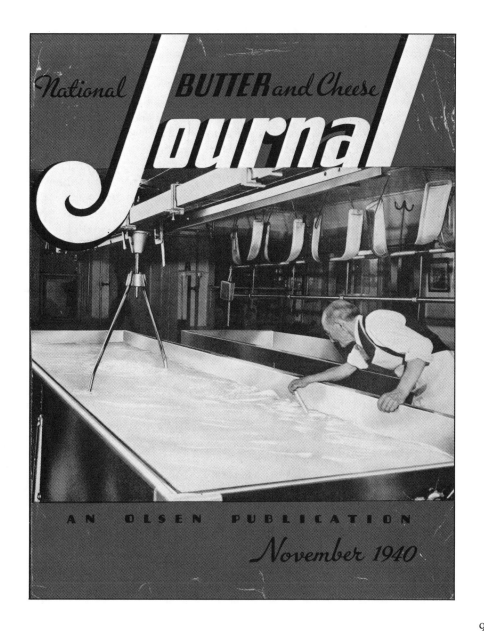

This cover of *National Butter and Cheese Journal* featured P. H. Kasper, grandfather of author Sara Rath, making some award-winning cheese at his Bear Creek, Wisconsin, factory. Ripley's "Believe It or Not" column reported that Kasper's cheese won more prizes than that of any other cheesemaker.

N ew Holstein,
Wisconsin is known as
Cowtown *and celebrates*
Cowtown Days *each year*
with sidewalk sales, a car
show, a dance, and a
Cowtown Race.

Stuarts' relatives were notified and they came from Willmar, twenty-two miles away, to witness the process. Finally the cheese was made and put in the press. Two hours later supper was announced and I was asked to bring some cheese for the table. When I said the cheese would not be ready to eat for ten days, there was a family consultation. They doubted that I knew how to make cheese, and I was told not to start a fire in the boiler the next day unless I received notice from Willmar to go ahead.

At Willmar there were two businessmen from Sheboygan. One operated a meat market, the other a furniture store, but they knew cheese. So they were consulted. That night Robert Stuart, who was managing the farm for his brothers, received a telegram, and came to me with a beaming face. "Start your fire and make cheese," he announced. All the milk from one hundred cows was in the vat, and the cheese I made that day I thought was the very best I had made in six years of experience. . . .
—*The Golden Jubilee of the World's Champion Cheesemaker*, 1941

Old Cheese, Good Cheese. Two elderly ladies stopped by my Grandpa Kasper's cheese factory one day. While he filled their orders, one of the women asked, "How often do you make old cheese?" Without cracking a smile, Grandpa replied, "Every other day."

When P. H. Kasper wasn't busy making old cheese, he was busy making plain everyday cheddar cheese—seven days a week for more than fifty years—cheese that was famous throughout the world. His natural cheddar won more than two hundred awards, and he was proclaimed "World's Greatest Cheesemaker" at the 1912 International Dairy Show. In fact, Ripley's "Believe It or Not" column once claimed that P. H. Kasper had won more prizes than any other cheesemaker.

Grandpa Kasper made his first cheese at the age of seventeen. In 1891 he opened his own factory near Bear Creek, Wisconsin. In 1893 he was awarded his first gold medal and diploma at Chicago's Columbian Exposition. Five years later he won the highest award at the Wisconsin State Fair, and in 1900 he won the Grand Prix at the Paris International Exposition. From then on he won nearly all the competitions he entered: The Pan American Exposition of 1901; the St. Louis Exposition of 1904; the National and International Dairy Shows of 1912; the Syracuse National Dairy Show in 1923; the Iowa Cattle Exposition in 1925 and 1926; and the Pacific Slope Fair in 1927. He won even though he was usually docked a point or two in competition due to the natural creamy color of his cheese—he seldom added artificial orange coloring.

P. H. Kasper was appointed by President Coolidge as a delegate to the International Dairy Conference in England in 1928. "It was the best time I ever had in my life," he recalled. After meeting King George V, he went on to Europe, where he spent months visiting other cheese factories and studying cheesemaking techniques. The key to Grandfather's success as a cheesemaker probably came from his patience. He claimed that he made prize-winning cheese every day and, in fact, once pulled a cheese at random from the racks in the curing room. It won the highest rating ever given to a cheese. "To make good cheese," he said, "You must stay with it, live with it from the milk can to the curing rack. Many young men nowadays are in too much of a hurry. I tell you, you can't make cheese in the morning and go to the ball game in the afternoon!"

In May of 1941 Grandpa Kasper was recognized by the Wisconsin legislature for his fifty years of cheesemaking and his award winning cheese. Shortly before his death in December of 1942 he wrote to my mother: "Was in the factory yesterday—it seemed good. They tell me I've made enough cheese, but what else should I do? I keep thinking about the cheese and all the things I've done with cheese, and now I've begun to get some ideas on how to make it better. I think I'll make the best cheese yet this summer. . . ."

—Sara Rath

The Pabst family—though better known for beer—also pioneered in the dairy industry. Fred Pabst established a farm near Oconomowoc, Wisconsin, in 1906 and began raising purebred Holsteins in 1907. He was a director of the Holstein-Friesian Association from 1918-1930. The Pabst breeding program was built around great sires. Beginning in 1940, Pabst Farms made their bulls available to other dairymen through artificial insemination. Pabst-bred cattle have been exported to countries as distant as Japan, Australia, and Italy. Photo courtesy Hoard Historical Museum and Pabst Farms, Incorporated.

Beefcake & Bulls

"We call them A.I.'s 'Bull Cheaters.'"
C. E. Neuenschwander,
Holstein Breeder

Historical Bull

On the cave walls of Lascaux, in southwest France, there are paintings of ferocious bulls thought to be representations of the *aurochs*, huge verile animals that once roamed throughout western Asia, Europe and northern Africa. The last known surviving auroch died in 1627 in Jaktorowka, a remote forest in Poland. Prehistoric skulls discovered in England and Scotland are three feet in length with the points of the cores of the horns three and a half feet apart. Anthropologists estimate the aurochs to have been around six feet tall, and powerfully built.

Caesar described the aurochs in 65 BC when he wrote, "In size these are but little inferior to elephants, although in appearance, colour, and form they are bulls. Their strength and their speed are great. They spare neither men nor beast when they see them. In the expanse of their horns, as well as in form and appearance, they differ much from our oxen."

To a pastoral people, bulls were the stuff of which legends were made, and thus classical legends about the beasts abound. A bull's virtues are all masculine. The bull's sexual organs are prominent and he is thought of as being fearless, powerful, combative, proud and potent—all characteristics men wish to emulate and women supposedly admire. From sex to religion was a small step for our primitive ancestors, and looking back it is sometimes difficult to see where one ended and the other began.

The Druids worshiped white bulls. Usually the Druids specialized in human sacrifice but when they were short of human victims they substituted bulls. Pliny described one of these occasions: "Having made preparation for sacrifice and a banquet beneath the trees, they bring thither two white bulls, whose horns are bound then for the first time. Clad in a white robe the priest ascends the tree and cuts the mistletoe with a golden sickle, and it is received by others in a white cloak. They then kill the victims, praying that God will render this gift of his propitious to those to whom he has granted it."

Where cattle were indigenous, the bull became an object of worship as a god, or the symbol of gods. His horns were regarded as peculiarly sacred and powerful. Fierce bulls appeared in mythology and in bull cults from India to Persia, Mesopotamia, Egypt, Greece and Rome all the way down through history to the present Spanish bullfights. The bull was an emblem of fertility and when it was killed in sacrifice, the eating of the flesh of the bull and the drinking of its blood were thought to confer the strength and vigor of the bull upon the celebrant.

Enlil, the Babylonian god of fertility and storm, was addressed as "overpowering ox, exalted overpowering ox." Gods of thunder, storm and rain were often depicted as bulls. In India the Aryan sky god *Dyaus,* the red bull who smiles through the clouds, "bellows downwards" (thunders) and several later Hindu gods had the form of a bull.

Mythological Bull

Bulls were felt to be responsible for the noise and destruction of earthquakes. The ancient Greek hero, Theseus, claimed his power was due to his special relationship with Poseidon, the god of the sea but was also the "shaker of the earth," and who often appeared in the form of a bull.

Apis was considered the most sacred bull of Egypt. He was kept in a temple at Memphis near the temple of Ptah. At a certain hour every day he was fed and watered in a courtyard attached to his temple while his devoted followers watched and worshipped. Apis was believed to be the reincarnation of the god named Ptah who had assumed the disguise of a celestial fire and inseminated a virgin heifer thus fathering a black bull calf with mystical markings who was actually Ptah returned to earth.

Whenever the bull calf that was *Apis* died, a calf with similar special markings that would identify it as the successor, had to be found. Then, for forty days the calf would be attended to by women who would display their genitalia to him. He would be brought by boat to Memphis in a gold-lined cabin.

Besides *Apis,* the Egyptians also worshiped another sacred bull, *Buchis,* whose hide supposedly changed color every hour.

Crete was dedicated to the worship of bulls. In Knossos, sacrifices and bull acrobatics were recorded in the murals of the palace. They believed the bull's virility was concentrated in his horns. Because the Minoan culture on Crete preceded that of Greece, many of Crete's legends became interwoven with Greek mythology.

A Mithraic sacrifice was included in *The Iconographic Encyclopaedia of Science, Literature, and Art*. This two-volume set, first published in 1851, was based on Friedrich Arnold Brockhaus's *Bilderatlas*, one of the finest encyclopedias of its day.

Zeus, the supreme god of Greek mythology (he became known as Jupiter to the Romans) possessed irresistible power and uninhibited sexuality. He could also manifest himself in various disguises, frequently choosing that of a bull whenever he was intent upon raping some unsuspecting woman. When Zeus desired Demeter and she refused him, he changed himself into a bull and raped her. From this union the goddess Persephone was born. Zeus became a bull again when he raped Europa, who then gave birth to Minos who became King of Crete.

Minos, perhaps because of his unusual conception, was somewhat haunted by bulls. His queen, Pasiphae, after having borne him several normal children, was overwhelmed with passion for a certain bull. Pasiphae asked Daedalus, the master-craftsman of Crete at that time, to construct a dummy cow. And Pasiphae hid herself in that cow, where she lay in wait to seduce the bull. Her ploy was a success. She eventually gave birth to the famous Minotaur, half-human and half-bull. Her husband Minos, however, was not pleased. He condemned the Minotaur to an underground labyrinth at Knossos where he could survive only upon a diet of human flesh which was provided by the annual tribute of seven Athenian youths and seven Athenian maidens. This, of course, came to an end when the hero Theseus met and slew the Minotaur.

The religion of *Mithraism* was born in Persia and was intimately involved with bull worship.

Mithra appeared on earth from the face of a rock on December 25, and sheperds watching their flocks heralded his birth. There are many other strange resemblances to Christ: Mithra was considered to be a god of light, justice and truth. After his death he ascended into Heaven, from whence he was to return on the Final Day of Judgment to judge the quick and the dead.

While on earth, Mithra performed many miracles. But his adventures with a white bull brought him the greatest

admiration and, in time, created the sacred symbol of his creed.

One day Mithra was walking through the pastures and saw a magnificent white bull grazing there. He decided to capture the bull alive, with his own bare hands. Mithra seized the bull by the horns and mounted him. He rode the bull and fought him until the bull collapsed, and then he dragged the bull to his cave. The painful journey of Mithra dragging the bull—over rugged terrain and against difficult odds—became symbolic of human suffering on earth.

The Mithraic religion grew out of a province of what we now know as Turkey. It spread to western Europe and finally to Rome, where it became quite powerful and threatened the birth of Christianity. According to Plutarch, Mithraism appeared in Rome in 67 BC and rose to its peak over three centuries later, in AD 308. At that time there was an Imperial edict that suppressed all pagan religions, and Christianity was able to triumph.

Mithraian shrines have been found wherever Roman legions marched, from the banks of the Black Sea to the mountains of Scotland and the borders of the Sahara Desert. But Germany claims the most numerous and richest of Mithraic relics.

An Irish epic, *Tain Bo Cualnge*, or "The Cattle-Raid of Cooley," concerned the attempt of Medb, Queen of Connacht, to capture the fabled bull, Donn Cualinge (the "Dark-horn") because her husband owned an equally fabled bull, Findbennach Ai (the "White-horn"). Medb ultimately failed in this endeavor, but near the end of the story there was a battle between the two bulls that was cast in terms of a titanic struggle between the two finest bulls that ever lived: "Each of the bulls caught sight of the other, and they pawed the ground and cast the earth over them. They dug up the ground [and threw it] over their shoulders and their withers, and their eyes blazed in their heads like distended balls of fire. Their cheeks and nostrils swelled like smith's bellows in a forge. And each collided with the other with a crashing noise. Each of them began to gore and to pierce and to slay and slaughter the other. . . ."

Heavenly Bull

The constellation of *Taurus*, the bull, forms the second sign of the zodiac. A V-shaped cluster called the *Hyades* marks the bull's face. The star *Aldebaran* is the right eye and two other stars form the tips of the horns. The cluster of stars called *Pleiades* composes the bull's shoulder, and Taurus also includes the *Crab Nebula*, a cloud of gas.

People born under the astrological sign of *Taurus, the Bull* (between 21 April and 22 May, when the sun is between 0 degrees and 29 degrees Taurus), are supposed to possess the bull-like characteristics of patience, persistence and obstinacy.

The Perfect Bull

A dairy bull should show an active, nervous disposition with little evidence of sluggishness. Sluggishness in a young bull is likely to indicate that he will take little exercise and will be slow in service as he gets older.

The importance of the bull in the herd must always be emphasized. He is by far the most important and valuable animal on the dairy farm, and better dairying will come about on farms more quickly through the use of good dairy sires than in any other way.

Management of older bulls—it is best to ring a bull at one year old. He is dangerous to handle as soon as he gets any size on him and it is better to be safe than sorry. Bulls that have gotten their growth should be fed sparingly on silage. . . . Bulls serving two or three cows a week need grain.

Bulls can probably handle as high as two hundred cows per year if properly fed and managed, if the cows are distributed. The trouble is that in most herds the calves are all wanted at a particular season, which makes it impossible to distribute the service to the

Cow Currency

In Africa it was common to purchase wives with cattle, even in the not-too-distant past. As recently as 1964, when the average Masai maiden was valued at $200 and twelve cows, a Masai chief offered to buy movie star Carroll Baker for 150 cows, 200 goats and sheep and $750 in cash. He didn't get her.

The classic volume *Prose and Poetry of the Live Stock Industry of the United States,* introduced in 1904 and reprinted in a limited edition in 1959, contained this illustration of the constellation Taurus. The "Great Celestial Bull" was reproduced from Huntington's *Plan of the Solar System.*

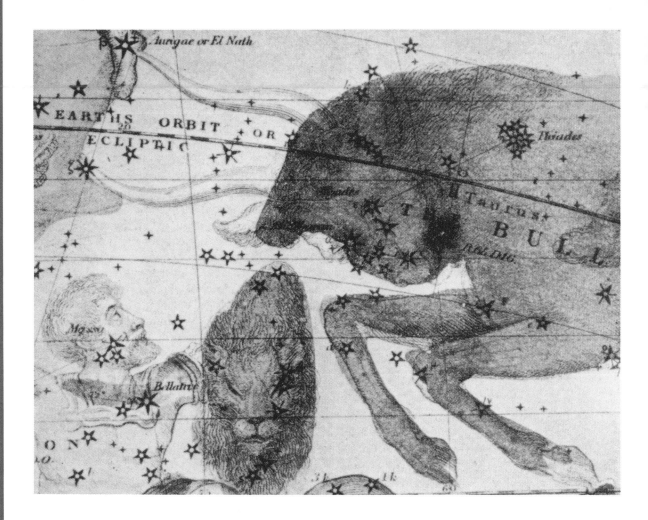

best advantage for the bull. In no case should a bull serve more than two cows in the same day and then these services should be as many hours apart as possible. One service to one cow is enough. Two services cannot possibly help in settling a cow and two services at one time are very hard on the bull."
—*Better Dairy Farming*, 1923

Dairy Bull Unified Score Card

General Appearance (55 points). Attractive individuality with masculinity, vigor, stretch, scale, and harmonious blending of all parts with impressive style and carriage.
(8) Breed Characteristics
(8) Stature—Height including moderate length in the leg bones with a long bone pattern throughout the body structure.
(8) Front End—Adequate constitution with strength and dairy refinement.
Shoulder Blades and Elbow—set firmly and smoothly against the chest wall and withers to form a smooth union with the neck and body.
Chest—Deep and full with ample width between front legs.
(8) Back—Straight and strong.
Loin—Broad, strong, and nearly level.
Rump—Long, wide, and nearly level with pin bones slightly lower than hip bones.
Thurls—High and wide apart.
Tail Head—Set nearly level with topline and with tail head and tail free from coarseness.
(23) Legs and Feet—Bone flat and strong. Front legs straight, wide apart, and squarely placed.
Hind Legs—Nearly perpendicular from hock to pastern from a side view and straight from the rear view.
Hocks—Cleanly molded and free from coarseness and puffiness.
Pasterns—Short and strong with some flexibility.
Feet—Short and well rounded with deep heel and level sole.
Dairy Character (25 points). Angularity and general openness without weakness, freedom from coarseness.
Neck—Long, lean, and blending smoothly into shoulders; clean-cut throat, dewlap, and brisket.
Withers—Sharp with chine prominent.
Ribs—Wide apart; rib bones wide, flat, and long.
Thighs—Incurving to flat and wide apart from the rear view.
Skin—Thin, loose, and pliable.
Body Capacity (20 points). Relatively large in proportion to size and age, providing ample capacity, strength, and vigor.
—*Purebred Dairy Cattle Ass'n*, 1984

Score of Another Sort

During a 1971 debate over the deleterious effects of supersonic transports on the atmosphere, Dr. S. Fred Singer pointed out that bovine flatulence sent an estimate 85 million tons of methane into the atmosphere each year.

Bull Shooters

There are approximately 300 photographers in the U.S. that specialize in racehorse and showhorse portraits; maybe 25 that professionally photograph dogs. But there are only around eight photographers that specialize in cattle.

Considering the fact that bulls must look their best for the camera, the job of a professional bull photographer is not an easy task. An innovative lensman can make a bull look especially fierce and macho.

A veteran photographer from Canada, Walter Browarny, brags that "Bulls I photograph look like they'll jump right out of the picture and start breeding your cows."

James Koch, beefcake photographer from Denver, Colorado, is a little more precise. He talks more about the science of his craft, of positioning the sun to cast shadows that can make a bull appear leaner or meatier. He insists that each leg, each ear, each nostril be posed with pinpoint precision.

Before the advent of the camera, bulls used to be romantically rendered by artists, who sometimes exaggerated a bull's fine points. Even the ensuing photographers tended to touch up their work, until the 1960's, when that practice went out of fashion. Still, some continue to artistically enhance the bull's testicles to suggest a good sperm producer.

Koch says there are other tricks to making a less than perfect bull look like a stud. Until the early 1970's, photographers often stood on fences to make the bulls seem plumper. But today cholesterol-conscious consumers want leaner beef, "So now, we have to shoot pictures from our bellies to make bulls look taller."

Bullfights

In Spain the bullfighting season extends from March to October. There are over a thousand bullfights held in over 350 bull rings per season. At least 200 ranches in Spain are devoted merely to the breeding and rearing of fighting bulls who will take to the ring when they are from three to five years of age.

In a bullfight the bull enters the ring and attacks, or is incited to attack, the picadors, men on horseback with pointed lances eight-feet long. The picadors prick the bull's crest with the small sharp tips, thus weakening the muscle with which the bull makes his toss. Frequently the horses are sacrificed in this preliminary encounter. The banderilleros stick darts in the bull's skin to stimulate his ferocity even further. Then the matador comes out to play with the bull, to tease him with his scarlet cloth and make the final sacrifice with the sword, driving it in high at the top of the angle between the two shoulder blades.

Hemingway described the fighting bull in his novel *Death in the Afternoon*: "The physical characteristics of the fighting bull are its thick and very strong hide with glossy pelt, small head, but wide forehead; strength and shape of horns, which curve forward; short, thick neck with the great hump of muscle which erects when the bull is angry, wide shoulders, very small hooves and length and slenderness of tail. The female of the fighting bull is not as heavily built as the male; has a smaller head, shorter and thinner horns; a longer neck, a less pronounced dewlap under the jaw; is not as wide through the chest, and has no visible udder."

Love-a-bull

A warm affection may go deeper and develop into a feeling not far removed from love. There is no need to elaborate on the subject of bestiality, although without question it must on occasion have occurred. Many a dairyman has had his favorite heifer, many a Bedouin his special goat and the Spanish shepherd in his lonely summer pilgrimage to the mountains his particular bell-wether to relieve the lonely watches of the night. Such things occur but do not mean so very much; much more significant is what

goes on in the mind. Many a boy watching the bull in service of the cow must have envied and admired the bull, wishing for the time and opportunity when, without seeking to be a bull himself, he might come to emulate it in lustful strength and masculinity. Again, although it might have required the genius of a Daedalus to assuage the unnatural yearning of Queen Pasiphae, there may have been women, burdened perhaps with weak, feeble or impotent husbands who, in their secret hearts, came to envy the cow her satisfaction by the bull. Or a shy and bashful maiden, closeted in dreams, may have sighed for the lover with the strength, courage, and sex-assurance of a masterful bull.

—Allan Fraser
The Bull

Super Bull, Valiant

S-W-D Valiant, super Holstein bull at American Breeders Service (ABS), whose semen sales produced $25 million for the company and 35,000 offspring worldwide, died August 9 of old age and other complications.

The bull was buried near the Holstein Hilton, a barn where top ABS bulls are housed. A marker commemorating his contribution to the company has been erected.

"Perhaps no bull in the history of any breed has caught the attention of

How Much?

To get the same amount of calcium provided by a quart of milk, you'd have to eat three and a half pounds of cooked spinach, eleven and a half pounds of carrots, sixteen pounds of peas, 22 oranges, 50 tomatoes or 50 slices of whole wheat bread.

cattle breeders or had the genetic impact of Valiant," according to Robert Walton, president of ABS. Walton said a supply of Valiant's frozen semen was still on hand—it sold for $125 per unit in late 1983.

Valiant's female offspring had a much greater volume of milk production than the average Holstein. Walton estimated the Valiant descendants have brought dairy farmers an additional $18 million in milk production revenues. The bull's financial value underwrote the testing of hundreds of other bulls, built several barns and paid a lot of taxes for American Breeders.

The company said 380 of Valiant's male offspring were being tested by the artificial insemination companies around the U.S. to find another which could have as much impact. Walton claims that with the frozen semen and the number of Valiant sons, the bull will "continue to have a direct genetic and economic impact throughout the remainder of this century."

—*Wisconsin State Journal*
August 16, 1984

Bull Long Dead; Calf's Just Born

Darlington, Wis.—Cow No. 126 gave birth to a calf Monday morning at the Harold and Charles Lattin farm. It's a bull calf, as yet unnamed.

The father, as often occurs in the bovine world, was not present at the delivery. But Cottonade Emmet has an especially good excuse. He has been dead for 30 years.

In fact, one of the last things the great old bull did on this earth was to produce the seed of his latest descendant. Old Cottonade died the very next day, on November 20, 1953. He had been employed at American Breeders Service, DeForest.

Old Cottonade was a diligent employee of the world's largest artificial insemination firm. There's still enough of him to produce 100 more little calves, ABS says.

The bull was a pioneer—one of the first in the U.S. whose semen was frozen for later use. In the early years the A-I technicians kept their semen in ice water and hoped their car batteries worked. Bull semen was no good after two days.

"I remember once the bus forgot to drop off a shipment," said Bob McDermott, an artificial inseminator since 1946. Rather than leave a cow unfertilized and lose a month's milk production he had a single engine airplane fly low over the Lafayette County Fairgrounds and drop a shipment from the air.

It was during Cottonade's five-year career in the early 1950's that Dr. Christopher Polge at Cambridge Uni-

112

Valiant, one of American Breeders Service's top Holstein bulls, was known for the dainty white butterfly on his flank. The names of registered cattle frequently include the breeder, the sire, and the dam. Minnehaha Matador DeKol, for example, was bred by the University of Minnesota, by the bull Valentine Matador, out of the dam Bess Burke DeKol. Photo courtesy American Breeders Service.

versity, U.K., discovered how to freeze semen using glycerine, a higher form of alcohol. Freezing in water had not worked; ice crystals snapped the microscopic tails off the sperm, rendering them immotile.

ABS brought Polge to DeForest. The first calf born of frozen sperm in America entered the world on a farm near Janesville on May 29, 1953. He was called "Frosty," for obvious reasons.

In those days alcohol and dry ice were the freezing agents. It was not until 1956 that the liquid nitrogen now in use was developed, with the help of animal physiologist F. I. Elliott, now retired and living in Monona.

As for old Cottonade, "He has no contribution whatsoever to make today to the dairy industry because the genetic germ plasm has passed him by," Dr. Elliott concluded Monday. The old bull was used this time only to provide living proof that "bovine semen, properly frozen, will last indefinitely."

At least they know it will last for 30 years.

—David Blaska
The Capital Times
May 3, 1984

New Breeds

In the area of beef cattle breeding, there was great interest in the mid-1960's in selecting strains of beef cattle that would grow more rapidly and produce more red meat with less fat on the carcass.

Other than the Holstein and Brown Swiss breeds, no major breeds of cattle had been imported from Europe to North America in this century. The quarantine against foot and mouth disease was primarily responsible for preventing any serious interest in any of the 200 different breeds of cattle on the continent.

Several breeds did look very promising though, and as interest intensified, the Canadian government built a maximum quarantine station in 1965 that was adequate to screen animals born in Europe for the foot and mouth virus and to introduce them into North America.

The first new imports were French Charolais cattle, with Simmental, Limousin, Maine-Anjou, Gelbvieh, Chianina and a host of about 20 breeds following in their path.

Most of the bulls imported had to remain in Canada for commercial reasons. Therefore, the only means of getting this sperm plasm into the United States for use in our herds was through frozen semen and artificial insemination.

With the tremendous interest these new breeds generated, soon there were hundreds of thousands of cows in the United States bred to bulls of these new breeds without one of the bulls having actually set foot in the United States. This was a remarkable technical achievement.

—Robert E. Walton, President
American Breeders Service

Sitting Bull

Tatanka Iyotanka, or Sitting Buffalo Bull was best known as Sitting Bull. Sitting Bull's childhood name was Jumping Badger, but he received his father's name in honor when he showed bravery against the Crow Indians. He became a famous medicine man and a leader of Hunkpapa Teton Sioux Indians. In fact, he was the leading medicine man in the Battle of Little Bighorn, June 25, 1876, where General George Custer was killed. The year before, Sitting Bull had had a vision that all his enemies would be delivered into his hands. In the spring of 1876 he told his people that they must change their way of fighting and instead of showing off their bravery they should fight to kill. The new tactic was successful.

After Little Bighorn, Sitting Bull and his tribe were driven into Canada. He returned to the United States in 1881 and toured with Buffalo Bill's Wild West Show, where he told Annie Oakley, "The white man knows how to make everything, but he does not know how to distribute it."

Sitting Bull and his son were killed in 1890, by Indian policemen sent on orders from the government who wrongly suspected that the elderly chief was attempting to renew the Indian wars.

Literary Bull

Perhaps someone once wrote of a rooster and a bull having a conversation, and because it was just too ridiculous to believe, it became known as a cock-and-bull story. Whatever the case, scholars have not come up with a better explanation despite years of trying. The phrase was first used in English literature around 1600 and means something concocted and incredible, something that stretches the imagination beyond the limits of credulity. The French say coq-a-l'ane, literally, cock to the donkey, and they use it in the same sense.

When we use the expression, Taking the bull by the horn, we refer to the need to take charge of a situation and face what might be unpleasant consequences. This may have derived from bullfighting imagery, in the part of the bullfight where the bull, after he has been stuck with darts, is threatened by the banderilloeros who rush at him with their cloaks, leap on his back and seize his horns.

In old England the sport of bull-running was popular, and the phrase may have originated there. Around the year 1200, during the reign of King John, the town of Stamford, Lincolnshire, turned a bull loose in the marketplace on November 13 at eleven o'clock. The idea of the sport was for men and boys to pursue the bull with clubs, trying to drive it up on the bridge where the most courageous of the crowd would seize the animal and grasp its horns, trying to make it fall into the river. Eventually the bull would swim to shore and there it would be slaughtered, its meat sold to the men and boys who'd been in the run. The sport of bull-running lasted for almost 650 years, until it was abolished in 1840.

Men or Mice

The average American eats one half ton of cheese during a lifetime.

As the home of *Hoard's Dairyman*, Fort Atkinson, Wisconsin, was on the cutting edge of dairy technology. The local firm of Cornish, Curtis & Greene offered this bull-powered cream separator, which was manufactured by Vermont's St. Albans Foundry Company, to its customers. Photo courtesy Hoard Historical Museum.

Another sport involving bulls and England was *bull-baiting*, in which bulls were teased by dogs:

I went with some friends to the Bear Garden, where was cock fighting, bull and bear baiting. One of the bulls tossed a dog full into a lady's lap as she sat in a box at a considerable height from the arena. Two poor dogs were killed . . . and I most heartily weary of the rude and dirty pastime.

—John Evelyn
Diary, 1670

From this association with bulls and bears in the bull-baiting and bear-baiting sports, it is possible that the terms *bears* and *bulls* evolved with regard to the stock market. A bear is a speculator who sells a stock he does not own in the belief that before he will have to deliver the stock to its purchaser, its price will have dropped, and he will be able to make a profit on the transaction. A bull is a speculator who is more optimistic about the possibility of a stock increasing in value, so he buys the stock at what he believes to be a low price and then encourages demand for it.

To shoot the bull is a term that nowadays means to sit around and talk. When it means to talk pretentiously, it refers back to its barnyard origins where "bull" can mean the male of the bovine species, or the smelly muck you happen to be standing in. A *bull ses-sion*, a peculiarly American institution, is an occasion for a group of (usually) young men to get together and air their opinions.

Bulling is a term used when a cow is in heat. At this time, she will put her fore legs on the back of another cow and pretend she is a bull—this is called bulling.

A ladyslipper is also called a *bull bag* in some parts of the country, since the ladyslipper looks like a bull's scrotum, or "bull's bag."

The tradition of giving a shivaree to a newlywed couple involves something called a *bull band*, or serenade. At this celebration the husband and wife are expected to come forth and give the noisy visitors a treat.

A *bullboat* is a boat made of a wood frame and stretched skins of cowhide, used by explorers or early pioneers. In 1859 it was said that "Green or soaked hides are cut into the proper shape to fit the frame and sewed together with buckskin strings. . . . Two men can easily build a bull-boat of three hides in two days which will carry ten men with perfect safety."

A *bull cook* was originally a term used for the man who fed the draft animals in logging camps. Then the name was used for the camp handyman and eventually for someone who had a strong back and weak head.

A *bull driver* or *bullwhacker* was a

man who drove oxen, usually without any lines, just by the use of his voice, especially in logging camps. *Bullwhacking* meant filled with rough activity. And a *bull train* was a wagon drawn by oxen in the old west, for hauling freight.

Bull Durham is a kind of tobacco, but it is also an exclamation used to mean "Nonsense!"

A *bull fiddle* is a bass viol. And a bull fiddler is one who plays the instrument.

The *Bull of Bashan* appeared in the Bible, Psalms XXII, verse 12: "Many bulls have compassed me: strong bulls of Bashan have beset me round. They gaped upon me with their mouths, as a ravening and a roaring lion." Moses overtook Bashan, which was known as the land of the giants (Deuteronomy III; 14) and the cattle there were immense. Thus the epithet "Bull of Bashan" is often given to someone with a deep voice and powerful physique.

In his book *Dombey and Son*, 1867, Charles Dickens commented that Mrs. Skewton's passion for cows and her desire "to retreat to a Swiss farm, and live entirely surrounded by cows and china," suggested to Mr. Dombey "a remembrance of the celebrated bull who got by mistake into a crockery shop." However, in real-life it seems that the only celebrated four-hooved animal to find itself loose in anything resembling a crockery shop is a donkey in Aesop's fable *The Ass in the Shop of the Potter*, in which the clumsy and stupid donkey breaks most of the pots in the place while trying to avoid them.

It has been suggested, however, that this phrase may refer to an early nineteenth century political cartoon involving Great Britain and China—and thus John Bull in a "China" shop.

A *bullpen* is, of course, the place where pitchers warm up before and/or during the baseball game. It is also the name of a children's game in which boys and girls stand in a circle and throw a ball at those who stand at the center and try to dodge being hit. The player then hit by the ball has to come out and is out of the game.

A *bull-roarer* is a children's toy, a noisemaker made by attaching a long, narrow piece of wood sharpened at both ends to a piece of string. This is then whirled rapidly in the air and makes a roaring sound.

The term *bull's-eye* has several definitions:

It used to be a kind of thick, small-faced old fashioned watch. The term is also used to describe a bull's-eye lantern which has a convex lens in one side. There used to be a penny candy that looked like a bull's eye, and so

Where there is a bullpen, can a cow catcher be far behind? Whimsical bovines appear on many of the handmade terra cotta tiles created by Ellie Hudovernik in her Cascade, Wisconsin, studio. The "Cow Catcher Cow" measures 4 inches square.

named. The same thing happened with a marble that had an eye-like appearance.

A game played by shooting marbles into a ring, or into a hole in the ground is called "bull's eye." It is also the target for darts, and a "bull's eye daisy" is another name for a black-eyed Susan.

If someone is *bull-shy*, he is usually bashful and timid. To be as *big as a*

beef bull is to be pompous. If you are wearing a new straw hat out in the barnyard someone may greet you by saying, "You have a new *bull's breakfast* today."

Miscellaneous Bull

The *Cephalopterus ornatus*, the bull bird of South America, has a voice that sounds like a cow.

From almost every farm a dreadful tale
Of what a bull had done made children
  quail. . .
How the bull, loose in meadow, chased and
  tossed
A little boy, who lived (with reason lost).
How one, pursued across a field, was torn:
'The bull had tatters of him on his horn'.

—John Masefield
Going to See the Bull, 1942

Bull Rider. Ted Terry rode his bull, Ohadi, from Ketchum, Idaho, to Times Square, New York. He began the trip in July 1937 and arrived in New York City on August 11, 1940.

Bull Driver. The Peck Meat Packing Corporation of Milwaukee, Wisconsin, has a fetish for crazy license plates. With a number of service and sales consultants on the road, these license plate/words can be observed:

TOP COW	HEIFER	BOLONY
COOKED	SALAMI	BEEF
BAD COW	COW	AU JUS
2 ROAST	BULL	OX TAIL

Bull-aim. I was herdsman for a pure breed Holstein herd here in Walworth County. The bull was kept in a small horse barn next to the road. House on one side of road, barns on the other. Cow came in "season." Helper led bull out to roadway, I led cow out. Bull mounted cow. Cow must have hugged tail down tight. Bull rubbed penis along side of tail next to pin bone, thus feeling he had reached the right spot. Made his leap. I was standing right side of cow's head. Charge flew thru the air, & landed on my right shoulder. However next try was successful. No laughing matter, but you may laugh if you wish.

—D. J. Getchell
Elkhorn, Wisconsin

Oxen

Oxen include domestic cattle, water buffalo, bison, musk oxen, brahman, yak, and other bovine family members. Most oxen originated in Asia and Europe. They have heavy bodies, long tails, divided hoofs and are ruminants. Domestic oxen give milk, provide meat and leather. In some parts of the world they are still used as beasts of burden. A dictionary definition is: "The adult castrated male of the genus *Bos*, used as a draft animal and for food."

Babe. Born in the Winter of the Blue Snow, faithful friend and companion to Paul Bunyan, Babe, the Blue Ox, measured 42 ax handles and a plug of Star Chewing Tobacco between the eyes. He could haul a whole forest of logs with a harness made of buckskin, which stretched when wet and shrank when dry. On a rainy day, Babe would start pulling his load and arrive in camp about noon, only to find that the stretched buckskin had left the sled

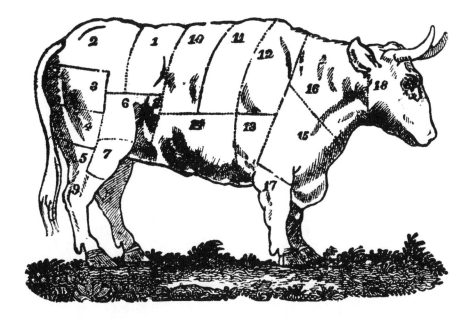

Miss E. Neil shared tips on preparing an ox in *The Everyday Cook-Book*, published in Chicago in 1892. Reporting in an 1850 issue, *Wisconsin and Iowa Farmer and Northwestern Cultivator* said: "The ox is not a showy animal, but he is a snug, well-fatted, useful beast. Depend upon it, he has made many a tender, dainty dish."

back in the forest. Then, as the sun came out and dried the harness, the shrinking action would pull the sled into camp. Every time Babe needed a new pair of shoes, Big Ole, the blacksmith, had to open a new iron mine in Minnesota. The Great Lakes were scooped out by big buddy Paul to provide drinking water for Babe.

Cows Worked as Oxen. A correspondent of the *Southern Cultivator* says: "I have worked cows in harness, not under the yoke, without detriment in any respect - on the contrary their calves were superior to the rest of the stock,—due, of course to the extra feed and attention the cows received. I should like to see this practice extended—for many of the poorer class have no other animal power to aid them in their farming operations."

—*Wisconsin Farmer*, 1849

Ox Power. To be 'as strong as an ox' long has implied possession of Herculean strength; and a full grown ox, or a bull, in good condition, truly is a powerful animal. In a 'dead pull' the ox is more than a match for any horse, excepting some of great weight and that have been especially bred for draft purposes. The strength characteristic of the ox was developed in its ancestors, partly in their long warfare with carnivorous animals, in which the fighting

121

As Robert Nesbit observed in *Wisconsin, A History*, slow, clumsy, but steady oxen were the mainstay of pioneer farmers, especially prized for the heavy task of breaking prairie sod. In Wisconsin, they outnumbered horses by a ratio of three to two in 1850. But reapers and mowers depended on the faster gait of horses to turn the working parts at satisfactory speeds. By 1870, horses outnumbered oxen by a ratio of five to one. Photo courtesy of Hoard Historical Museum.

122

was done at close quarters; the cattle depending solely upon goring, ripping, and tossing their antagonists—methods that required great muscularity in their necks and shoulder-parts. In the process of 'natural selection' in this work the weak or undersized cattle went down before their enemies, while the larger and stronger vanquished their foes and transmitted to their descendants the qualities that had made them victors. But another and contemporary great factor in the development of their astonishing strength of neck and forequarters was the strife for mastery between rival bulls, the reward of the successful one being the lordship of the herd. In these desperate encounters, the heavier, stronger, and more agile usually would win the battle; and as their fighting was done by furiously charging upon each other, and by each endeavoring to rip with his strong horns the body of the other and to toss it by main strength, their muscular system thereby became very highly developed, and the practice of applying their weight and energy by 'pushing' was fixed. Captivity has not deprived the bull of its martial spirit nor of its strength for fighting, and the old warfare for the lordship of the herd still goes on.

—*Prose and Poetry of the Live Stock Industry*, 1905

How Long?   It was in college and not on the farm that I first learned how long a furlong is, namely, a furrow long, namely, the length of a furrow an ox was expected to plow between rests. It was then I first realized that it was the stamina of the medieval English ox that gave us the measure of the familiar but arbitrary English mile we live by, namely, eight furlongs. The furlong was first.

—Ronald Jager
Country Journal

Ox Words.   The saying, *Adam's Off Ox* is probably a reference to the ox on the righthand side of Adam's pair of oxen (assuming Adam drove a team of oxen, which is questionable). The "off" ox is the one farthest from the driver, and because it cannot be seen as well by the driver, it may get poor footing. Thus, the term "off ox" may be used to designate an awkward person.

But not knowing someone *from Adam's off ox* means not knowing anything about that person. Nobody seems to know how Adam got involved with this, anyway, except that in 1848, a book titled *Nantucketisms* included the saying "poor as God's off ox," which meant very poor, indeed. It's possible that Adam was substituted for God.

The Black Ox is a mythological creature. If he steps on your foot, it symbolizes dire events, such as the death

123

of a near relative or a similar calamity. Lucky is the one of whom it can be said, "The black ox ne'er trod on his foot."

Beefcake

The Spanish Connection. The Spaniards introduced cattle into South America before the middle of the sixteenth century, and prior to its close there were wild descendants of these animals ranging over the pampas in the central-southern parts of that division of the New World. The regions they occupied were especially favorable to them, and they increased until the herds became enormous in size. It has been asserted by several Spanish writers that these cattle all sprang from seven cows and a bull that were brought from Andalusia to Paraguay about the year 1556.

—*Prose and Poetry of the Live Stock Industry,* 1905

Herefords. They are usually of a darker red; some of them are brown, and even yellow, and a few are brindled; but they are principally distinguished by their white faces, throats and bellies. In a few the white extends to the shoulders. The old Herefords were brown or red-brown with not a spot of white about them. It is only within the last fifty or sixty years that it has been the fashion to breed for white faces.

They are not as good milkers as the Devons. This is so generally acknowledged, that while there are many dairies of Devon cows in various parts of the country, a dairy of Herefords is rarely to be found. To compensate for this, they are even more kindly feeders than the Devons. Their beef may be objected to by some as being occasionally a little too large in the bone, and the fore-quarters being coarse and heavy; but the meat of the best pieces is often very fine-grained and beautifully marbled. There are few cattle more prized in the market than the genuine Herefords.

—*Wisconsin & Iowa Farmer* November 1854

Wild Beef. The rhythm of ranch life was determined by the manner in which the cattle were collected, fattened, and marketed. Texas was the breeding ground for numberless thousands of longhorns, and at a time when steak sold for 25 cents a pound in New York City a steer on the range could be bought for $1 or $2. The animals that farsighted cattlemen began driving north after the Civil War were the lean, rangy descendants of cattle brought to America by the Spaniards, and which had escaped from missions in the eighteenth century and had run wild through southern Texas; they were, first and last, virtually untamable. 'We have seen some buffaloes that

Greetings from longhorn country, circa 1930.

were more civilized,' a St. Louis newspaper noted in 1854. It was estimated that five million of these beasts, untended, were ranging the Texas frontier when the Civil War's end released thousands of men who returned home, looking for work and opportunity. And, simultaneously, the North and the Rocky Mountain West were clamoring for beef.

—*Will Rogers: The Man and His Times*

Comic Beef. The following exchange was included in *Roy Rogers & Trigger Comics*, published in 1960.

Dear Roy:

I'm always reading about branding and brands on cattle, but I really don't understand what they're for. Can you explain it for me?

Don

Dear Don:

In the early days, before there were fences on the range, cattle from all the ranches wandered freely over the pastureland. So, it became necessary for each rancher to identify his own cattle. Branding was the method they used.

Let me tell you a little more about branding, though, because it's one of the most interesting features of cowboy work. Did you know, for instance, that branding started way back . . . about 2,000 years before the birth of Christ? Drawings have been found on ancient Egyptian tombs picturing the process, and, believe it or not, their methods did not differ too much from ours! So, maybe it's true that "there's nothing new under the sun."

Your friend,
Roy Rogers

To Be a Successful Cattleman.

1. A wide-brimmed hat, a pair of tight pants, and a pair of $200 boots.
2. At least two head of livestock, preferably cattle, one male, one female.
3. A new air-conditioned pickup truck with automatic transmission, power steering, trailer hitch, and push-button radio for listening to football games.
4. A gun rack, big enough to hold walking stick and rope, for rear window of the pickup.
5. Two Border Collie dogs to ride in bed of truck.
6. A $40 horse and a $400 saddle.
7. A gooseneck trailer small enough to park in front of cafe.
8. A place to keep the cows, a little land too poor to grow crops.
9. A spool of barbed wire, six cedar posts, and a bale of prairie grass hay to haul around in the truck at all times.
10. A descriptive name for your ranch, such as Melodie Acres or Wagon Track Ranch, and a fancy brand, such as Circle O upside down. Brand on the side nearest corral fence.
11. Breed at least one female a year to an exotic bull—any bull that is unknown and whose breed name you are unable to pronounce.
12. Should you need credit at the bank, be sure to park pickup and dogs in front of bank president's window.

—Clarence C. Olson, Professor
Dairy Science Department
University of Wisconsin

Milk and Beef. Veal calves are immature milk-fed calves, usually not over three months of age. There are three classes: lightweights are 110 pounds or less; mediumweights are 110 to 180 pounds; and heavyweights are 180 pounds or more. One of the requisites of veal is that the flesh must be nearly white. To produce veal of this color, it is essential that no hay or grain be fed—only milk will maintain the desired color, and nothing but whole milk will produce veal of the highest quality.

Americans eat an average of about 110 pounds of beef per person per year. The average steer yields around 450 pounds of meat, so the typical American family eats a cow a year.

Holsteins are usually raised for their milk production, but with the oversupply of dairy products, more and more Holsteins are ending up on the butcher's block. Can the consumer tell the difference between a Holstein steak and a T-bone from a Black Angus? Norval Dvorak, vice president of Packerland Packing Company of Green Bay, Wisconsin, says, "Holstein beef now has all the eating qualities of traditional choice beef. There is not a person who, in a blindfold test, could tell the difference between a six-ounce steak from the finest choice Angus and one from a choice Holstein." He claims that Holstein beef is six to ten percent leaner than meat from traditional beef cattle and thus accommodates current consumer demands.

Cow Congestion

It is reported that the greatest concentration of cows in the United States is in Calumet County, Wisconsin, where there are 94 cows per square mile. Kewaunee County, Wisconsin runs a close second, with 90 cows per square mile.

In America's Dairyland, the number of cows peaked at 2,367,000 in 1944. Since then, although the number of dairy cows and dairy farms has declined, milk production has increased because of higher output per cow. Chart reprinted from *1984 Wisconsin Dairy Facts.*

Opposite page:
The Schuster Barn—Bruce Fritz

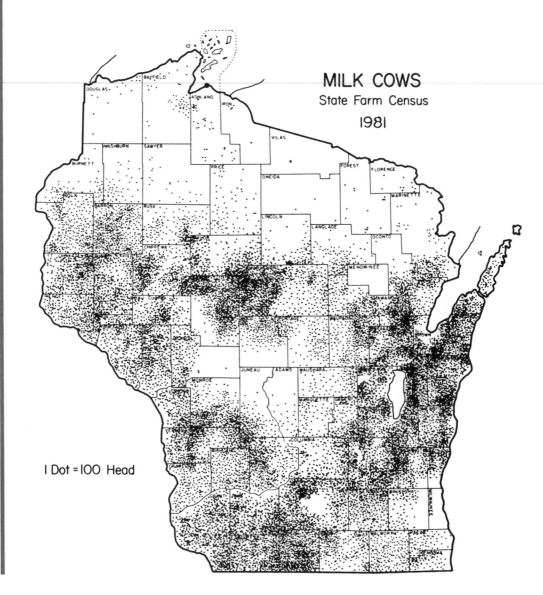

MILK COWS
State Farm Census
1981

I Dot = 100 Head

Brave New Bovine World

"I heard that some folks never seen a cow. Hell, they gotta be blind."
—William Peterson,
Wisconsin farmer

Not only have some folks never seen a cow, most bulls these days have never seen a cow. And cows almost never see a bull. More and more calves have never known their real mother, almost none ever see their father, and a lot of calves are not just a twin of a brother or sister, but a clone. Computers are deciding what to feed cattle, when to breed cattle, and cows can be brought into heat at the convenience of the dairyman. The dairy business is getting to be high-tech business. The small dairy farmer faces a bigger challenge than ever, not only because of risky economic circumstances but because his competition is the huge corporate farm.

The basic function of the cow remains the same: to produce milk. But for the past two centuries, since the 1760's, that function has been constantly tampered with and refined.

Now we have cows that are bigger and better, cows that produce more milk than ever, and cows that multiply by the hundreds.

In 1922 cows produced an average of 5,000 pounds of milk per year. In 1985 the average cow produced 13,000 pounds of milk and by 2083 scientists hope to have cows producing over 30,000 pounds of milk per year; that's over eleven gallons per day!

With advancements in artificial insemination and embryo transfer techniques, a cow with a high quality bloodline can be flushed of 100 embryos a year, embryos which are then fertilized with semen from a top-of-the-line bull and which are then carried through gestation by a herd of plain old everyday cows.

Experiments in embryo-splitting, or cloning, have successfully brought about duplicate fertilized embryos and have resulted in many births of identical twin calves, carried to term in non-identical surrogate mothers. So the 100 embryos flushed from that high-quality donor can become 200 calves per year from one cow.

As individual cows have become heavier producers, the number of cattle on U.S. dairy farms has diminished. As an example, in 1944 we had 2,367,000 cows in Wisconsin. In 1985 we had 1,825,000 cows and predictions are that that number will be reduced substantially as milk production increases. More milk from fewer cows, but those cows will be bred for it and therefore more expensive.

At the same time, farmers are giving up. In 1970 there were 647,860 dairy farms in the U.S. and that number had been reduced by 1984 to 285,740. To reach this total, almost 26,000 farms go out of business every year. Meanwhile, there is an overabundance of milk and the government is paying farmers to cut back on production or slaughter their cows.

Somehow this does not make sense. If you think we've come a long way from "The friendly cow all red and white, / I love with all my heart," you're right. As with so many things in our new and modern world, we've let Technology run away with the Cow. And there's no way to call either of them back anymore.

This Is a Test

Recording milk and fat production of individual cows was observed in the United States as early as 1854 with a Jersey cow, Flora 13, producing 511 pounds, two ounces of churned butter in 350 days. Most records reported after this were based on a short period of seven days and involved weighing of feed consumed and milk produced under the supervision of a "tester." This type of test was popular during the early 1900's and became the official program for various breed associations under the name of Advance Registry. With this program, a dairyman could select individual cows to be tested.

With the advent of the Babcock test for percent butterfat in milk in 1890, dramatic changes occurred in methods for evaluating dairy cows. Not only was there a shift away from measuring the pounds of churned butter to determine the percent butterfat in milk, but also to reporting of annual production of milk and fat. Reporting of complete lactations of up to 365 days in length was stressed, rather than seven day totals.

The first cow testing associations (CTA) in the U.S. were formed in Michigan following a meeting of six to eight dairy farmers in September of 1905. This meeting was called by a Danish immigrant, Helmer Rabild, who had previous experience with cow testing associations in Denmark. This cow testing association began operation in January 1906 with 31 herds and 239 cows. The size of a CTA was limited by the amount of work a tester could do alone. Typically, he would arrive at a farm in time for the evening meal, weigh and take samples that night and the next morning (after sleeping at the farm). After breakfast, the samples would be tested on the farm, bottles cleaned, and, while these bottles were drying, the tester would calculate and enter production figures in the record book.

The concept of cow testing associations spread to other states with Wisconsin in May 1906, Maine and New York in 1908, Vermont, Iowa, California, and Nebraska in 1909, and a total of 40 states by 1920. All 48 states had testing programs by 1929.

—Wisconsin Dairy Herd
Improvement Cooperative
Madison, Wisconsin

Test Cream. This writer can remember, as a youngster, watching with interest as his father carefully weighed the milk from each of his five or six cows using the cumbersome old steelyard. Milk from each cow was poured into tumblers to uniform depth and these allowed to stand in a cool place until morning when the comparative depths of cream could be noted.

—Roy T. Harris
Assistant in Charge of
Official Testing, 1906–1948

Test Scores. The average production of all cows tested by the Dairy Herd Improvement Association is now 15,400 pounds of milk a year, and that figure is expected to reach 17,000 pounds within the next six years. The 265,000 cows on the Holstein Association's Dairy Herd Improvement Registry averaged more than 18,890 pounds of milk in 1983, up almost 1,000 pounds since 1979.

Of course milk consumption hasn't come close to keeping pace with milk production, so those gigantic increases in per-cow production require a corresponding decrease in the number of cows. There were only half as many dairy cows in the United States in 1977 as there were in 1950, but they produced more than twice as much milk. The Dairy Herd Improvement Association estimates that by 1990 national milk production needs can be met with only 8.5 million cows—23 per cent fewer than there are on American farms right now.

—*Blair & Ketchum's Country Journal*
July 1985

The Day the Tester Comes
The cows are in a shady place,
(The day is sultry hot)
Not even lured by tender grass
To leave their comfort spot

The water tank seems far away,
And their ambition lags;
They're more concerned with idle ease
Than filling up their bags.

The pesky flies chew constantly
On men and cows alike;
And, though the men work as they swat,
The cows are on a strike!

The ones which last week filled the pail
Now this week seem near dry;

131

And though the milker tugs and pulls,
The cows won't even try.

Between the rains—between repairs—
The men put up the hay;
It's bound to rain again and then
There'll be some more delay.

The morning milking was quite late—
(The farmer overslept)
Besides all else, there's feed to grind;
Someone had better step!

A salesman comes and wants to talk—
Has nothing more to do;
A fence breaks down and calves get out—
Emergencies anew!

What day is this? So trouble-filled
It seems to be all thumbs.
Why any dairy farmer knows
The day the TESTER comes!
—Frances B. Koehler
Cow Testing Association, Annual Report
Viola, Wisconsin, 1922

Cow Education

When the State of Wisconsin was created in 1848, the constitution called for the creation of a strong educational system all the way from the primary schools to a state university to be built in Madison. In 1850, the Board of Regents to the University, in their third annual report, made this statement:

Agricultural science, like all other sciences, can only be acquired by study and research. The discipline of the school is essential to its acquisition. Without it, the farming processes fall to the low level of routine and drudgery. With it, agriculture rises to the dignity of a profession, and indicates its undoubted claim to stand not only in the front rank of the experimental arts, but side by side with the learned professions in interest and honor, as well as in profit.

The Regents created a professorship of agriculture and attempted to find someone to fill the chair. This was not an easy matter. In 1866 the president of the University of Vermont wrote that they also had a department of agriculture but knew of no one who could fill the post. In 1868 W. W. Daniells was hired as a professor of agriculture and analytical chemistry. His "experimental farm" consisted of an orchard and vineyard but neither the University president nor the Regents paid much attention. In the 1870's the University seemed to consider the experimental farm as a source for firewood, and needy students saw it as a place where they could usually find work (at 12½ cents an hour). The citizens of Madison saw it as a kind of public park.

Finally, in 1878, the Board of Regents was asked to appoint a farmer to the Board in the hope that he might be of some help. Hiram Smith, a successful dairy farmer, gave the new school much needed direction. He also helped convince the University that they needed a full-time professor of agricul-

The class of 1900 at the University of Wisconsin's cheesemakers' school was photographed in Hiram Smith Hall. Cheesemaking practices developed and tested at the University and its Agricultural Experiment Station beginning in 1890 helped make Wisconsin the nation's leading cheese producer. Photo courtesy of Agricultural Journalism Department, University of Wisconsin-Madison.

ture with the result that William A. Henry was hired in 1880. Henry, in turn, soon hired Stephen Babcock, and Wisconsin's influence on the nation's agriculture and dairying was assured.

On the 27th of March, 1883, the Wisconsin Assembly passed a bill which increased the state property tax . . . with the funds earmarked for the University to establish an Agricultural Experiment Station. Four days later, the Senate approved the measure which was promptly signed into law by Governor Jeremiah Rusk. Thus began one of the great facets of the University of Wisconsin. Thus began a program of economic and academic development that no other University, no other state has matched.

Wisconsin, since about 1850, had been a major wheat-producing state. By growing wheat after wheat, it soon depleted its soils and had a major need of soil renovation technology. It, thus, joined the Eastern States in experiencing a serious decline of soil productivity. The need to increase soil fertility was . . . the most salient force behind the Agricultural Experiment Station movement in the United States and earlier in Europe. A national movement toward a network of state experiment stations had been underway since about 1872, and it was natural for Wisconsin to move along this line.

After the Civil War, livestock production, particularly dairying, replaced wheat as the underpinning economy of the State. There was a virtual void of industrial technology for dairying, a situation that was both an opportunity and a problem for Wisconsin and its State University.

The rapid shift from wheat to dairying and the great need for dairying technology were accompanied by an almost complete failure of the University's curriculum in agriculture (begun in 1868) to attract students. Farmers expressed a basic fear that if they sent their sons to Madison, they would be educated into non-farming professions. The farmers needed help and they knew it, but they sensed something that academia didn't understand; namely, that the University did not have an information base to teach agricultural technology. This was, perhaps, a blessing in disguise for it inadvertently oriented the University to research to an unusual degree. It is of no little significance that the establishment of the Experiment Station preceded that of the College of Agriculture by six years.

—Glen S. Pound, Former Dean
College of Agricultural
and Life Sciences
University of Wisconsin-Madison

Bashful Babcock.   Stephen Moulton Babcock, hired as an agricultural chemist at the University of Wisconsin in

Stephen Moulton Babcock, best known for inventing a quick and simple butterfat test for milk, was a native New Yorker. A graduate of Tufts, he taught at Cornell and worked at the New York Agricultural Experiment Station before being hired by the University of Wisconsin in 1888. Though serious about his scientific work, Babcock was very friendly and had a boisterous laugh. M. E. Diemer photographed him milking a cow in 1928. State Historical of Wisconsin photo.

1888 proved himself quickly with his development of the butterfat test in 1890 that permitted fair and equal marketing of milk based on quality.

But Babcock would not accept full credit for his discovery, stating that this was based entirely on the findings of others and that he had merely perfected a simple and inexpensive test already in use in the dairy industry.

While at the University, Babcock conducted experiments in animal nutrition. He was skeptical of the value of chemical analysis in determining the nutritional value of feeds for dairy cattle, and pointed out that one could construct a diet of entirely organic and inorganic substances that could easily conform with the proximate analysis claimed for a nutritionally adequate diet. Once he inquired why leather might not be ground up and used as cattle feed, since it was rich in nitrogenous material. Nevertheless, his skepticism was fully justified and his point was well taken; namely, that mere analyses of protein, carbohydrate, and fat together with minerals could not be used to predict the nutritional value of a diet.

In his work with George C. Humphrey of the Animal Husbandry Department, Babcock was able to prove the importance of salt for dairy cattle. The University herd was divided in half: one-half received salt in the usual manner and the other received an unsalted basal ration. Eventually the salt-starved cattle changed in behavior, appearance and production. In fact, when they were being driven to their pasture in what is now the Camp Randall football stadium, the salt-starved cows would often block the streetcar tracks at University Avenue and Breese Terrace where they would lick the salt that remained there from use during the winter to improve the traction for the streetcars. This brought complaints from Madison citizens and a warning to the University concerning control of its animals. To make matters worse, in those days, before the invention of mechanical refrigeration, ice cream had to be stored in heavily insulated boxes inside metal containers filled with a salt and ice mixture called brine, that held the temperature well below freezing. One day the cows were put back on the Camp Randall pasture after a circus had appeared there, and the cows ate a cubic-yard hole in the sod where the brine from an ice-cream freezer had been dumped.

Won't Replace Bossy.   An artificial cow that gives real milk is holding down a laboratory stall at University Farm school.

The mechanical bovine, constructed and operated by Prof. W. E. Petersen of the dairy husbandry department, is yielding up secrets about the inside of

G enuine buttermilk is not always available, due to variations in the manufacture of butter, so cultured buttermilk (practically the only kind the consumer is able to find these days) is made by the fermentation of milk or skim milk with lactic acid bacteria.

a cow—once termed the darkest place on earth.

To Petersen's knowledge, the cow is the only one of its kind in the world. . . A product of research that began in 1927, the milk-giving artificial animal little resembles Bossy in the flesh, but produces just as much and just as good milk as its live counterpart.

Petersen used the pulsator of a milking machine for the artificial cow's heart, two vacuum-expanding rubber devices corresponding to the right and left sides of the heart, and a large bottle for the lungs.

The parts are connected with glass and rubber tubing.

The udder from a slaughtered cow is attached to the device and the cow's blood is started through the pumping machinery.

Occasionally the artificial cow has suffered "heart trouble," said Petersen. The udder can go for some time without damage while repairs to the heart are made.

The laboratory animal, however, is purely experimental, the professor said, and there is no likelihood of its replacing the life-and-blood cow.

Petersen explained that the milk, produced from elements in the blood, is manufactured in the udder. It is secreted in tiny tubes, known as alveoli, of which there are about 1,000,000 in a cubic inch of udder tissue.

Four hundred gallons of blood have to be pumped through the udder to make one gallon of milk, Petersen explained. In the case of the artificial cow, depleted elements are added to the blood at correct intervals.

Letdown of the milk in the artificial cow was solved by Petersen through the injection of a hormone called oxytocin.

Until Petersen made his demonstration with the hormone, little was understood about the reasons why a cow fails to let down her milk.

The hormone is manufactured in the posterior pituitary gland in a cow's skull. When a cow is contented and correctly stimulated, Petersen said, oxytocin flows normally into the blood and the milk is released freely.

The idea that a cow can "hold up her milk" is incorrect, Petersen said. The letdown, as proved by his experiments, is not voluntary but automatic, and involves the sensory nerves which carry the stimulus to the pituitary.

It in turn ejects the hormone into the blood.

"If the cow is frightened or angry or has her attention called to any strange factor, there will be but partial or no response to milking," he said.

He has caused this in experiments in which rats were placed in the manger, inflated paper bags were exploded, a cat placed on the cow's back, or the

New Ideas

Softer butter is the current challenge before the Wisconsin Milk Marketing Board. They have approved a study to develop butter that won't turn solid when it gets cold. The butter-softening process involves taking butter apart chemically and recombining the components. Other research projects aim to develop milk and ice cream with a longer shelf life; study the effects of artificial sweeteners on the taste of yogurt; and a study that will allow cheesemakers to turn cheese whey into fuel alcohol. But the best idea of all, currently in the works, is the development of a dairy-based candy bar that would be nutritious instead of providing empty calories.

Professor W. E. Petersen of the University of Minnesota developed a mechanical cow in the 1940's. Graduate students like Max Dawdy, shown here, rigged the artificial bovine. To conduct experiments on nutrition and the physiology of milk secretion, udders were obtained from a local packing plant. Dr. Clarence C. Olson of Madison, Wisconsin, one of Petersen's former graduate students, took the photo.

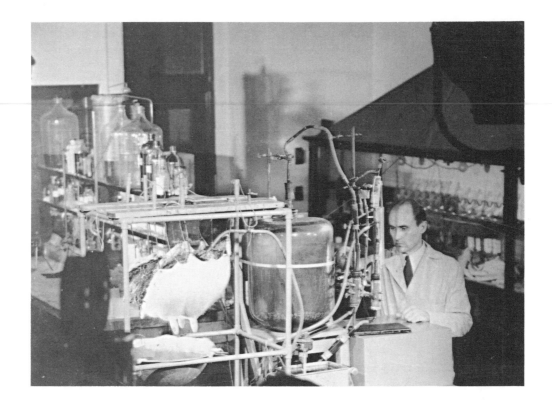

cow stuck with needles. The milk flow has then been restored with an injection of oxytocin.

In other experiments, Petersen has been able to obtain milk from sterile heifers, and even from bulls, through injection of a chemical substance known as diethylstilbestrol. "In most cases with sterile heifers," he said, "as large udders and levels of milk flow can be attained artificially as would be expected following a normal calving."

"A fair percentage of animals so treated subsequently conceive, making the treatment practical, at least in the case of well bred sterile heifers," he said.

Other studies conducted by the professor have shown that cows have a definite social order, ranging from the queen who holds her position by out-butting the others, down to the cows which have no aspirations to the throne and thus are the most contented.

At present Petersen is engaged in another experiment. While still a secret, if successful it will be an important contribution in the birth of healthy calves.

—University of Minnesota
Minneapolis Sunday Tribune
March 7, 1946

Artificial Insemination

Artificial insemination (AI) is the artificial introduction of semen into the genital tract of the female. The practice of artificial insemination of farm animals is not new, nor did it originate in the United States.

An Italian scientist, Spallanzani, working with dogs, conducted the first reported scientific experiments with this technique in 1780. The Russians, after several decades of experimentation, (in 1893 M. F. Ivanov first accomplished artificial insemination with cattle and sheep), began using the technique in the 1930's to breed millions of sheep and cattle. In the mid- to late- 1930's, the technique was first reported in use in the U.S. Dr. Clarence L. Cole at the University of Minnesota, Pabst Farms in Wisconsin, and Enos Perry of New Jersey were among the earliest practitioners.

The idea began to spread rapidly, and nearly 100 recognized A.I. units were operating by 1950. Most were cooperatives that were formed at county and district levels. Mergers reflecting the pressures of cost and competition in the '50's and '60's began to take their toll. Today there are about 15 effective operating units in the United States.

During the early days of the industry, there was no means of preserving semen other than in a liquid form for a few days at 35° to 38°. Thus, semen had to be shipped usually on an every-other-day basis to the field technicians scattered across the country where the cows were located. Semen not used within 2 to 3 days had to be discarded because of the decline in fertility.

—Robert E. Walton, President
American Breeders Service
DeForest, Wisconsin, 1985

Artificial Breeding Won't Work.

Farm Journal, March 1950
"Artificial breeding won't work. It simply won't work!"

Farmers in five important dairy states have told *Farm Journal* to tell you that. Not just a few farmers either—but 147 of them. They're from New York, Washington, Tennessee, Ohio and Wisconsin. What kind of farmers are these? They're good dairymen, good enough to belong to a Dairy Herd Improvement Association. About half of them have used artificial breeding, but quit for one reason or another. The others never started . . .

Most of these dairymen agreed on certain general complaints. . .

"We've had too much trouble getting our cows with calf. I tell you there are just too many repeat breedings."

"A neighbor got only one calf from 25 cows in a whole year's trial with artificial breeding."

"Your calving gets off schedule, your freshening dates get later each year. I had fall calves to start with, but ended up with winter and summer calves."

"Funny thing, I had trouble getting my cows settled with the breeding thing; but when I used my own bull on these same cows, they settled on the first service."

"Heifers from artificial breeding don't look enough alike."

"The calves from artificial breeding are weaker."

"One of my neighbors got a Jersey calf from a Holstein cow. And I know one fellow who got mostly bull calves."

"Cows will not respond to this breeding more than three years. After that, you've got to use a bull."

. . . and one farmer complained, "We can't use artificial breeding because we have poor telephone service—sometimes no service at all."

[The magazine's response:]

"In some places where there is no phone service, farmers tie a yellow tag on their milk cans. The tag gives the man's name, tells how many cows are in heat, when they came in heat, and their breed. These tags are taken off at the milk plant, and the information is phoned to the technician. Sometimes local gas stations and grocery stores keep a record of farmers who have cows to be bred. The inseminator drives by the store and picks up his calls."

We'll Never Keep Another Bull.

Farm Journal, April 1950

Last month, 147 farmers said "Artificial breeding won't work!" Here's a quick answer from 243 of their neighbors who say. . . . "We'll Never Keep Another Bull"

. . .Dairymen from Washington to New York say that breeding the neighbor's cows has always been a sore spot—a risk if you do, and likely to make you unpopular if you don't.

Just ask the man with a barn full of artificially sired heifers what he thinks of artificial breeding. He's very likely to tell you that it's the best thing that ever happened to dairying.

. . . for the first time in history, . . . the average dairyman has a chance to breed his cows to the best bulls in the country—better bulls than he could afford to own, or than he'd have time to find.

. . . It's little wonder that one of the

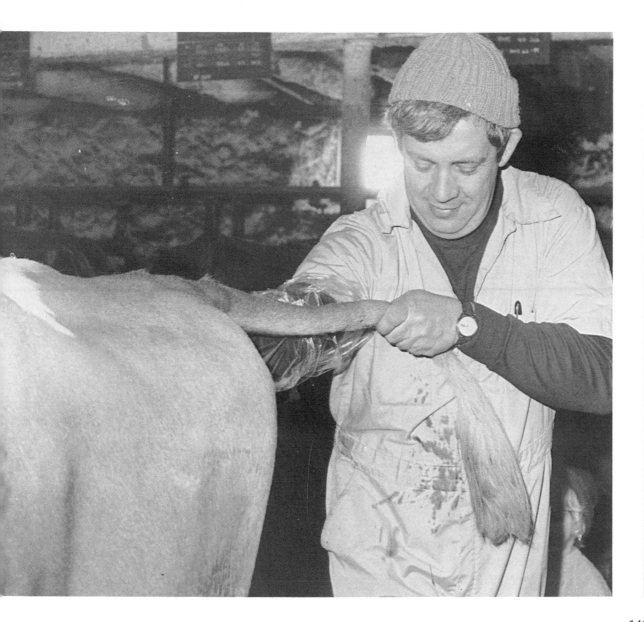

Cows that are ready to be inseminated can be identified using chin-ball markers worn by surgically altered bulls or androgenized cows. The marker acts like a giant ball-point pen and leaves a blaze on the back of a cow in heat when she is mounted. Ray Mueller of Chilton, Wisconsin, captured the gentle touch of veterinarian Paul Berge in this photo.

most popular reasons in favor of artificial breeding is *safety*. It is a relief not to have to argue with a bull about who's boss. As John Albrecht, a farmer from Tioga County, N.Y., puts it:

"I'm very allergic to bulls. I used to love the devils and gloried in my ability to handle the mean ones. Then one day one of the most gentle bulls I ever owned put me through the barn door—without even opening it.

The door and I both needed fixing after that.

Our inseminator has always been well behaved, and I doubt if he'll ever try pushing me around."

. . . After years of watching artificial breeding grow, *Farm Journal* believes—along with this month's farmers—that it is one of the greatest things that ever came along for the dairyman. But, like last month's farmers, we don't think for a minute that it's as good as it could be—or ever will be. It simply isn't. But despite its faults, if we were to vote for the outstanding dairy achievement of the last half century, artificial breeding would be it."

Instructions to Inseminators. Always protect the syringe from cooler temperatures and direct sunlight. The best place to keep a loaded syringe is in the coveralls, shirt or jacket that you're wearing. Body heat protects the semen from temperature extremes. Plus, putting the loaded syringe in your coveralls or shirt keeps the semen from direct sunlight. Once the straw is properly loaded in the sheath and syringe, there's little chance semen will flow out, unless the inseminator accidently hits the plunger.

Next, put a plastic shoulder-length glove on the arm that you'll be working with in the cow. Make sure it's stretched all the way up the arm and that the fingers are well-filled and fairly tight. Also, have two or three clean paper towels opened up in your pocket.

Generally, lubricants are not necessary when you use a plastic glove. But for an occasional problem cow or heifer, mix a small amount of lubricant with water and smear it over the gloved hand and arm.

Then pick up the cow's tail and move it toward the outside of the arm that will enter the cow. Do this with the hand that does not have the glove on. Use a paper towel to avoid direct contact with manure or genital discharge.

. . .Always remember to handle the syringe like a feather, not a sword.

—American Breeders Service

From Moos to Moola. Embryo transplants may be only the beginning of the reproductive wizardry science is unleashing.

Such advances are making an already valuable cow's worth astronomical. When Ontario interests purchased the Thomas Pearson cow Allendairy Glamourous Ivy for $1,025,000 on November 20, 1982, they said embryo transplant technology had enhanced its value.

How does embryo transplantation work?

Cows are injected with fertility drugs to make them super-ovulate; one week after injection they are artificially inseminated. Another week later, the fertilized embryos—not quite visible to the naked eye—are flushed out with saline water solution and transferred to the recipient cows. Meanwhile, the drug

lutalyse has been given to the donor cows to make them come into estrus. The host cows then carry the calves to term (nine months).

Cows can be flushed successfully about twice a year, says Raymond Bula, former director of the U.S. Dairy Forage Research Center. As many as 25 embryos have been recovered during such flushing. Through embryo transplantation, Bula says, the center will build up a prize herd in three years instead of the generation normally necessary.

Embryo transplants were first performed in the late 1960's on the exotic beef breeds like the French Charolais to overcome import bans due to hoof-and-mouth disease. Embryo transplants do not carry the disease.

Robert Rowe, who has a veterinary practice in Middleton, Wisconsin, developed in 1976 the nonsurgical method of embryo transplantation now in use. He has carried a valise full of embryos aboard jetliners to such countries as Hungary and Columbia. Embryos can live on their own for 36 hours.

Cloning. University of Wisconsin reproductive physiologist Neal L. First conducted the cloning three weeks ago. Seven embryos were obtained; each was split in two by a fine surgical blade connected to a micro-manipulator device.

In the process of embryo transplantation, cows from superior bloodlines are injected with fertility drugs and then artificially inseminated. About a week later, the fertilized embryos are flushed out of the uterus and transferred to other cows, who carry the embryos to term. In this way, top cows can produce several calves in a single year. Jim Larison photo courtesy of Agricultural Journalism Department, University of Wisconsin-Madison.

I*f you let milk stand before it's homogenized, cream will rise to the top. Or it can be separated by means of a centrifugal separator. Sometimes this is sold directly to a manufacturer for ice cream or butter, but if it's sold for consumption as "cream," it is called market cream. When we purchase cream we might think that heavy, thick cream is of higher fat content than thin cream, but actually the viscosity or thickness is not necessarily an indication of its richness. Homogenized cream is thicker than non-homogenized, and pasteurized cream does not thicken as it ages although raw cream does. Heating cream increases its viscosity.*

First said embryos could be split three or four ways, "but your success goes way down." The embryos are then transplanted. The result nine months later is seven sets of perfect twins—twice as many animals as would have resulted had nature been allowed to take its course.

The first cloning was done in Cambridge, England, in 1981 with cattle, sheep and horses. It has also been done in France and at Colorado State University.

Another fun thing about embryo transplantation and cloning is that an Angus beef cow can give birth to a Holstein dairy animal, or perhaps an endangered species of the same family, such as the European bison. The populations of such endangered species could be increased dramatically in a relatively short time. . . . The next phase is further away—genetic manipulation to re-program the cells themselves to provide tailor-made cattle. Or people.

—*The Capital Times*
Madison, Wisconsin
November 24, 1982

Brave New World of Bovines

Professor Neal First and his colleagues at UW-Madison are busy creating a brave new world of bovines which will someday change the face of the dairy industry in Wisconsin.

What First is trying to do is to clone cattle embryos so that the new cows will be able to produce far more milk than the average cow today produces. He is also working on gene-transfer programs that will someday allow farmers to change a cow's feeding program and have the cow produce extra milk during periods when milk production normally would slack off. First admits that methods to increase milk production may frustrate dairy economists and government cost-cutters who see American farmers producing far more milk than can be sold today. But he suggests, "the ultimate beneficiary of technological advances in agriculture is the consumer, who over the years has been able to purchase food at reasonable prices because farmers have become more efficient.

The cloned cattle that will be produced through First's research will probably be purchased by corporations, rather than individual farmers.

"In the dairy industry, the nature of who owns the valuable cows has changed considerably," he said. "It's gone from the hands of individual dairy farmers to corporations that own investor herds.

Those corporations will pay thousands of dollars for a cow that can produce 30,000 pounds of milk a year because the calves from that cow will also produce far more milk than the average cow—especially if scientists can develop cloning methods to make sure that happens. . . ."

—*Wisconsin State Journal*
Madison, Wisconsin
June 23, 1985

Identical Twins.   American Breeders Service, DeForest, Wisconsin, has a two-year contract and research agreement with the U.S. Dairy Forage Research Center and the University of Wisconsin-Madison to use embryo splitting in an effort to get identical twin bulls. Fertilized embryos are being collected from exceptional cows mated to top bulls in select herds around the nation. A week after the cows are bred artificially, the fertilized embryos are collected nonsurgically in the morning, flown to Madison and moved to the dairy-forage center north of Prairie du Sac. In less than 12 hours from the time of the collection, the embryos are split and transferred to recipient females.

Then the waiting begins. There are eight pairs of identical twins (calves from the same embryo) now being carried by recipient animals. The only unknown factor is the sex of the calves.

The embryos are split by University of Wisconsin research specialist David Northey. Moments later, veterinarian Robert Rowe checks the embryos for quality and transfers them to recipient females. In splitting the embryos, Northey uses a powerful microscope and has instruments with remote controls to do the delicate surgery for division of the cells. The embryo is about one-fourth the size of a grain of salt.

Northey "anchors" the embryo against a suction tube. He first cuts the "shell" of the embryo, a tough circle of growth surrounding the embryo cells. Then he carefully splits the interior cell mass, making his cut between the connected cells. One half of the embryo is drawn into a pipette so it can be lifted and moved to a shell of an unfertilized embryo. The other half is kept in the original shell from the donor cow.

Individual embryos from the split are put into plastic tubes, called straws, and then transferred to the reproductive systems of recipient animals—one per cow.

ABS [hopes to] double the normal supply of frozen semen for generations to come.

Right now the success rate from current technology is not what is expected . . . the ability to sex the embryos to determine which will have bull calves will be the greatest advance.

—*Wisconsin State Journal*
Madison, Wisconsin
August 5, 1984

Divide and Duplicate.   The first pair of identical twin Holstein bulls produced by splitting an embryo have en-

Benefits of Higher Education

T*he amount of ice cream eaten increases with income and education.*

145

Staffer Josephine Lewandowski poses with Maggie, a Holstein cow, and some of Maggie's embryo-transplanted offspring. The calves are full brothers and sisters. Photo courtesy U.S. Dairy Forage Research Center, U.S. Department of Agriculture, Agricultural Research Services. The Center is located in Prairie du Sac, Wisconsin.

tered the ABS Progeny Test Program. . . .

The most visible nongenetic differences between Divide and Duplicate are size and color markings. The difference in size results from the calves being carried to birth by different cows.

The twin's color markings are similar, but not identical, because pigment cells within developing animals do not settle in exactly the same position. . . .

—American Breeders Service
Technology Rampant. And now technology has broken an ancient link

that, for many ages and among many peoples, for good and for ill, bound the bull and mankind so closely together. The great body of the full-grown bull has become a mere encumbrance. His strength, his courage, his potency are no longer required. Fertility has become divorced from valor, potency prostituted to unnatural usage. Fewer and fewer bulls ever meet with a cow. To ensure the burden of conception a cow must suffer the intrusion of a plastic straw bearing a mere half cubic centimetre of deep-frozen bull's semen from an unseen donor. She is denied everything in sex that people clamour for, bearing the unwanted and unasked offspring without the pleasure copulation provides. Mankind caught up in the slave chains of technology is fast converting the helpless animals he exploits into the image of machines, sacrificed in the service of a modern idolatry. Cattle, both bull and cow, are fast losing all pride of breed, all individuality, all that ever gave a measure of meaning to their enjoyment of life. The bull of proud title, the cow with poetical name—they are doomed to become mere numbers on a filing card system. Man, in his sacrifice to Technology, has degraded his sacrificial substitutes, the cow and the bull; the cow to the level of mere incubating test-tube; the bull to that of a masturbating machine. Must man, himself, follow as the su-

preme sacrifice? Or will it so happen that in a revolt of nature and in the shadow of a fading cross, the bull with head down and dewlap sweeping the ground, may charge and bellow again? After all is said and done it may not always be the meek who inherit the earth.

—Allen Fraser
The Bull

Automation. Just about everything you might imagine being done on dairy farms by the turn of the century is already being done—or at least researched—on a University of Illinois dairy research farm. The research program there, titled "Automation and Electronics for Dairy Management," is a joint University of Illinois and USDA ARS project. It is being conducted by Sidney Spahr, a U of I dairy scientist, and Hoyle Puckett, a research agricultural engineer with USDA.

The heart of the computerized dairy farm will be what Spahr calls automatic data collection.

"The farmer will have a central management computer on the farm, probably something like the personal computers we're seeing right now," he notes. "There will be data collection points all around the farm, feeding information to this central computer to be recorded in the appropriate file and then used by the farmer to better manage his herd."

Otis Bunratty, dairyman of the 1980's, is the creation of Port Edwards, Wisconsin, artist Jeffrey Johannes. The Bunratty panel and five other tongue-in-cheek commentaries on cow lore make up a watercolor entitled "Bovine-ities," which appeared in a 1984 issue of *Agri-View*. Jon Bolton photo courtesy Wustum Museum of Fine Arts.

Otis Bunratty did the walking in his old dairy barn. Changing to a new dairy barn and new work methods saved him 475 hours, 234 miles and 31,490 full knee bends a year. Otis also gained 87 pounds.

Each cow will be considered as a collection point, since each must have some kind of electronic identification.

Spahr envisions a small transponder implanted in the cow's reproductive tract as a form of permanent identification.

"The reason for implanting the transponder in the reproductive tract rather than hanging it by a chain around the neck or in an ear tag is for heat detection. . . . Information collected by the sensor in the reproductive tract would be fed into the farm's management computer and the farmer could get an up to the minute report any time he wanted it.

"There is also an on-farm test being perfected to judge the amount of progesterone in milk. Normally, when a cow begins her estrus cycle, the progesterone level will go down. If she's pregnant, the level will stay high. A sensor could take a reading on progesterone level while the cow is being milked, too."

As part of his degree work at Illinois, Jim Leverich developed a program that considers a cow's milk production and her stage of lactation and adjusts her grain ration accordingly.

"With the computer measuring and recording the amount of milk produced, it's fairly simple to feed the cow for what's she's producing now rather than what we expect her to produce or what she produced during the last testing period," he says.

"Another part of this system will be data feedback from the electronic feeders to tell the computer how much feed the cow is consuming. With an electronic ID in the cow's reproductive tract, a pedometer, a sensor in the milk line, and one at the feeder, we can tell how much feed she's eating, how much she's producing, whether she's bred or in heat, and whether she has or is developing a subclinical mastitis.

"Take this one more step and let the computer actually turn belt feeders on and off for you.

"Something a little further off is the use of robots to milk cows," Leverich continues. "Work is currently underway in Germany to develop a robot that can put a milker on a cow. If this is successful, it's possible the dairy farmer could devote nearly all of his energies to managing the system and cut physical labor."

—*Wisconsin Agriculturist*
September 8, 1984

Georgia O'Keeffe's "Cow's Skull: Red, White, and Blue," painted in 1931, may have inspired photographer Grant Gill. Like O'Keeffe, Gill was born and raised in Wisconsin. He currently lives in New York City, where he works as an associate producer with an advertising agency and takes freelance photographs.

Cows in the Arts

The cow has been a part of the history of art since its beginnings, with paintings of bison and bulls created in the caves of Lascaux in France between 15,000 and 10,000 BC. Cattle appear in Egyptian tomb paintings. Mycenaean Greeks depicted cattle grazing on their gold cups and the Minoans of Crete created wall paintings of bull-vaulting games. Later in Europe, Pieter Breughel the Elder depicted the lives of peasants with warmth and attention to the details of rural life. Landscapes by Rembrandt, Lorraine, Poussin, and Constable often contained cattle. In the twentieth century, Picasso used the minotaur in his paintings and graphic work, and his sculpture "Bull's Head," created from a bicycle seat and handlebars, is a modern classic. Dubuffet created an entire series of expressionistic pieces devoted to cows which manage to be both ridiculous and sympathetic.

—Bruce W. Pepich, Director
Charles A. Wustum
Museum of Fine Arts

In *Georgia O'Keeffe*, the artist described one of her most famous paintings as follows: "When I arrived at Lake George I painted a horse's skull—then another horse's skull and then another horse's skull. After that came a cow's skull on blue. In my Amarillo days cows had been so much a part of the country I couldn't think of it without them. As I was working I thought of the city men I had been seeing in the East. They talked so often of writing the Great American Novel—the Great American Play—the Great American Poetry. I am not sure that they aspired to the Great American Painting . . . . I was quite excited over our country and I knew that at that time almost any one of those great minds would have been living in Europe if it had been possible for them. They didn't even want to live in New York—how was the Great American Thing going to happen? So as I painted along on my cow's skull on blue I thought to myself, 'I'll make it an American painting. They will not think it great with the red stripes down the sides—Red, White and Blue—but they will notice it.' "

Marc Gallant, writing in *The Cow Book*, a spoof on history as viewed by cows, discusses other celebrated artists' associations with cows. "Pierre Auguste Renoir, a well-known painter of

151

Inspired by French artist Jean-Auguste Dominique Ingres's reclining nude entitled "La Grande Odalisque," Lois Mogensen of Kenosha, Wisconsin, created "La Grande Moo-Dalisque," a charcoal work (24" by 36") copyrighted in 1984. Jon Bolton photo courtesy Wustum Museum of Fine Arts.

sensuous nudes, completes a canvas entitled 'The Return from the Fields'; Renoir's painting depicts a young dairymaid with a beautiful French cow. The following year Alfred Philippe Roll paints 'Farmer's Wife,' a large painting with girl, milk pail, and cow. French cows believe both these artists are on the right track."

H. W. Janson, an art historian for real, included this commentary about one of Picasso's bulls in *History of Art*. "Now let us look at the striking 'Bull's Head' by Picasso which consists of nothing but the seat and handlebars of an old bicycle . . . . Of course the materials used by Picasso are man-made, but it would be absurd to insist that Picasso must share the credit with the manufacturer, since the seat and handlebars in themselves are not works of art. While we feel a certain jolt when we first recognize the ingredients of this visual pun, we also sense that it was a stroke of genius to put them together in this unique way, and we cannot very well deny that it is a work of art. Yet the handiwork—the mounting of the seat on the handlebars—is ridiculously simple. What is far from simple is the leap of the imagination by which Picasso recognized a bull's head in these unlikely objects; that, we feel, only he could have done. Clearly, then, we must be careful not to confuse the making of a work of art with manual skill or craftsmanship. And even the most painstaking piece of craft does not deserve to be called a work of art unless it involves a leap of the imagination. But if this is true, are we not forced to conclude that the real making of the 'Bull's Head' took place in the artist's mind? No, that is not so, either. Suppose that, instead of actually putting the two pieces together and showing them to us, Picasso merely told us, 'You know, today I saw a bicycle seat and handlebars that looked just like a bull's head to me.' Then there would be no work of art and his remark would not even strike us as an interesting bit of conversation."

James Gardener is a designer, living in London, known generally as G. The July 1985 issue of *Connoisseur* magazine featured an article about G and mentioned that among his unusual artworks is a mechanical cow that gives real milk. The cow is located at the Commonwealth Institute in London, where troops of schoolchildren visit educational exhibits designed to enlighten them in the ways of the various nations the make up the British Commonwealth. The so-called New Zealand Cow is a stylized transparent bovine with insides made of found objects—bellows for lungs, bagpipes for the first stomach, and an oil filter for the liver. At the press of a button, the cow's pituitary gland lights up in its forehead, nerves ignite all the way through the body, and a glass calf is born. At the same time, lactic glands made of Spontex squirt milk out of the glass udder into a pail.

Cows in Music

During the early 1900's a plethora of tunes appeared, involving cows in one way or another, particularly in the genre of ragtime and early jazz:

"Who Let the Cows Out?" Published by the Howard & Browne Music Company of St. Louis in 1910, this tune by Charles Humfeld (known as "Humpy") was subtitled "A Bully Rag," and included a challenge to the pianist to "Make a noise like a cow" in a one-bar break. This was probably a local vaudeville feature.

"The Cows." "The Cows" was a difficult, form-free, unorthodox and unpredictable piece of what is sometimes called "roll and tumble blues." Robert Shaw was born in Stafford, Texas in

153

1908 and he wrote this piece which is much like the tunes played in back-country barrelhouses in the 1920's.

"Cows May Come and Cows May Go." This delightful tune was composed by Harry Von Tilzer in 1915 and didn't seem to make much of a splash until it was recorded nearly sixty years later by the St. Louis Ragtimers. The verse depicts a love scene between a fellow named Joey and his sweetheart, Jane. Joey watches the cows come over the hill and whispers to Jane that he loves her just as much as that cow loves her calf. Jane, however, is not moved. And in the chorus she replies:

Cows may come,
And cows may go
But the bull goes on forever.
Down in Mexico I know that you'll make a
*   hit,*
No one else can shoot the bull like you, I'll
*   admit.*
I may be a little green, you see,
You won't fool me, no never—
Modern love is just a bluff,
Nothing new, the same old stuff.
Cows may come
And cows may go
But the bull goes on forever.

"Cow Cow Blues." Charles Davenport, born in 1894, made his living playing a barrelhouse/boogie piano in brothels around Chicago's South Side,

Picasso is not the only artist to sense the kinship between bovine and bicycle. Raymond L. Gloeckler's woodcut "Dane County Damsel" combines elements familiar in the home of the University of Wisconsin (Gloeckler's alma mater)—cows, bicycles, and letter sweaters. Meanwhile, a laid-back bovine from Davis, California, pedals across the front of a T-shirt.

Cows have firmly planted their hoof-prints on music. Charlie Byrd and Ella Fitzgerald both recorded "Cow Cow Boogie," and the New Lost City Ramblers included "Milk 'Em in the Evening Blues" on the Flying Fish label. The *Complete Tommy Dorsey* album by Victor features Dorsey's rendition of "Milkman's Matinee." "Whoa You Heifer," a ragtime piece written by Al Verges, was recorded by the Columbia Orchestra.

Detroit, and Cleveland. He was the son of an Alabama Baptist minister. During his travels he came upon the blues called "The Cows," and adapted it into a piano showpiece that he called "Cow Cow Blues," which he recorded in 1928. After this, his first big hit, Charles became known as Cow Cow Davenport. Except for the title, the piece doesn't mention a single bovine. Perhaps we are to assume the woman ran off and took the early morning "milk train."

"Hookin' Cow Blues." A blues tune with words and music by Douglass Williams from Greenville, Mississippi, with "jazz" (including the bellows of a cow played on the piano) and other embellishments by W. C. Handy, in the Dixieland tradition of "Livery Stable," and copyrighted in 1917.

"Cow-Cow Boogie." With words and music by Don Raye, Gene de Paul and Benny Carter, this tune was copyrighted in the early 1940's when boogie-woogie had become so well established that songwriters were looking for different gimmicks to use with the twelve-bar blues phrase. Cow-Cow Boogie tells the story of a hip cowboy, and it was recorded by Freddie Slack and his band and a vocalist named Ella Mae Morse, who also sang the tune in the movie *Reveille With Beverly* (RKO 1943). The tune was a big hit.

"Milk Cow Blues" This tune was written by Kokomo Arnold and recorded by various artists with a variety of different lyrics, such as these by Elvis Presley on his album, *Sun Sessions* (1954) and called, in this version, "Milk Cow Blues Boogie":

> I woke up this mornin'
> And I looked out the door
> I can tell that old milkcow
> By the way she lowed.
> Now if you seen my old milk cow
> Rock her up on home
> I ain't had no milk and butter
> Since that cow's been gone. . . .

This seems to be yet another of the "cow" tunes to rely on the cow/woman allusion, and "Milk Cow Blues Boogie" continues, with Elvis singing "I tried to treat you right" and "you're gonna need your lovin' daddy, gonna need him some day. . . ."

"Milk Cow Blues" was a popular blues tune and was recorded by a lot of other musicians:

Ricky Nelson, on his albums *Souvenirs* and *Legendary Masters*;

Doc & Merle Watson, on their album *Alive and Pickin*;

Bob Wills and the Texas Playboys on their album, *Texas Fiddle Milk Cow Blues*; and others.

"Milk Cow Blues" can also be found on the album *Best of the Chocolate Watchband* (RHI-108); on the albums

Reunion and *Dance All Night* by John-nie Lee Wills; and on the album *Draw the Line* by Aerosmith. Harlow Wilcox included it on his album, *Cripple Cricket*.

"Barnyard Blues," a/k/a "Livery Stable Blues."   This was the first jazz recording (Victor Records, 1917) by The Original Dixieland Jazz Band, a white New Orleans band with strong ragtime influence. In this number the trombone imitated the cow; the clarinet was the rooster; the cornet was the horse. There was a lawsuit over the au-thorship of the tune, and the judge asked The Original Dixieland Jazz Band to play it right in the courtroom, after which he covered his ears and de-clared, "That's not music!"

"At the Jazz Band Ball."   This piece was not strictly about cows, but it was recorded in 1927 by Bix Beider-becke and his band, Bix and His Gang. Critics found drummer Chauncy More-house's syncopated use of the cowbell, which was attached to his drum set, rather unusual.

Cowboy Songs

We'd be remiss if we did not pay at least minimum homage to the songs of the cowboy. The first cowboys were Spanish-speaking Mexicans and Indi-ans. They were called *vaqueros* from the Spanish word, *vaca*, meaning "cow."

Next to his cow pony, the cowboy's songs were his most prized posses-sions. He sang as he rode alone, he sang to keep the herd quiet at night, he sang to give himself courage in the wind and the rain or, most of all, just to pass the time because he was alone in a world of prairie and cattle and al-most nothing else.

The cowboy sang of *dogies*, little calves that lost their mothers. The cow-boys used to say "A dogie is a calf whose mammy has got lost, and whose pappy has took up with another cow." The longhorn cattle they herded were then among the largest, fiercest and most dangerous animals in the land. A full-grown longhorn weighed well over a thousand pounds and had tough sharp hoofs, pointed horns and a fight-ing spirit. He (she) was wilder than the deer, almost as fast and much stronger.

"I'm Bound to Follow the Longhorn Cow."   The lyric to this old favorite goes like so:

*I'm bound to follow the longhorn cow until
   I get too old,
Although I work for wages, boys, and get
   my pay in gold.
My bosses they all like me boys, and say
   I'm hard to beat,
I always give 'em the brave stand-off, they
   say I've got the cheek. . . .*

*I'm bound to follow the longhorn cow,
   where'er the critter goes,*

"Dolly was milking her cow one day," begins this song from *Mother Goose's Nursery Rhymes*, a collection of alphabets, rhymes, tales, and jingles published by M. A. Donohue and Company of Chicago.

159

Moon-hour

Point Reys Station,
California is located in a
dairy area and has replaced
its noon whistle with a
noon "Moo."

In desert heat and rain and sleet, and winter's icy snows.
The dogies and the moss-back steers, I'll fol-
  low all my life,
I'll follow the longhorns through the year,
  and never have a wife.

What about cowgirls? Well, here's the
chorus of a folk tune, "I'd Like to Be a
Cowgirl but Oooo I'm Scared of
Cows," sung by Kathy Fink on her album *Grandma Slid Down the Mountain*:

I'd like to be a cowgirl
But oooh I'm scared of cows,
Moo, moo, moo, how they scare me;
I often try to face them
While in the fields they browse,
Moo, moo, moo, how they scare me.
[yodeling] . . .moo, how they scare me.

Special Cow Songs

Two familiar children's tunes with
cows in the lyrics:

"Old MacDonald Had a Farm."

Old MacDonald had a farm,
  E-I-E-I-O.
And on that farm he had a cow,
  E-I-E-I-O.
With a moo, moo, here
And a moo, moo, there
Here a moo, there a moo,
Everywhere a moo, moo.
Old MacDonald had a farm,
  E-I-E-I-O.

"Away in a Manger."

(final verse)
The cattle are lowing, the poor baby wakes,
But little Lord Jesus, no crying He makes.
I love thee Lord Jesus
Look down from the sky
And stay by my cradle til
Morning is nigh.

And a cow-tune not so familiar:
"The Bovine Cantata."
Each year
on February 18, Elm Farm Ollie Day is
celebrated in Madison, Wisconsin, by
her champion, Barry Levenson. On that
day Levenson has been known to dress
in cow costume (with a small pink
udder/purse) and visit his colleagues in
the Wisconsin Department of Justice to
promote the observance of Elm Farm
Ollie's flight in 1930. [See "Famous
Cows in History."] In honor of his heroine, this bovine advocate has composed a libretto for *The Bovine Cantata*,
excerpts of which follow:

In 1930, on a cold winter day,
Elm Farm Ollie was munching on her hay.
The skies above St. Louis were cloudless and
  deep blue-ie
'Though Ollie was a trooper, the hens just
  wouldn't lay.

Elm Farm was in trouble. Poor old farmer
  Brown!
His debts were increasing, his profits were
  way down.

If only, friend, you knew how, he loved that
little moo-cow,
You'd weep in your beer, you'd shed a tear,
you'd wear a heavy frown.
Near St. Louis city, where calves are so
pretty,
'Twas there I first met my sweet Ollie the
cow.
Through streets old and cobbled
With her dainty hooves she hobbled,
Crying: "Whole milk and butter, pasteur-
ized-O!"

Cows in Hollywood

In addition to the hundreds of westerns that starred thousands of head of beef cattle, these movies—which featured actual cows—stand out.

Go West, starring Brown Eyes and Buster Keaton. A docile Jersy named Brown Eyes stars with Keaton in this film. Keaton plays a greenhorn cowboy named Friendless, newly arrived in Arizona, who removes a pebble from the cleft of Brown Eye's hoof and thus earns her undying devotion. But Friendless is also the love object of the ranch owner's daughter, and when the mortgage on the ranch is to be foreclosed all sorts of dilemmas pop up. The plot has Friendless and Brown Eyes leading hundreds of steers through crowded downtown streets, through a barbershop and into a Turkish bath. In the end, Friendless delivers the herd to the stockyards, the owner and his daughter arrive just as the cattle are being consigned, the ranch is saved and Brown Eyes is the hero's reward.

This was not the best of the Keaton-directed comedies, but even in his old age the comedian continued to speak fondly of Brown Eyes, clearly one of Buster's favorite leading ladies.

Little Men, with Elmer the Bull (standing in for Elsie the Cow). In 1940 the publicity given Elsie the Cow, a cartoon character invented by Borden, Inc. in the 1930s and frequently exhibited in the flesh as You'll Do's Lobelia, so intrigued RKO pictures that Elsie was offered a costarring role with Jack Oakie and Kay Francis in an epic entitled "Little Men." Elsie was to play the role of a cow named Butter Cup, but she was tied up at the World's Fair at the time (and also just then in what was delicately termed an "interesting condition"), so a husband named Elmer was invented for her. Elmer was actually a very meek bull (staggering under the real name of Sybil's Dreaming Royalist), but he traveled to Hollywood in her stead and carried the show forward. *Little Men* was a sequel to *Little Women*, both based on the books of Louisa May Alcott.

The Milky Way, with Harold Lloyd. The most impressive Harold

Whipping Cream

The whipping of cream is the first step toward making butter, but if you stop whipping it before the emulsion is broken and the fat globules separate, you'll have a semi-stable foam with an increase in volume. For best results, both the bowl and the cream to be whipped should be at a temperature below 45° F. Only small amounts should be whipped at one time. Aged cream whips better than fresh cream. Sugar should not be added until the cream is whipped because it inhibits coagulation of the milk proteins and thus reduces the stability and stiffness of the cream.

Keaton and costar in the 1925 release *Go West*. Buster trained his leading lady, a Jersey named Brown Eyes, in ten days. He patiently led her around by a stout halter, then a narrow rope, then a length of cord. When shooting began, Brown Eyes fell in step behind him without a sign of restraint. Invisible to the camera was a fine black cotton thread leading from the comedian's elbow to the Jersey's neck. State Historical Society of Wisconsin photo.

Lloyd "talkie," this film also stars Adolphe Menjou and Helen Mack. It is based on a 1934 play of the same name and was filmed in 1936. The opening credits of this Paramount classic set a precedent for the comedy: The logo, based on the well-known MGM roaring lion features instead a cow's head and a lovely "Moo."

Harold plays a milkman who happens to knock down the champion milkman in a brawl and a multitude of gags result.

The Kid From Brooklyn. A Samuel Goldwyn 1946 remake of *The Milky Way*, "and not as good," according to reviewers. The movie, starring Danny Kaye, Virginia Mayo and Vera-Ellen, concerns the evolution of a milkman to prizefighter. This version is a musical, and the "Sunflower Dairymaids" (the Goldwyn Girls) perform a dance number with a handful of Holsteins in their "dreamery-creamery."

Ferdinand the Bull. This short cartoon made in 1938 by Walt Disney is based on the 1936 book by Munro Leaf and adapted from the original illustrations by Robert Lawson.

The story of Ferdinand is one of nonviolence: Ferdinand is born in Spain, to a mother who allows him to sit under his favorite tree every day and smell the nearby flowers, even though this is not usual bull-behavior. "His mother saw that he was not lonesome, and because she was an understanding mother, even though she was a cow, she let him just sit there and be happy." However, soon the men come to gather up bulls for the bullfights. Ferdinand sits quietly while his fellow bulls snort and butt and leap and jump, putting on their best display of fearsome energy. Then Ferdinand is stung by a bee. The men think that Ferdinand's crazy reaction means he is the fiercest bull of all, just the one for the bull fights in Madrid. So they take him there. The day of the bullfight dawns and flags fly and bands play, and the ladies all wear flowers in their hair. And when Ferdinand gets in the middle of the bull ring he sits down and looks at the beautiful ladies and their flowers. No matter what the Banderilleros or the Picadores or the Matador do, Ferdinand will not move. So they take him home in disgrace. But Ferdinand is not disgraced. He is happy to go back to his favorite tree, sit down, and quietly smell the flowers.

The film won an Academy Award.

Clarabelle Cow. Another Walt Disney creation, Clarabelle was not a featured star but served as one of the supporting cast to Mickey and Minnie Mouse. Clarabelle was created in 1929 for the eighth Mickey Mouse animated film, *The Plowboy*.

At that time she was paired with a fellow character named Horace Horse-

Holsteins starred in *The Kid from Brooklyn*, a 1946 Samuel Goldwyn musical. The Technicolor comedy also featured Danny Kaye, Virginia Mayo, Eve Arden, and Fay Bainter. State Historical Society of Wisconsin photo.

collar, and Disney, who apparently was trying to play matchmaker for the two, issued this memo to his staff on July 20, 1931 regarding their first appearance together: "Clarabelle and Horsecollar could do a dance together, or individually . . . could work up a hillbilly act with Clarabelle, Horsecollar, Mickey and Minnie as the hillbillies."

Clarabelle and Horace became a duo, albeit secondary, and appeared in several Disney animated films until Donald Duck and Goofy were introduced, at which time the couple kind of fell by the wayside. According to Disney scholars, Clarabelle and Horace had never been well developed and their personalities were too limited to do much with. Movie critic Richard Schickel agreed that "Clarabelle Cow and Horace Horsecollar were serviceable but not memorable. And who were, in any case, the product of a style of animation Disney wanted to move beyond."

However, despite the fact that she was dumped from Disney's films, Clarabelle managed to stay alive in Disney comic strips and comic books. Even as recently as 1973 Clarabelle could be found in a comic book with her new boyfriend, Goofy (something apparently occurred behind the scenes). Clarabelle is still very much concerned about her youthful appearance and in this scenario she encounters a fellow bovine on the street. Clarabelle is astonished and thinks to herself, "Here comes Mamie McMoo in a hat *just like mine!*" And she tells her boyfriend, "Quick, Goofy . . . take me away from here!" Goofy, always ready to oblige, replies, "Gawrsh! Heh! Hop in, Clarabelle!"

The Cow and I. A French film, made in 1960 and starring Fernandel. The story concerns a French prisoner of war who escapes from a German labor farm and encounters a series of adventures en route to France. According to reviewers, "There are many charming sequences in this off-beat comedy," and, of course, there was a cow.

Zarda, Cow From Hell! An April 1984 *Esquire* article on Duck's Breath, a five-man, new-age, San Francisco comedy team, said the zany quintent was working on a screenplay called "Zarda, Cow from Hell!" The story purportedly was to feature a giant cow that invades a nuclear power plant in Iowa. Repeated inquiries to Duck's Breath for more details of this potential classic have been unsuccessful.

Woody Woodpecker. Of course Woody Woodpecker was not a cow, he was a bird. But he was involved with a cow at one time, in a scene that caused the censors to sharpen their scissors with zeal. The scene simply involved Woody, milking. Creator Walter Lantz was furious. "You see women on the

Cows as art, circa 1800s. Just as breeder's photographs today are designed to highlight certain special features of their breeding stock, engraved portraits of cows in olden times often depicted them with a "square" body to show off the ideal of bovine health.

screen today with their breasts hanging out, and we couldn't even show the udders on a cow!'' he complained in 1971.

Cows in Poetry

Cows appear frequently in poetry, especially in verses written for children. But the presence of cows in our con-

cept of the picturesque idyll seems to lend a tone of peace, natural charm and contentment to these works, despite their intended audience or era.

The Cow

The friendly cow all red and white,
I love with all my heart:
She gives me cream with all her might,
To eat with apple-tart.

She wanders lowing here and there,
And yet she cannot stray,
All in the pleasant open air,
The pleasant light of day;
And blown by all the winds that pass
And wet with all the showers,
She walks among the meadow grass
And eats the meadow flowers.

—Robert Louis Stevenson

The Pasture

I'm going out to clean the pasture spring;
I'll only stop to rake the leaves away
(And wait to watch the water clear, I may);
I shan't be gone long. You come too.

I'm going out to fetch the little calf
That's standing by the mother. It's so young
It totters when she licks it with her tongue.
I shan't be gone long. You come too.

— Robert Frost

The New Cow

The new cow came through the gate,
and her calf came after, a little late.
No longer willing to be led,
the calf went on ahead,
while she stood to look around
over the hills and lower ground
stood shyly, defiantly there,
smelling flower-fragrant air,
and gazed toward the old cows grouped on
   the way
before.
Knowing not how she might stay
among them, stranger still,

she hestitated yet, now they had turned
at the foot of the hill
and seemed to wait for her at the gate,
to wait for her who was strange and thin,
till she came on,
and they opened their ranks
to take her in.

—August Derleth

The following sampling of excerpts
indicate the wealth of poetic works
written about cows:

A Pen-pictur' of a Certin Frivvolus Old Man

...."Oh!" he says, "to wake and be
Bare-foot, in the airly dawn
In the pastur!—there," says he,
"Standin' whare the cow's slep' on
The cold, dewy grass that's got
Print of her jest steamy hot
Fer to warm a feller's heels
In a while!—How good it feels!...

—James Whitcomb Riley

The Young Calves

A hush had fallen on the birds
And it was almost night,
When I came round a turn and saw
A whole year's loveliest sight.

Two calves that thought their month of life
Meant June through all the year
Were coming down the grassy road
As slender as young deer....

—Robert P. Tristram Coffin
Saltwater Farm

167

Thomas Hart Benton's lithograph "The White Calf," from the collection of The Madison Art Center.

The New Baby Calf

Buttercup, the cow, had a new baby calf,
a fine baby calf,
a strong baby calf,
Not strong like his mother
But strong for a calf,
For this baby calf was so new . . .
—Edith H. Newlin
Very Young Verses

Green Afternoon

The mother cow looked up and great sur-
prise
Darkened her soft eyes
To see a spotted fawn come out to play
With her young calf that day . . .
—Frances M. Frost
The Little Naturalist

Here is a classic cow-poem much loved
and often quoted:

The Cow

The cow is of the bovine ilk:
One end is moo, the other milk.
—Ogden Nash

This poem appeared in *The Lark*, San
Francisco, May 1895. It was Gelett Burgess' first appearance in print:

I never saw a PURPLE COW
I never HOPE to see one;
But I can tell you, anyhow,
I'd rather SEE than BE one.

And five years later he wrote:

Ah, yes, I wrote the "Purple Cow"—
I'm sorry, now, I wrote it!
But I can tell you, anyhow,
I'll kill you if you quote it.
—F. Gelett Burgess

Various and Sundry Historic Excerpts

An herd of bulles, whom kindly rage doth
sting,
Doe for the milky mothers want complaine.
—Spenser
The Faerie Queene, 1590

The curfew tolls the knell of parting day,
The lowing herd wind slowly o'er the lea,
The ploughman homeward plods his weary
way,
And leaves the world to darkness, and to
me . . .
—Thomas Gray
Elegy Written in a Country
Churchyard, 1750

A little after two o'clock the people in
the royal Exchange were much alarmed
by the appearance of a cow, hard driven for Smithfield . . . and great confusion ensued, some losing hats and
wigs, and some their shoes, while
others lay about the ground in heaps.
—*Annual Register*
London, January 1761

A cow is a very good animal in the field; but we turn her out of a garden.
—Samuel Johnson
Life of Boswell, 1791

Straight to the meadow then he whistling
   goes;
With well-known halloo calls his lazy
   cows;
Down the rich pasture heedlessly they
   graze,
Or hear the summons with an idle
   gaze. . . .
—Robert Bloomfield
The Farmer's Boy, 1800

—A tender, timid maid! who knew not
how
To pass a pig-sty, or to face a cow.
—George Crabbe,
The Widow's Tale, 1817

I am she, O most bucolic juvnal, under whose charge are placed the milky mothers of the herd.
—Walter Scott
The Monastery, 1825

"If you mean Paradise, Mama, you had better say so, to render yourself intelligible," said the younger lady.

"My dearest Edith," returned Mrs. Skewton, "you know that I am wholly dependent upon you for those odious names. I assure you, Mr. Dombey, Nature intended me for an Arcadian. I am thrown away in society. Cows are my passion. What I have ever sighed for, has been to retreat to a Swiss farm, and live entirely surrounded by cows and china."
—Charles Dickens
Dombey and Son, 1867

The cows were brought over [from Alderney] on the Channel cutters, the other cargo usually consisting of cider. One boat was thirteen days out, and the captain, running short of water, tapped the cider casks. The cows enjoyed it so much that for three days they would drink nothing else.
—C. J. Cornish
Animals of To-day, 1898

Nowhere can I think so happily as in a train . . . I see a cow, and I wonder what it is like to be a cow, and I wonder whether the cow wonders what it is like to be me.
—A. A. Milne
If I May, 1920

I always feel at home in a cow byre . . . I like to stand in front of a cow and look into her rather staring eyes, laugh at the sideways waggle of her jaws, and wait for the inevitable hiccup after turnips which is part of the mealtime ritual in cowland.
—David Thurston Smith
Thistledown, 1933

The two happiest moments of my life at Bath Farm were the first time I was left to milk Bess on my own, and the first time she came across the pasture

Basic Truths

Country girl: *"If you treat a cow with affection, it'll give more milk."* City girl: *"Big deal, so will the milkman."*

when I called her . . . Bess was a lovely little creature . . . She had a rich, honey-coloured hide . . . brown velvet eyes, a shiny black nose, and slim fine legs. She was one of the prettiest animals I have ever seen.

—Rachel Knappett
A Pullet on the Midden, 1946

Upavon is a nice clean village with a very pleasant smell of cows.

—Brian Vesey-Fitzgerald
The Hampshire Avon, 1950

I decided I would break in one of the heifers, to be ridden. The light roan one was my choice, and I found her extremely amenable . . . I rode her all round the roads just like a pony.

I met my match with a mad cow. She had come to me a few days before calving, and had then seemed a nice quiet creature. Unfortunately she calved in the field, and when I tried to get her in she went mad. . . She just lowered her head and came at me at a pace which Spanish bullfighters would have welcomed.

I milked the cows with a great love for them, and found that I had only to milk a cow myself for its yield to go up.

—Barbara Woodhouse
Talking to Animals, 1954

He saw a calf that had just been born on the steep slope of a field. As he stopped to look, the new-born calf began to slide helplessly down the grassy hill. The mother cow gave a strange cry and at once six other cows ran and stood in a line on the hill and stopped the calf sliding any further.

—Maurice Burton
Just Like an Animal

You do de pullin', Sis Cow, en I'll do de gruntin'.

—Joel Chandler Harris
Uncle Remus and his Friends

God's jolly cafeteria
With four legs and a tail.

—E. M. Root
The Cow

Stories of exhausted landgirls [in England during the Second World War] were almost universal. . . . My favourite was of a kindly cow, who, as the weary landgirl staggered in to milk her, said sympathetically: "You just hang on, dearie, and I'll jump up and down!"

—Jilly Cooper
Animals in War, 1983

Cows in Nursery Rhymes and Stories

*I heard a cow low, a bonnie cow low
And a cow low down in yon glen;
Long, long will my young son greet,
Or his mother bid him come ben.*

*I heard a cow low, a bonnie cow low,
And a cow low down in yon fold;
Long, long will my young son greet,
Or his mother shield him from cold.*

—Scottish Nursery Rhyme

171

Dairying is a major industry in Hokkaido, Japan's northernmost island. This color woodcut from the collection of The Madison Art Center is by Hiroshi Yoshida and is entitled "Noonday Rest, Namazaki."

Bigger

The cow is big. Her eyes are round.
She makes a very scary sound.

I'm rather glad the fence is tall,
I don't feel quite so weak and small.

And yet I'm not afraid. You see,
I'm six years old and she's just three.
            —Dorothy Brown Thompson

Hey Diddle Diddle.

Here is the original
rhyme and its original moral.
High diddle diddle,
The cat and the fiddle,
The cow jump'd over the moon;
The little dog laugh'd
To see such craft,
And the dish ran away with the spoon.

Moral: *It must be a little dog that laugh'd for a great dog would be ashamed to laugh at such nonsense.*

And now here is the rhyme as amended by the Quakers.

Hey diddle diddle
The cat and the fiddle
(Yes, thee may say that, for that is nonsense)
The cow jumped over the moon.
(Oh no, Mary, thee mustn't say that, for that is a falsehood; thee knows a cow could never jump over the moon; but a cow may jump under it, so thee ought to say the cow jumped under the moon.)
The little dog laughed . . .
(Oh, Mary, stop, How can a little dog laugh? Thee knows a little dog can't laugh. Thee ought to say, the little dog barked . . .)
And the dish ran after the spoon . . .
(Stop, Mary, stop! A dish could never run after a Spoon. Thee had better say . . .)
—from *The Authentic Mother Goose*
and quoting *Mother Goose Exposed*

Hey Diddle Diddle is one of the best known nonsense verses in the English language, and the editors of *The Oxford Dictionary of Nursery Rhymes* say that a considerable amount of nonsense has been written about it. For instance, the refrain, *Hey Diddle Diddle* is quite ancient. A line from a play printed in 1569 indicates that it was a tune played for dancing. The *Cat* from line two seems to refer to Elizabeth I, as she was often thought of in this man-ner because she toyed with her cabinet as if the ministers were so many mice. And, at the supposedly sedate age of forty-eight this Cat was frequently sighted in her apartments, spiritedly dancing to the music of her beloved fiddle.

The *Cow* is also thought to be connected with Elizabeth I, through the elaborate charades she played at Whitehall and Hampton Court. Other theories about the rhyme, stemming from the line *The Cow jump'd over the Moon*, are that (1) it is connected with the worship of Hathor, the Egyptian goddess of love, sometimes represented as having a cow's head; (2) it refers to the constellations of Taurus the Bull and Canis Minor; (3) it describes the periodic flight of the Egyptians from the rising waters of the Nile. And you thought this was a simple nursery rhyme!

Little Boy Blue.   This rhyme shows similar complications.

Little Boy Blue, come blow your horn,
The sheep's in the meadow, the cow's in the corn.
But where is the little boy tending the sheep?
He's under the hay-cock fast asleep.
Will you wake him? No, not I,
For if I do, he's sure to cry.

Boy Blue is identified with Thomas, Cardinal Wolsey (1475–1530), chief

173

minister of Henry VIII, a scornful man who compelled bishops to tie his shoelaces and forced dukes to hold basins of water while he washed his hands. He was also the son of a well-to-do Ipswich butcher, and, as a boy, undoubtedly did look after his father's flocks.

Little Miss Muffet.   Is there anyone who is not familiar with this tale?

> *Little Miss Muffet*
> *Sat on a tuffet,*
> *Eating her curds and whey;*
> *There came a big spider,*
> *Who sat down beside her*
> *And frightened Miss Muffet away.*

It is widely thought that *Muffet* is Mary Queen of Scots, and the *big spider* is John Knox, who denounced the frivolous Miss Muffet from the pulpit. Of course, it is possible that the heroine could be someone named Patience Muffet, whose father, Dr. Thomas Muffet (he died in 1604) was an entomologist who admired spiders and who wrote a verse called *The Silkewormes and their flies.*

Incidently, there is no such word as *tuffet*, and illustrators usually depict the maid sitting on a three-legged stool or perched on a grassy hillock.

Milk Made.   Not all dialogues are as inconsequential as they seem.

"Where are you going to, my pretty maid?"
"I am going a-milking, sir," she said.

"May I go with you, my pretty maid?"
"You're kindly welcome, sir," she said.

or

"Little maid, pretty maid, whither goest
*   thou?"*
"Down in the forest to milk my cow."
"Shall I go with thee?"—"No, not now;
When I send for thee, then come thou."

In some parts of England, to ask a girl if one might go milking with her was considered tantamount to a proposal of marriage. According to a manuscript in the British Museum, Henry VIII is said to have sung a song,

Hey, troly, loly, lo;
Maid, whither go you?
I go to the meadowe to mylke my cowe...

And it's a safe bet that in this case the young man's intentions were strictly dishonorable.

Rashin Coatie.   This Scottish tale is mentioned as early as 1540. A loving mother dies and leaves her daughter, Rashin Coatie, a little red calf who gives the girl everything she desires. The stepmother discovers this and orders the calf butchered. The girl is desperate but the dead calf tells her to pick up its bones and bury them under a gray stone. She obeys, and henceforth receives whatever she wishes by going to the stone and talking with the calf. At Yuletide, when everybody puts on their best clothes to go to church,

Rashin Coatie is told by her step-mother that she is too dirty to join them. However, the dead calf provides her with beautiful clothes, and as Rashin Coatie goes to church a handsome prince falls in love with her. On their third meeting she loses her slipper, etc.

The Mad Cow—La Vache Folle. Once upon a time there was in a village a great, ugly, lean, dirty, cross-grained cow, with crooked horns, that frightened everybody. She had made her appearance suddenly, one winter's day, just after a great wedding, at which the guests had sat for three days and nights at the table, only rising now and then to dance. A poor laboring man, who was at the wedding, reeled home with her, without troubling himself much about whence she came, and she had a hard life with him. He made her work all day, sometimes at plowing up a field full of stones, and sometimes at carting dung for the rich peasants. At evening he sent her to seek her food along the road, where she found nothing but coarse, muddy, unsavory grass, and at night he shut her up in a wretched hovel, open to the winds, which was never cleaned, and which exhaled an infectious odor. With all this she was milked four times a day— just double what is required of cows

When the French lad Zephyr planted a kiss between the horns of the mad cow, she turned into a fairy right before his eyes. The fateful moment is depicted in this illustration from *Home Fairy Tales,* a translation of Jean Mace's *Contes du Petit-Chateau,* published by Harper & Brothers in 1867.

175

bountifully fed, that live in idleness, and lodged in good, warm, clean stables.

Now this unhappy cow was nothing less than a fairy—the fairy Good Appetite, the godmother of the bride at the wedding where the guests had eaten so much. The other fairies, indignant at such gluttony, had metamorphosed her in this manner to punish her for having in some sort authorized the feasting by her presence, and her present bad cheer was an expiation of the fault. To leave her some hope, she had been told that she should resume her original shape whenever she had reformed a thoroughly bad child. With this design, a part of her former power had been left her. She was permitted to do what she liked with the child, but she had no power over his heart; he must change of himself; and again, in token of his reformation, he must give her a hearty kiss between the horns: This would break the enchantment. . .

—Jean Macé
Home Fairy Tales,
Contes du Petit-Chateau, 1867
translated by Mary L. Booth

The Proverbial Cow

To every cow its calf; to every book its copy. According to a history of Irish proverbs, this is King Diarmuid's famous judgment, given around 560 AD, on the ownership of a copy of a manuscript made by St. Colmcille of a manuscript belonging to St. Finnian. It is probably one of our first copyright laws.

The English philosopher Francis Bacon once said "the genius, wit, and spirit of a nation are discovered in their proverbs." For centuries, cows have been used to give enriched dimension to proverbs and proverbial phrases, especially in Great Britain. Proverbs frequently say one thing and mean another, often with pungency and surprise, almost always with a smile.

Take, for instance, these unfortunate comparisons:

Awkward as a cow.
Awkward as a cow on a crutch.
Awkward as a cow on roller skates.
Awkward as a cow with her first calf.
Clumsy as a town cow.
Ornery as an old cow.
Nervous as a cow in deer hunting season.
Big as a cow.
   or even
Big as the side of a cow.

These all seem to be rather contemporary sayings, but they have origins in the distant past.

If you thought the sly comment, *Why buy the cow when you can get the milk for free* is something relatively recent, compare it with, "Who would keep a cow of their own, that can have a quart of milk for a penny? Meaning, who would be at the change to have a wife, that can have a whore when he listeth?" John Bunyan wrote those words in 1680, in *The Life and Death of Mr. Badman.*

In 1771 Lady Anne Bonnard wrote:

". . .When the sheep are in the fauld
  and the kyes come home,
And a' the weary warld to
  rest are gone . . ."

referring to *when the cows come home* in a positive sense. This saying is usually alluded to in a negative manner, meaning "not for a very long time, if at all," or, as in *It's time the cows came home*, meaning "It's time that something a person has done is found out." A century and a half before Lady Anne, Beaumont and Fletcher used this line in their play *The Scornful Lady*:

"Kiss till the cows come home . . .," which, I suppose, could be taken either way. Again, using this proverb in a romantic fashion, Langdon Mitchell wrote these lines for his comedy in four acts, *The New York Idea*, in 1906:

VIDA: "Don't you realize she's jealous of you? Why did she come to my house this morning? She's jealous—and all you have to do—

JOHN: "If I can make her wince, I'll make love to you till the Heavenly cows come home!"

When the Cows Come Home
When the cows come home the milk is coming
Honey's made while the bees are humming;
Duck and drake on the rushy lake,
And the deer live safe in the breezy brake;
And timid, funny, brisk little bunny
Winks his nose and sits all sunny.
                    —Christina Rossetti

The anatomy of the cow is frequently alluded to in proverbs. Let's start at the tail:
Haec colonia retroversus crescit tanquam coda vituli "This town goes downhill like the calf's tail," and *Tanquam coda vituli*, or "Always behind, like a cow's tail," were written by Petronius in *Satyricon* in AD 60.
Cows don't know the good of the tail till fly time.
The cow knows not what her tail is worth until she has lost it.
The old cow needs her tail more than once. (The worth of a thing is known when it is lost.)

This herd of whimsical bovines (copyright 1974) is the work of Milwaukee, Wisconsin, artist Schomer Lichtner. In America's Dairyland, the opportunity to work directly from the model abounds, and cows have been a dominant theme in Lichtner's art for decades.

177

A scene from "Swan Lake, Minnesota," a 1983 PBS production based on Tchaikovsky's classic nineteenth-century ballet. Videotaped on Minnesota and Wisconsin farms, it featured ballerinas waiting to be milked and other spoofs of the rural scene, yet managed to capture the essence of the original. *Time* called it one of the ten best TV productions of the year, and *The New York Times* dance critic noted soberly, "it impressively tells a simple story about real people."

The cow may want her tail yet. (You may want my kindness hereafter although you may deny me yours just now.)

Il ne fault q'une queue au'elle soit bien longue. (Only one cow's tail is needed to reach the sky, but it must be a very long one.)

D'une vache perdue c'est quelque chose de recouvrer la queue, (Of a lost cow it is something to recover the tail.)

He that aughts [owns] the cow gaes nearest her tail. (Every man is busy and careful about his proper interest.)

It is idle to swallow the cow and choke on the tail, and *It's a shame to eat the cow and worry on the tail,* both meaning it is senseless to give up when a great task is almost completed.

And then, consider the other end of the cow, the horns:

A Latin proverb of the year 1000 goes, *Dat Deus immiti cornua curta bovi,* or God gives short horns to the fierce ox. This is meant to say that Providence so disposes that they who have the will, want the power or the means to hurt. But it has also been interpreted to mean that angry men cannot do all the mischief they wish: *Curst cows have curst horns*. Shakespeare wrote "It is said 'God sends a curst cow short horns; but to a cow too curst he sends none,'" in *Much Ado About Nothing*, 1599. In 1588, Robert Greene wrote, *A curst cow hath oftentimes short hornes, and a wiling minde but a weake arm.*

Hooves? Feet? Or, as in these proverbs, *heels*:

A-milking, a-milking my maid,
"Cow, take care of your heels," she said;
And you shall have some nice new hay,
If you'll quietly let me milk away."
—Nursery Rhyme

If you live in Scotland and have a cow that is stubborn and tricky and kicks when she is milked, you might say, *She has an ill paut wi' her hind foot.* John Heywood wrote in 1546 that *Margery good coowe (quoth he) gaue a good meele, But than she cast it downe again with hir heele.* In his *Historie of the Holy Warre*, 1639, Thomas Fuller wrote, *These Italians . . . as at first they gave good milk, so they kicked it down with their heel.* And Samuel Richardson said *You are a pretty cow, my love; you give good store of milk, but you have a very careless heel.* All of these play on the term "to lift up the heel against," which means to spurn someone physi-

cally or figuratively, to treat with contempt or to become an enemy. And then there's the Scottish proverb, *Shame fa' the couple, 'quo' the cow to her feet*, which seems to imply the same thing albeit from a different point of view.

Proverbs about calves often feature a simple mother/daughter allusion, as in *Pet the cow to get the calf*, or *Gawsie cow, gudely calf*. But calves are often referred to in proverbs about love: *Calf love, half love; old love, cold love. Bad as a cow with a weaning calf*, and *A bellowing cow soon forgets her calf*, suggest that emotional display is not necessarily a sign of true feelings.

More calf-proverbs: *Show the fatted calf, but not the thing that fattened him. He eats the calf in the cow's womb* (He spends his rent before it's due). *The cow has calved*, a smuggler's phrase, meaning the ship has successfully landed her cargo. This is applied to any kind of good fortune.

Perception of size is relative in Scotland where a proverb states, *They think the calf a muckle [large] beast that never saw a cow*. In France one might say "Il a pris la vache et le veau," if you wanted to imply that someone who has married a pregnant girl, *has caught the cow and the calf*. On the other hand, the Germans say "Manche gute Kuh hat ein ubel Kalb;" or *Many a good cow bringeth forth a sorry calf*. John Ray,

Cheese Boxes

Cheeseboxes used to be a common item in the early 1900's, and cheese box companies were plentiful, too. Now there are only about 340 cheese factories remaining in Wisconsin, and only 3 manufacturers of wooden cheeseboxes. The style and appearance of the boxes, as well as the manner in which they are made, has not varied much over the years. The boxes are approximately 15 inches in diameter for cheddar, and others are made to order. Tops and bottoms of the boxes are made of Eastern aspen, popple and basswood, but the sides of each box are made of elm veneer which is more difficult to obtain these days.

in his book *English Proverbs*, 1670, explains this proverb to mean, "Many a good cow hath but a bad calf . . . Men famous for learning, virtue, valour, success, have for the most part either left behind them no children, or such as that it had been more for their honour and the interest of humane affairs, that they had died childless."

His calves are gone to grass is said of a man with spindly legs. Another mocking taunt is *Veal will be dear, because there are no calves.* In England and Scotland cold veal is called "Kiss your sister," for what they feel is its insipid nature. And when women kiss each other they use the saying, *Butter to butter's nae kitchen.*

Nay, I am told you meet together with as mych Love, as there is between the old Cow and the Hay-Stack.
　　　　　　　　　—Jonathan Swift

Feeding and milking have been a natural focus of proverbial content, as in *It's by the head that the cow gies the milk. A collier's cow and an alewife's sow are always well fed. To thrive as a cow does on wet clover,* meaning not at all; and *The cow may die ere the grass grow,* implying that she can't wait forever. *The cow that little givith that hardly liveth,* has a similar message.

Milk the cow that standeth still; why follow you her that flyeth away? is a proverb from 1688 and succeeding generations.

Local tradition gave birth to this proverb from Scotland, *Ye may as weel try to lift the milkin' stane o' Dumbarton,* which refers to the "milking stone," an enormous mass of rock which was purported to have fallen from the castle of Dumbarton onto the cow park beneath, smothering a number of women who were milking their cows there. The saying is used to indicate something that's impossible.

Many of the most colorful cow proverbs relate to dairy products. In Russia you might say to a greedy person, *You would like to eat milk with a needle if you could.* And the seasons get involved, too: *A soft-dropping April brings milk to cows and sheep. In winter the milk goes to the cow's horns.*

Jonathan Swift wrote a running commentary on the use of proverbs and proverbial phrases in 1704, in the form of dialogues. These conversations are typical:

Miss Notable: Colonel, don't you love Bread and Butter with your Tea? Colonel: Yes, in a Morning, Miss, for they say Butter is gold in a Morning, and Silver at Noon, but it is Lead at Night. This referred to the alleged affect of butter on one's digestion.

Miss Notable: The Weather is so hot, that my butter melts on my Bread.

Lady Answerall: Why, Butter I've heard 'em say, is mad twice a year. In other words, it's too soft in mid-summer and too hard in mid-winter.

Dairy-product proverbs sometimes get kind of personal:
Swift wrote,

Lady Answerall: She looks as if Butter would not melt in her Mouth; but I warrant Cheese won't choak her. The first half of this proverb was said of both men and women, but the second half implied a woman's physical intimacy with a man.

Ye hae got butter in a burd, is said to someone who sings, speaks or calls with a loud voice and alludes to the chickens raised by Scottish housewives to be their house roosters because they will crow more loudly.

Butter and burn trouts are kittle meat for maidens. Butter is the king o' a' creesh (grease). *As sure as it were sealed with butter.*

Like Orkney butter, neither gude to eat nor to creesh woo', grease wool. *The oldest cheeses have most mites. The juice of the cow alive or dead is good.*

According to a book of ancient English proverbs *All is not butter the cow shites.* And *They that have a good store of butter may lay it thick on their bread. Or put it in their shoes.* It does not explain why.

If you live in Scotland and pledge never to do what you say you won't do, you might state *May I never chew cheese again.*

Measuring a man's wealth by the number of cows he owns goes back to Egyptian times. Perhaps that's why selling ones cows has given rise to so many proverbs:

Ye canna sell the cow and sop the milk too.
There's little value in the single cow.
A man of one cow—a man of no cow.
Nae cows, nae care.
Steal my cow and give away the hide.
It's better to keep a cow than an ass.
One who is without cows must be his own dog.

Put a cow in a clout and she will soon run out. (A "clout" refers to a rag, in which the price of the cow is wrapped. This proverb says the money for the cow is soon spent.)

The cow that's first up greets the first o' the dew. And the early bird gets the first worm.

Bring a cow to the hall and she'll run to the byre (barn). This is a popular proverb and means that it is impossible to change or conceal a person's true character.

Often a cow does not take after its breed.

As cows come to town, some good, some bad.

Many a time the man with ten cows has overtaken the man with four.

Better a good cow than a cow of a good kind, meaning a good character is better than a distinguished family.

The whiter the cow the surer it is to go to the altar, is perhaps an allusion to

Mo, Ni, and Que are three polyester cows—two of whom appear in this photo by Dennis Darmek—created by Swiss sculptor Samuel Buri. The cows graze in the Bradley Sculpture Garden in River Hills, Wisconsin, part of a collection of 60 outdoor works by the world's leading sculptors, assembled by Peg and Harry Lynde Bradley. Bradley Sculpture Garden is open to the public once every summer and by appointment through the Milwaukee Art Museum.

the sacrifice of white cattle by the Druids and thus the richer the spoil, the greater the chance of its confiscation.

...*Quoth the good man when that he kissed his cow.*

That kiss, (quoth one), doth well her, by God a vow!

But how can she give a kiss, sour or sweet?

Her chin and her nose within half an inch meet...

—John Heywood, 1562

Cow proverbs are sometimes used to make comparisons.

I ken by my cog how my cow's milked or, I know by my bucket, by the appearance of something, if it's properly done.

It can't be both curds and whey with you.

He's like a cow in an unco loan in a strange lane.

You're as white as a loan soup, milk given to strangers who come at milking time, and said to flatterers who are called "white folks."

If you can't be the bell cow, fall in behind.

As nimble as a cow in a cage.

Learn your gudedame to make milk kail. Teach your grandmother to suck eggs. (Said in anger, and goes back to early 16th century).

He picked it up at his ain hand as the cow learned the flinging.

He hasna as muckle sense as a cow could hauld in her faulded nieve, her folded fist.

To reprimand a noisy girl in Scotland you would say *Loud i' the loan was ne'er a gude milk coo.*

And a sly comment might be, *More hair than tit, like a mountain heifer.*

Where comes a cow, the wise man lay down. There follows a woman, and where comes a woman follows trouble.

Truisms popular in Ireland and Scotland even today:

Three traits of a bull: a bold walk, a strong neck and a hard forehead

The three ugliest things of their own kind: a thin red-haired woman, a thin yellow horse and a thin white cow.

Four things an Irishman should not trust: a cow's horn, a horse's hoof, a dog's snarl and an Englishman's laugh.

Three things that don't remain: a white cow, a handsome woman, and a house on a height.

Three sauciest by nature: a ram, a bull and a tailor.

Take care o' an ox before, an ass behind, and a monk on all sides.

A crooning (singing) cow, a cawing hen and a whistling maiden were ne'er very chancy (fortunate, happy).

A horse on a cliff or a cow in a swamp, two in danger.

Take a man by his word and a cow by the horn.

By their tongues people are caught, and by their horns, cattle.

Look to the cow, and the sow, and the wheat mow, and all will be well enow.

There must be one or two of these proverbial phrases that will fall conveniently into your conversation someday. If not, here are two more:

Dinna cast awa' the cog (bucket) when the cow flings.

and,

A bumblebee in a cow-turd thinks himself a king.

In 1939, Ralph Quinney helped water purebred Jerseys on the southern Wisconsin farm settled by his Irish-English forebears in the 1860's and still owned by the Quinney family. Photo by Alice Quinney reproduced courtesy of Richard Quinney.

With Love & Affection

"Cows—I know the sound, the touch, the smells of them. . . ."

Norma Hoffman,
who grew up on a
Wisconsin dairy farm

In the middle of this project I sent out a press release to a number of rural newspapers requesting readers to submit their favorite cow anecdotes for a "light-hearted, whimsical, affectionately humorous" book about cows. Farmers and former farmers, farm women and children, responded with cow stories from their past and present that were funny, sad, tender and silly.

As I sorted through the letters it became obvious that these memories were important documents of a special time and way of life. "I'll never forget a Guernsey cow named Babe, even though it's been 40 plus years since she has been around," one woman wrote. "Because my story happened 80 years ago I don't have any pictures," another apologized.

"Cows are a pretty tough subject to write about unless you have lived with them," warned a farm woman friend who had seen the clipping. And that's the real reason for this chapter. Because cows and I have never been close, I'm leaving these concluding pages to the experts.

Cows Are Not As Dumb

I had two small farms and had some cows on both of them. And I know they can be trained, as I had mine trained so they didn't leave droppings in the barn while I was milking them; they waited until they got outside. Cows are not as dumb as they look.

—*Bertrain W. Zellmer*

Cows Are Not As Smart

Cows are smart. Aside from knowing and telling each other that half the farm away there is a hole in the fence, hidden from you by five gooseberry bushes and a wild grape vine, cows are also smart up close.

For example, they know there is feed in the barn and if they will come in, stick their heads in the stanchions and be detained, they can eat it. They also know that late in the evening one of us will come to the barn and fork up to them any hay they have pushed too far away. But they know what I should be wearing. They like familiar things, peo-

185

ple and clothes. Let me wear something different, like an old white sweater, and Polly and probably Sadie too will snort and lunge back, starting an epidemic of attempted stampede.

I say, "Come on, girls, don't you know me?" and the whole line will be at ease. Well, not exactly. As I make my way down the feed alley with the pitchfork they stretch forward, sniffing and even tasting. The more affectionate ones give a gentle, friendly bunt with their polls.

Stepping in between the cows without a milker in hand is inviting a two-way pinch. It's easily prevented by staying out, but now and then a stanchion needs more secure closing, a trainer needs adjusting and just like that the two rear ends swing together and the harder I push, the tighter they squeeze. Then the only possible victory is a retreat and I crawl between the stanchions and out in front of the cows—in the meantime telling them what I think of them. Gently, of course, and in a ladylike manner.

But cows can step on their own teats. And they do. And a good illustration of violent indignation is a cow still needing to be milked in spite of her injury.

Cows can step on your foot, then forget completely how to shift their weight to the opposite side. And they will. Pushing, shoving and screaming can get her so upset she is apt to stand on just one foot. Yours.

Cows can stick their heads in the crotch of a tree and die there. And they have, too stupid or stubborn to wiggle their heads around to the position that got them into that position.

There are times for two cents and a bottle of stove polish I'd let the whole herd go. But there is something about an approaching end of a situation that puts it in a different perspective. Then I wonder, after four decades of morning and night milking, what would next summer be like without the cows around?

—Pearl Swiggum

In Disguise

At the time my father purchased the 100-acre farm in 1910 from two bachelors, my parents had not yet married. The property had suddenly become available as the previous owners had violently argued one day in June and the brothers had decided to part company. A reasonable offer was extended to my father and by noon his acceptance made him the proud possessor of a dilapidated dairy farm, lock, stock and barrel.

Being without a wife and faced with the prospect of milking a dozen cows alone, he prevailed upon his unmarried sister to assist in the first evening's chores. Pride turned to dismay as the cows protested violently when the sister approached them with pail, wooden milking stool, flopping sunbonnet and flowing dress. Never in the cows' lifetime had such an apparition appeared in the bachelors' milking barn! Any attempt at milking the gyrating animals was futile, until my aunt finally slipped into a pair of overalls and donned an old felt hat. Disguised as a man, and after a lengthy struggle, she and Father eventually crossed the first of many challenging hurdles.

—Roland Schomberg

Suspicion

My father, Ned Place of Wapakoneta, Ohio, has been a purebred breeder of Shorthorn cattle since 1947. He has raised nearly all of his replacement heifers from the ten original cows he bought back then. He can trace each cow's family history all the way back and give interesting insights about their personalities, births, etc. These cattle are the love of his life and he is immensely proud of them. They return this love by their gentleness and attentiveness.

Two years ago my sister and I took over the training preparations when Dad had a heart attack just two weeks before the Ohio State Fair. My husband got into the act and donned Dad's bib overalls to help. One heifer, whom my husband was holding by the halter, started sniffing at his feet and continued all the way up to my husband's shoulder. Then she stepped aside and gave him a long searching look. Evidently she wasn't fooled by the disguise for one minute.

When Dad heard this, he was delighted. Just following my father around as a child, I learned to love these animals as he does. He has said many times that he relaxes at the day's end just by walking through his herd. He doesn't need golf to achieve relaxation. And he says the best music in the world is a cow bawling for her calf.

—Sandra Kattman

Particular Cows

My grandfather kept a small herd of cows and a feisty bull which served the neighbor's cows, but we were never sure, as children, just what went on because we were sent to the house when a restless cow was brought into the barnyard.

We asked Grandpa to teach us to milk, but he refused, saying the cows would give down their milk only for him, as they knew his touch. On the few occasions when Grandpa was sick and a neighbor or our Uncle Martin did the milking, we found Grandpa was partly right. The cows did give some milk, but not as much as with Grandpa. They were definitely partial

Yogurt

Also known as yoghurt, this is a Turkish name for a fermented milk. It is known by different names according to the place where it is made: in Armenia it is known as Matzoon; in Egypt it is called Leben; in Bulgaria, Naja; in Italy, Gioddu; Tiaourti in Greece; and Dadhi in India. The Russians call it Varenetz; Yugoslavians call it Kisselo mleko. In almost every one of these countries yogurt is associated with long life. And in many parts of the world this is the only way milk is consumed. The protein in yogurt is partially predigested and the lactic acid has dissolved some of the calcium, thus these are more easily absorbed during digestion and therefore good for sick people and babies.

As *Hoard's Dairyman* observed in 1945, there is something in the touch of a woman that brings out the best in a cow. This Wisconsin milkmaid was photographed in 1929 on the farm of G. L. Harmon. State Historical Society of Wisconsin photo.

to his touch. Once a cow who didn't like a stranger on the stool kicked over the milk pail and this did not please Grandma who depended on the cream for her buttermaking! But Grandpa was never sick for long and soon the milk flow was back to normal.

We girls still wanted to try milking a cow. Uncle Martin said he had a cow he'd let us milk. So we went over to his farm, sat on the stool and tried to imitate Grandpa's hand movements. We must have done it correctly as we soon had half a pail of milk. We were very proud of ourselves until Uncle Martin deflated us by saying, "Any fool can milk that cow. She ain't particular like your grandfather's."

—*Josephine Austin*

Musical Bovines

Way back in about 1910 we lived across from what is now Ochner's Park in Baraboo, Wisconsin. At that time a family by the name of Weber lived there in a big red brick house. They had several cows that roamed the large area. It had a barbed wire fence around it to keep them in. It was hot summertime and we had our front door open to get a little breeze. When my sister was about fifteen she would sit down at the organ and play and the cows would line up along the fence and just stand and listen. When she'd quit they would walk away, so they must have liked music way back then.

—*Marjorie Brescia*

Dime

My older brother, Lloyd, and I had a tame bull calf, named Dime, who would pull our sled with us on it, up the hill after a slide. Hitched to a little wagon which Lloyd had made, and fitted with a harness of sorts, Lloyd would try to drive Dime up town to be in the parade on the Fourth of July each year. But when Dime heard the bands playing he would turn around and much to Lloyd's disgust, hurry for home. I wonder whatever became of our tame Dime. Is he now a ferocious bull feared by everyone?

—*Roberta Anderson Smith*

Names

When we started farming we found it was easier to identify the cow we were talking about by its character name rather than the number in its ear. Some of the names our girls have earned are:

Miss Piggy—she is always the dirtiest cow in the barn.

Dolly—named after Dolly Parton, for the obvious reason.

Stubby Ears—she had small ears due to frost bite when she was a calf.

Jumper—always has the jitters; you don't want to surprise her.

Sonny—short for Son of a _____!
We didn't have her very long. She had
the bad habit of kicking the milking
machine off.

Meathead—we bought her from a
neighbor real cheap because she had a
bad disposition, but she milked good
so we thought we could break her bad
habits with some TLC. We have had
her a year now because she's a good
producer, but she is also on the verge
of getting the middle name, "Sonny."
—*Rosalind Gausman*

Bessie

It was a clear, fall evening and Father
and Brother were readying to milk the
cows. I asked my father if he would
teach me to milk, for it was the common belief that all farm women knew
how to milk. I didn't. "Come along,"
my father said. I tagged along but
when Bessie saw someone in a skirt,
she rolled her eyes. Even though being
the most gentle of the herd, she was
suspicious of me.

Father gave me a three legged stool
and a milk pail. He demonstrated how
you squeeze the teat and then release
in a sort of rhythm. I sat down, and after a couple squeezes, Bessie decided
she'd have to do something about this.
She raised up her left hind leg and
stepped squarely into the pail. I

jumped up, the stool fell over, and I
ran. Bessie thought, "I got rid of her."
I'll bet she smiled to herself, our
Gentle Bessie. And I remained the
farmer's daughter that never learned to
milk cows.
—*Alletta L. Baxter*

Self-Image

One time the question was passed
around, "Knowing what you do of
your own personality, character and
mindset, what animal do you most resemble?"

> *My friends are all badgers,*
> *or leopards or wolves,*
> *or foxes, or eagles, and how*
> *can I ever reveal*
> *to such glamorous folk*
> *that I'm only a Brown Swiss cow?*
> —*Evelyn Melotte*

Cowlick

Our daughter's name was Christine,
but we called her "Tootsie." She was
two years old at the time and her big
brother, Mark, was three and a half.
One summer afternoon Mark came
running, screaming, to tell us that
Tootsie was stuck. He pulled us to the
far back yard where we found she was,
indeed, "stuck." She had placed her
head through the square-wire fence of

Inside Milk

Milk is about 87
*percent water and thirteen
percent solids. The solids
consist of fat and the fat-
soluble vitamins it contains,
and the solids not fat,
which include protein,
carbohydrate, water-soluble
vitamins, and minerals. The
minimum amounts of fat
and the solids not fat in
milk that is shipped in
interstate commerce are
specified by federal
standards.*

the pasture and the "friendly" cow was licking her face. Tootsie's screams should have reached downtown, and she had good reason. Have you ever felt the courseness of a cow's tongue?

—Carol Hunter

Cows Recalled

My family lived on a farm; there were seven children and we all loved the animals. We had twenty-five cows. Each cow had a name and personality of her own. We each had a very favorite cow: some of the names were Dardanella, Gwendolyn, Black Spot, Mooley, Hook-a-Rock, Maria, Lucy, Lump Jaw, Rosalie, Brindel, Fawn, Fifi, etc.

Fifi was a red, agile cow with short curled horns. She was a leader and very clever. In the winter when the cows were let out of the stable for sunshine and exercise, Fifi would hook her horn into the threshing floor door and slide it open. The herd would follow her so they could feast on the hay from the mow.

We had another cow we called the "Noon Cow." In the summer, when the cows were in the pasture, she'd leave the herd at noon and stand at the house gate and moo until she was milked.

—Ann Wellner

High on Silage

This happened many years ago—in the twenties. We had eight or ten cows and a small wood silo. Well, the silage sprouted and would you believe we had a herd of drunken cows, and I mean lit. We tried so hard to get them back in the barn—they were out to get water, and we ran so hard after them, just ahollering so, tails over their backs. Boy, was it ever a circus. But we did get them in.

—Mrs. Marvin Gordon

Lightning

My father farmed four miles north of town, and one summer morning he went to the pasture to check his livestock. He found one Holstein calf with all of its black hair gone, and all of the white hair intact! We wondered what could or would destroy only the black hair and came to no decision. So our local veterinarian was called to the farm. He made the diagnosis that lightning from the storm that day had "burned" off all the black hair when lightning had struck nearby, as black absorbs heat. Eventually, all the black hair grew back but what a funny patchwork job that lightning bolt did, and it followed every spot so very,

Milk Processing

The main steps in milk processing are: after vitamin D is added (and vitamin A in lowfat and skim milk), the milk is pasteurized, usually at 161°F for 15 seconds. Ultra-pasteurized milk and ultra high temperature (UHT) processed milk are heated to 280° F for at least two seconds, which increases shelf life.

As it flows out of the pasteurizer, most milk is homogenized by being pumped through extremely tiny openings that break up the milkfat and mix the tiny particles throughout the milk rather than rising to the top as cream.

The pasteurized, ultra-pasteurized or UHT processed milk is cooled rapidly. The UHT milk is packaged into pre-sterilized containers and aseptically sealed. Since bacteria cannot enter the UHT milk it can be kept unrefrigerated for at least three months. The pasteurized and ultra-pasteurized milks are packaged and stored in a refrigerated room until loaded into an insulated delivery truck.

very exactly that not one black hair was left on that calf.

—Lucille Hirsch Frick

Lousy Liz

Back in 1944 we lived on a tenant farm in Harmony Township. We farmed on shares and the owner lived in town. One day he went to a consignment sale and brought back two cows. One cow always kicked when you put the milking machine on her; the other was the gentlest cow you ever saw, but very nervous. My husband checked her over and found she had lice. So that's probably why their owners got rid of them. We were told her name was "Elizabeth."

My husband said, "I'm going to get rid of those lice." He took four pails and mixed some Creosote dip with water. He filled the pails half full, then put one of the cow's feet in each pail. He washed the cow down with the water in the pails and you should have seen what happened—the lice were on the move. They all traveled down into the pails and that was the end of them. But the poor cow shed all her hair and was as bald as a blister. My husband said, "I guess I made the solution too strong."

Elizabeth's hair came back in a hurry, however, and she was the slickest cow in the barn. The kids just loved her and she was known from that day on as "Lousy Liz."

—Mary Zillmer

Poor Franz

This happened in Switzerland: Franz Tauferer, a farmer and restaurant owner in South Tirol, Italy, got his cows drunk to get more milk from them. When he got caught, he said his family did this for generations and it helped a lot. He made the schnapps from berries, and when he stopped giving them the daily ration they only gave half as much milk and some even died. He was sentenced to two months in jail and was fined 350,000 lira.

—Alois and Alice Huber

S(mash)ed

The funniest thing I ever saw was when I was a girl. A herd of cows got drunk. Some of our neighbors had a moonshine still and got word that the "revenuers" were coming. So they dumped out their barrel of mash and the cows licked it up. They were really loaded.

—Olga E. Knapp

Daisy

This incident occurred one hot August day in the early 1940's. It had been quite a dry summer but events proceeded more or less as normal on the farm. One of my parents' Guernsey cows, Daisy, had given birth to a fine calf the day before. The calf had been placed in a calf pen in the barn. Daisy was very disturbed to be separated from her offspring. She would not stay with the rest of the herd in the pasture but ran frantically back and forth outside the barn. She bellowed and called to her calf, who answered from inside the barn.

I was out in our bean patch picking green beans which we raised for the Stokely Canning Company—my earnings were used to help pay for my college education. On this particular day I happened to look up and saw a large black bear standing upon his hind legs looking at Daisy over the pasture fence, where he'd apparently been eating blackberries.

Daisy must have seen the bear at approximately the same time I did. She looked terrified, then broke through the barnyard fence and into an oat field where my parents and I had stacked the oat bundles into shocks on the previous day. The cow ran to an oat shock, grabbed a bundle of oats in her mouth and headed out to join the other cows in the pasture, as fast as she could go. I've often thought about Daisy—she knew fear, but wherever she was going, she was bringing her own lunch!

—Margaret Palmer

Babe

I'll never forget a Guernsey cow named Babe, even though it's been 40-plus years since she's been around.

Some friends of our family had a farm in northern Wisconsin where I spent many wonderful childhood days. When Babe was born she became an instant pet of my girlfriend's father. Bill taught her to put her front feet on his shoulders whenever he stood with his back to her. This was fine when she was young, but calves have a habit of growing into rather large animals. This didn't stop Babe, even when she was a hefty heifer. All Bill had to do was bend over in front of her and she'd have her forefeet on his back in a flash.

—Jean Luehr

Lessons

About 1907 a bad case of diphtheria had left my young brother, Henry, so weak that our parents were badly alarmed. The family doctor advised fresh country air and fresh milk. So, with our mother, we were boarded for the summer with relatives in Pennsylvania. We were three and six, inquisitive and therefore underfoot at milking time.

Between the house and the pasture was an apple orchard. One evening, as the cows were being driven home, one of them started making the most

Cows and Booze

There are cows in County Cork, Ireland, that produce a bottle of gin a day. A plant that manufactures Irish cheddar cheese transforms the solid matter in whey into an alcohol base used by gin distilleries. Similar experiments are being carried out in the Netherlands. Dutch chemist Dr. Frans Nieuwenhoff says, "The average cow gives about 1,250 gallons of milk every year. This is enough to produce about two hundred bottles of whiskey or gin."

In Germany—Bavaria—beef cattle are fed on schlempe, a kind of high protein sludge which is a by-product of the manufacture of schnapps and is often piped directly from the distillery to the feeding trough.

Cordly Jackson and friends—a pair of doe-eyed Guernseys—on Milwaukee Avenue East. Photo courtesy Hoard Historical Museum.

unearthly noises. She was choking on an apple stuck in her throat. To make matters worse, the kids got scared and all started screaming.

Details are blurred, but I can still hear that poor animal. I can see the two older boys restraining the cow while their father calmly thrust his arm down her throat and brought out the apple. His arm was bloody to the elbow.

After that it was easier for me to gracefully accept the many "don'ts" of my elders—"Don't pile so much food on your fork," "Don't drink your milk so fast," and, "Don't swallow so much food at once!"

—Gertrude S. Lubke

Princess

Princess was the first Jersey cow we ever owned. We bought her at a farm auction in 1962 for the staggering price of $150. She had been a 4-H animal and was very tame, having been raised by children, pampered by them and exhibited at the local county fair.

When winter came, my husband laid aside his farm cap and wore a tassel cap instead. One night while he was hand-milking Princess, she kept turning her head, looking at him. Finally she could stand it no longer and whipped her head around, grabbed the tassel cap in her teeth and pulled it off

his head. It became a regular game with her and she often played it from that time on.

This same Princess had a great curiosity about other things, too. One day when I was hoeing the garden she came over to the fence to see what I was doing. It wasn't the strongest fence in the world, and she leaned on the fence post with all her weight. The post bent and Princess stepped into the garden to join me. "Get out of here!" I shouted, but she kept right on coming. Then she discovered the bean plants and systematically went down the row, scooping them up in her big mouth as neatly as a vacuum cleaner.

My husband and sons came to my rescue when they saw me trying to push Princess out of the garden and crying at the same time.

The beans had to be replanted that year.

—Bernice Abrahamzon

Guilt

This incident happened in Richmond township, Walworth County, when I was about fourteen. I was driving the cows to pasture while on my way to the corn field to cut some corn. I had the corn cutter in my hand and there was one cow that lingered, took her time, would stop and wait. In my frustration I threw the corn cutter at her. I didn't intend to cause any harm, but the blade hit her leg. The cut was deep enough to cause her to limp.

I was worried that I might have a dead cow on my hands. But when I told my dad about it, he told me that he'd had the same experience when he was about my age. The limp only lasted a few weeks and then everything was back to normal.

—James Kestol

No Malice Toward Alice

In summertime during the depression years, I was the farmer's daughter who faithfully watched cows grazing in grass along side roads.

One day while doing this dastardly duty, a friend rode over on horseback to see me. I rode horseback, too.

Alice and I gabbed awhile that day and then decided to have a race riding our trusty steeds. The cows were busy chewing the lush greenery so why not put some spirit into our boring day? Off we went, riding bareback, the wind in our hair, both determined to be the winner.

But alas, it turned out to be a tie and we laughed until we cried. Suddenly I screamed, "Alice, where are the cows?!"

"I don't know," she answered. "We better look for 'em."

We began to search, and soon I was really crying. Finally, we discovered them in a field of barley—owned by Alice's father.

I don't remember how we herded them out of there, or even how we got them home. I do recall how our fathers, who hadn't ever been very neighborly, were even less friendly after that.

—Dorothy Schwenkner

Grandmother's Cows

The summers could be hot in Wisconsin's Jackson County, where my family spent two weeks each summer vacationing on my grandmother's farm. I was accustomed to swimming everyday, and found myself desperately looking for a place to cool off when I remembered the huge wooden water tank in the barnyard.

I hopped into that tank and had a good cooling off, and thought nothing more about it—until my uncle started asking questions. He wanted to know why his thirsty cows were standing around the water tank just looking, not drinking.

My uncle had to drain the tank and clean it in order to get them to drink, and that was the end of my barnyard pool.

—Donna Latshaw Peterson

Cow IDs

In the 1980's it was reported that identity cards had been issued for all of Israel's 300,000 cattle.

Cousin Geneva

After my marriage in 1917, we moved to a large farm. Many of my city friends were very curious when they visited us since they'd had little contact with farm life. One weekend Cousin Geneva and her husband came to visit us.

The week before we had received a notice from the State Department of Agriculture, informing us that all our cattle would be tested for bovine tuberculosis. The day before our guests arrived the examiner checked our cows. He marked those that passed the test by placing a metal tag on their ear.

At midday, Geneva and her husband arrived. When it was time to milk the cows they followed us into the barn to watch. Geneva spied one of the tags and asked, "What is that thing in your cow's ear?" Jokingly my husband Perry replied, "Oh, that's her wedding ring."

Geneva rushed along the rows of stanchions and examined every cow. "Oh, all of your cows are married, aren't they, Perry?" she exclaimed.

As we were leaving the barn she said in an excited voice, "You forgot to milk that big one tied up in the corner!" My husband, a bit embarrassed at her naivete, replied in a low voice, "I only milk that one on Sunday."

—*Mae Roets*

Eartags

As my three-year-old saw me putting my earrings in my newly pierced ears he said, "Mom, are you putting in your heifer ear tag?"

—*Linda Breuckman*

Old Bessie & Other Cows

When my husband, Emery, bought our farm in 1931 we had a herd with each one named. They went by the alphabet—Anna, Bertha, etc. We loved those cows dearly. We saw some hard times during the depression and at one time had a chattel mortgage on them. It was for $650. The mortgage came due and we thought we could renew it, but the relative we had borrowed it from had different ideas. We were shocked when he sold our herd. He did leave us one cow for milk.

We bought a new herd, paying half the milk check for them. It put us back five years. And they weren't the cows we'd had before.

One time a cow had a calf born in the woods and Emery went back to bring it in, but no matter how much he looked for it, he couldn't find it. So the next morning we kept the cow in and followed her. Still, no calf was found. Emery thought if we kept the cows in another pasture the calf would be hun-

Sour Cream

Sour cream is a cultured-milk product, made by ripening pasteurized cream of about eighteen to twenty percent butterfat with a lactic culture in the same way cultured buttermilk is made. The cream is pasteurized at 180° F. for 30 minutes, cooled to 155° and homogenized at 2000 pounds of pressure. After cooling to 70° F, from one to three percent starter is added and mixed with the cream.

gry and show up. We looked all over for that poor calf, but no use. We finally thought someone had stolen it or something. A week went by. Then one morning Emery told me to get out of bed, quick. A calf was there in the yard. A deer bounded away while we looked out the window, and we decided that deer must have been caring for the calf, because the calf was fat and healthy as could be.

—Olga E. Knapp

In The Nursery

One spring, after most of the expected mixed Herefords had made their appearances, a young heifer was obviously about to drop her calf. She seemed to be running about and making more noise than necessary. After putting up with this performance for awhile, the cows surrounded her and seemed to be saying, "Now just calm down and grunt a few times." Each "aunt" seemed to low or moo a piece of advice, and were ever so proud when the new arrival was finally pushed out; they helped to lick it and get the calf on its feet.

We would often see the cows grazing far from the pod of little calves napping on a sunny slope out of the wind. The cows were unconcerned since the calves were under the care of a "baby sitter," perhaps a brand new mother. It

was most amusing to see that sometimes Sandy, the huge herd bull, was the baby sitter while the cows were contentedly off in the back pasture. I never knew which wife of the harem made the arrangements for this sharing of duty or family-life, nor how.

—Lee DeVitt

Old Brindle

As a six-year-old I found Grandpa's farm a fascinating place. It was fun to go to the barn at milking time and see the cows march in orderly procession to their appointed stalls. After being anchored there with necks in stanchions, they would contentedly eat the hay put before them.

I recall one time when Aunt Lois sat on a low stool and begin milking "Old Brindle." Brindle was so named because of the streaky dark spots on her brown coat; she was gentle and that was why my aunt chose her.

I stood with my tin cup ready for a helping of warm fresh milk and listened to the "pings" as the first streams hit the shiny metal pail.

Like all cows, Brindle would flick her tail this way and that to shoo the flies from her back. Her tail seemed unusually long and often Aunt Lois would feel it swishing across the back of her neck as it returned to position.

Suddenly Auntie stood up, carefully

The Basics

R egardless of the flavor, all ice cream has most of the following ingredients: milk and cream to give it substance and prevent crystallization during freezing (the butterfat in the cream adds smoothness and richness); eggs, to bind and stabilize the mixture; sugar and/or honey, to sweeten.

set her pail down and decided on a remedy for the annoyance. She found a piece of heavy board and tied it securely to Brindle's tail. Then she went back to her task.

Alas, Brindle's tail was not only long—it was strong! Luckily the cow's aim was poor and Aunt Lois had only a bruised shoulder, but my uncles had one more taunt to use when they wanted to tease her.

—Evelyn Sherwood

Cow's Cradle

A friend tells me that like most young farm wives she went to the barn for milking, even with a small baby to tend. But she had her own unique way of handling the situation. They were fortunate to have an old fashioned cradle that she took down to the barn. The baby was placed in the cradle, with one end of a rope tied to the cradle and the other end of the rope tied to a cow's tail. And as the cow switched her tail the cradle was rocked. And the cow was milked.

—Norma Hoffman

Chores

One of the most pleasant chores of June was taking the cows down a dirt road to the night pasture a quarter of a mile away. The cows, relieved of their milk, ambled in a state of bovine bliss.

Their tedious winter of parched hay was past, and summer heat and stinging, clinging flies were still in the future. For both kids and cows, time was timeless. After the gate was closed on the cows, the walk home was even slower, for timelessness would end abruptly in bedtime once we reached home. Dawdling was the best way to delay the inevitable. If it got so dark that we inadvertently stepped into cowpies, it really did not matter. Unlike the Schmidt kids, whom we envied fiercely, we always had to wash our feet before going to bed, cowpies or not.

During August a chore that fell to the youngest of us was holding the tails of the cows being milked by Father and the older brothers. Even the most docile animals became so fly-maddened in August that they lashed their tails in a furious attempt to drive the tormentors from their flanks. The milker, perched on a three-legged stool, hands occupied with squeezing milk out of the cow's teats and into a pail clamped between his knees, was the vulnerable victim of this clubbing. What hit him was not the mop of hair at the end of the tail but the tough sinewy muscles of the "mop handle." Even though the cow had no mean designs on the man, she could inflict a real clout unless a tailholder was on duty.

Early Version

A form of ice cream was mentioned in a log kept by Marco Polo; he described seeing Mongolians eating fruit-flavored ice when he visited Mongolia in the late 1200's.

BEN & JERRY'S
VERMONT'S FINEST ALL NATURAL ICE CREAM

Ice cream connoisseurs can recognize the pride of Vermont, Ben & Jerry's, by Woody Jackson's herd of Holsteins ambling through a bucolic scene. Ice cream firms abound. Many, like Widemire's, whose single shop serves customers in Mobile, Alabama, remain genuinely local for decades. A handful of others, like Ben & Jerry's, grow into industry giants whose ice cream is distributed nationwide.

Another cow-related chore assigned to kids in August was keeping the cows out of the corn. Cornfields and hayfields often bordered each other, and if cows were pastured on the hay, it was up to us to see that they did not discover the sorghum-sweetness of corn. Once they did, their lust was lunatic, and it took all the lung and leg power of kids and dogs to keep them out. But if they were kept unacquainted and uninformed, they grazed in numskull contentment, allowing us to create our own pastimes. Long periods of cow-sitting in a hayfield in the heat of August forced us to improvise our own amusements. What we contrived proved, among other things, the creative power inherent in boredom.

—Edna Hatlestad Hong

Dairy Heritage

Over one hundred years ago, George W. Witter delivered the first milk in Wausau. When his horse and wagon traveled down the street with bell ringing, anyone interested in fresh milk would come out with a container. The fresh Jersey milk was measured from a 10-gallon can.

On June 6, 1905, George joined the Holstein Freisian Association of America, Certificate No. 1323.

The dairy farm operation stayed in the family. Harry, Earl, Gene and now Tom currently have a herd of 70 purebred Holsteins. We process, bottle and sell our milk from our own farm store.

—Gene Witter

Old Toppy

She was gorgeous, and she really brought home the gold. *Yeksa's Tops of Gold's Fannie* was her name. I thought she was the most beautiful Guernsey cow in the world (and still do), although she was long gone when I sat on my grandfather's knee and heard the stories about her. Our favorite game was for him to turn the pages of the *Guernsey Breeders Journal* and see if I would recognize our cows. When I'd come to the famous one I'd say, "There's old Toppy."

My grandfather, William M. Jones, was one of the early Wisconsin dairy farmers who imported Guernseys from the Island of Guernsey, built up purebred herds, kept production records and showed their cattle at state and national dairy shows. Waukesha County called itself the Guernsey Capital of America and it may well have been just that during the first quarter of the twentieth century when our Guernsey breeders were walking off with all the prizes.

I was only three years old when my grandfather died but I remember his office, which was probably meant to be the pantry of the Victorian house. It was a long narrow room with one north window and a big roll-top desk. The shelves were full of Guernsey journals, Guernsey sale catalogues, record books and so forth; and the walls were covered with pictures of cows and bulls wearing blue ribbons.

The height of Grandfather's glory and prestige probably was attained in 1913 when a picture of Sunny Valley Farm made the cover of the *Guernsey Breeders Journal* and a story of his herd appeared inside. In 1916, a photograph of Yeksa's Tops of Gold's Fannie was on the cover. Her record was the third best in butterfat production and second best in milk production in the list of Guernseys up to that time. Her record remained in the top ten of the class of mature cows until 1927, the year Grandfather died.

—Lois M. Jones

Blackie

We had a cow named Blackie. She was a Holstein but was completely black except for the top of her tail and three white feet. She was a strong, heavy-set cow and could kick with might and fury. When my husband fell ill, it became my responsibility to milk her twice a day. Her first calf arrived without a problem. Her second calf also arrived strong and healthy.

But when her third calf was due it was early summer and the cattle were out on pasture. The pasture was in a hilly area without available water so my husband's brother, who lived with us, brought the cows home for milking and took them back again afterward. We kept an eye on Blackie as we knew when she was about to freshen.

Our barn doors were split so the top half of each door could be left open for fresh air and light but the bottom half was securely fastened with a turn latch. When we noted a feeling of excitement in Blackie, we looked for a calf but couldn't find one. So we decided to keep her in the barn overnight and follow her in the morning when the rest of the herd went back to the pasture, figuring she'd lead us to her calf. But in the morning we noticed that Blackie came to the barn with the rest of the herd as usual. How had she escaped from the barn?

My brother-in-law followed her back to the pasture and discovered her calf, which was promptly brought back to the barn and penned in with Blackie. She licked and soothed the calf all along the way. We thought this would be the end of the ordeal. But the next morning Blackie was mysteriously gone again. How she'd made her leap over that barn door without injuring herself or breaking the door, we never did determine. But this time when we looked for her we found a second calf, safely hidden among some cedar trees and

This photograph of Yeksa's Tops of Gold's Fannie—"Toppy" to her friends—appeared on the cover of the September 1916 issue of *Guernsey Breeders' Journal.* Her records for milk production and butterfat content lasted for more than a decade.

berry brush in another part of the pasture.

—*Ada Federman*

George & Daisy & Mittens

On September 25, 1983, we received our first herd of twenty cows. I remember that date so well because it was the day after my birthday. And the next day, on the 26th of September, we had our first calf born. It happened to be a bull calf but he was our first and I just couldn't sell him. I named him George. Two and a half weeks later we had another calf. Well, by this time wherever I went, George was right behind me.

So Daisy tagged along with us. We never had to fence them in—they would stay by the house.

After about seven months had passed they weren't so little anymore, and they would ram us with their heads to get us to play with them. We would chase them around and they would chase us.

When winter set in my husband wanted to take George to market, so I rode in the back of the truck with George all the way there. When we arrived the trucker told us George wasn't worth anything and I was never so happy in my life. We got to keep him.

I made the biggest birthday cake for George on his first birthday. We all shared cake that day with George and Daisy. I couldn't believe they ate it, but they did.

We moved to a bigger barn soon after that and my father-in-law said we could bring our heifers down to his house and let them graze in his pasture. They kept growing, of course, and finally he sold George. I never found out until three weeks later.

But I still have Daisy and she is the biggest baby in the barn. I can sit down by her and she'll lay her head on my lap, or if I walk out into the pasture to get the cows she'll come running and I have to walk back with her head under my arm all the way.

Daisy is a good little milker, but one of her ears is only half there because George sucked on it and it froze off. Because of that I enjoy putting mittens on the cow's ears in winter. Our whole herd of 32 cows always stands there so proud when they have my mittens on their ears, and that makes me really happy, except that I still miss George a lot.

—Julie Bauerfield

The Christian Cow

My father always had Ayrshire cows, which are rather large anyhow. Well, he had one exceptionally large and muscular Ayrshire that looked something like a horse and, come to think of it, kicked like a horse. We all dreaded the times when Dad was gone and someone else had to milk that monster. We not so lovingly referred to that cow as the "Christian Cow," as everyone who had to milk her prayed a lot. She also helped explain Einstein's theory of relativity: When a good looking gal sits on your lap, two hours seems like two minutes. But when we milked that cow, two minutes seemed like two hours.

—Peter Dale Weber

Fond Memories

Cows—I know the sound, the touch, the smells of them.

I was raised on a small farm where we had fewer than ten cows, a couple of calves, a team of horses, two or three pigs and a small flock of chickens. Along with our garden and orchard we grew most of our own food supply. This was a good thing as our cream check was sometimes less than $5.00 for two weeks, but that income was supplemented by Dad's cream route and part-time work. We were never aware there were so many things in the world to be had if we could have afforded them.

Dad drove that route with his horses, Rack and Maid, until he later got a truck. A grand outing was to ride along on the cream route, picking up the cans to take to the creamery. Each patron had their own butter crocks that were filled for their use and the rest was sold in the store. There was a tin dipper where we drank fresh buttermilk.

At home, after milking our own cows, the milk was run through the hand cranked DeLaval separator that stood in the kitchen corner beneath the kerosene bracket lamp. I remember well the twice daily chore of washing that machine with all its disks. It was an interesting piece of equipment.

The cows were kept close to the buildings and at night they went to what we called the night pasture. After the morning milking they were let out to the woods to forage. A most pleasant time of day was to go out to bring them back for the evening milking. The dog and I could take a wonderful hike each day. I knew where the different wildflowers, nuts and berries grew, or where I could drink from the small cold spring that came out of shale rock. I still dream of the large flat sun-warmed rock with the small crescent of sparkling stones in it; my favorite place to stop and contemplate the joys and sounds and smells of each season. There were burdocks to stick together for pink and green doll chairs, acorns to make their cups and saucers, birchbark for their canoes and tepees. I had things money couldn't buy. I may have been lacking in social graces but not in basic values.

The 40 acre farm we lived on most of the time, where mother, my brother and I were all born, didn't have a spring. We had to hand pump water for our house, the laundry, and the cattle. My brother and I counted a hundred or two hundred strokes and made sure the other did the same amount.

The cows were pets—each had her own name and the bell cow was always Belle. Because they were so tame we just pulled up a milk stool beside them right out in the cow yard and

Butter

The origin of butter goes back to the Hindu Veda, written over 3500 years ago, when Hindus valued their cows according to the amount of butter that could be obtained from their milk. Butter was used as a medicine with the ancient Greeks and Romans who applied it to their hair or used it as an ointment. The soot of burned butter was supposed to be good for sore eyes.

Four hundred years ago butter was indicative of the owner's wealth in Scotland and Ireland. And when the butter-owner died, his butter, contained in casks, was buried with him. Sometimes the butter was buried for safekeeping and when it was unearthed it was known as "bog butter," rancid and inedible.

The first creamery to produce butter was built in Manchester, Iowa, in 1871. The churn is the oldest form of dairy equipment. In prehistoric times it might have been a bag of skin hung on the back of a horse or camel and as the animal moved, the motion of the bag would cause the milk or cream to form butter.

milked outside when the weather permitted. The cats were always around waiting to get squirted.

Once a year Dad led each cow to a neighboring farm. He said they needed spring water. I was a grown young woman before it occurred to me that not only did we not have a spring, we didn't have a bull, either.

— *Norma Hoffman*

Sally Rand

I named her Sally Rand. My aunt always talked about Sally Rand the Fan Dancer, but being only eight I didn't really know what a fan dancer did. I only heard that she was pretty and popular and I thought that was a good name for my favorite cow.

My Sally Rand was a "blonde" Guernsey with light tan hide blending into the white. Her brown eyes would look at me affectionately whenever I came near. If she was in her stanchion in the barn and I'd walk by, her head would rise and she'd stretch out her long neck for a little pat. When my uncle wasn't looking, I'd give her a couple extra handfuls of ground corn and oats. She'd nod her head thankfully and pull the feed into her mouth with her long tongue.

In my eyes Sally Rand could do no wrong. I never saw her lean hard against fences for a blade of grass on the other side. She never kicked up her heels and ran the other way when I called. She didn't try to bunt me over just because I was a little kid!

I always made sure the grownups handled my Sally with care. Almost every evening after she'd been milked I'd brush and comb her with the curry comb. Sometimes I'd even wash her tail in a pail of warm, sudsy water. The tail would come out white and clean as a whistle and she'd look like a show cow standing so proudly. My uncle said I was spoiling Sally Rand, but I didn't care. She added lots of fun to my life on the farm.

—*Virginia Krogwold*

My Cow Bonnie

I was the "city slicker," six years old and looking like Shirley Temple in "Rebecca of Sunnybrook Farm." My mother had a thing about shiny white dress shoes, ruffles, and a head full of curls. So, to my deep humiliation, that was my uniform on those visits to the farm.

The farm belonged to my grandmother and could be found in the deep, rolling wooded hills west of Baraboo, Wisconsin. It held many mysteries . . . a trout stream, a bog where many of my cats went hunting never to return, and a century-old farmhouse equipped with a labyrinth of small rooms upstairs, unfamiliar to a child of the "ranch house" generation.

"My dog Trixie is like a hired hand when it comes to chasing the cows out of the barn," reports fourteen-year-old photographer Hans Gausman. "She does that with all the new animals. She doesn't like them." Gausman's picture was among fifty images exhibited at the Madison Art Center in 1986. In a locally funded project, a dozen children were given 35mm cameras, instruction in their use, and plenty of film. They were asked to photograph their families, friends, and farm life from their unique point of view.

Dairy Numbers

CONVERSION FACTORS:
One quart of milk weighs
2.15 pounds
One gallon of milk weighs
8.6 pounds
46½ quarts of milk equals
100 pounds
The Specific gravity of milk
at 60 degrees F. is 1.032.

100 pounds of whole milk
will yield approximately:
10 pounds of cheese and 90
pounds whey or
5 pounds butter and 90
pounds of skim milk or
13 pounds dried whole milk
and 1¼ pounds 40% cream.

100 pounds of skim milk
will yield approximately:
16 pounds cottage cheese
and 84 pounds whey or
3 pounds casein and 94
pounds whey or
9 pounds non-fat dry milk

100 pounds whey will yield
approximately;
5 pounds of lactose
1 pound of protein
⅓ pound of milkfat

But best of all, the farm was the residence of My Cow Bonnie. She was a beautiful Jersey and the family favorite, clearly the most beautiful cow in my uncle's small, mixed herd. And she liked me best of all—I was certain of it.

We spent many hours gazing into each other's eyes, Bonnie and I. Those great, double-lashed, brown Bambi-eyes. And Bonnie was so gentle; I knew she could never hurt me. I would follow her fearlessly out to the field, her great clumsy hooves just inches from my sandal-clad feet. Lying in the cool grass I would dream up adventures for Bonnie and me. We were going to be the "Timmy and Lassie" of the rural Baraboo community. I would be the cute star of the show, and Bonnie would be my talented, intuitive sidekick.

My Cow Bonnie. That had such a ring to it back home in the city, especially when my playfriends were bragging about that trip to Yellowstone or the new hula-hoop or the big station wagon on order. Always one for swaggering a bit under the right circumstances, I would then deliver a lengthy report on my Bonnie days and the health and well-being of My Cow Bonnie.

— Kathy Durrant

Rosie

On one of the coldest days in 1941 I was alone in the house and getting ready to bake a cake. I needed an extra egg or two so I dashed to the thief-proof henhouse without taking time to put on any wraps. On the way I met our favorite cow. Rosie was such a pet that we never passed her by without making over her.

That day she was so warm that I nestled my face against her nice warm hide and she walked with me to the henhouse door. Since I didn't want her trampling up the place I shut the door between us.

I ran back to the laying section, gathered up a few eggs in my apron, and hustled back to the door.

I put my hand to the door and pushed. The door didn't open. I pushed and banged and then realized that Rosie had locked me in by rubbing the hasp of the lock. There was no way for me to get out. The windows were protected inside and out by heavy galvanized netting which I had no hopes of loosening.

I looked around me getting more exasperated and chilled with every minute but I could see nothing that would enable me to pry open that heavy door. It was only nine o'clock and the children would not be home from school until four that evening and my husband not until nearer six.

Rosie had wandered off to join the other cows on the sheltered side of the barn. But since she had locked me in, maybe she would help me out.

I started yelling to Rosie. Over and over I called and begged her to come. I fervently prayed that for once in her bovine life she'd answer my call.

Then I heard Rosie bumping along through the hard-crusted snow, mooing softly as she came. She peered in at the window seeming to sense something was wrong. I went over to the window talking to her in my most caressing tones and then I moved to another window and another hoping she wouldn't lose interest until I had tried out my plan.

I moved to the door and began tapping on it. Rosie followed. If only old Rosie would start rubbing her head and neck against the door, she might lift the latch as she had lowered it. I talked and waited and then it came— the sweetest sound I ever expect to hear. Rosie was beginning to rub against the door, while I gently pushed against the door. And then old Rosie pushed the latch up and the door swung out against her fat warm side.

I waited only long enough to plunk a kiss of appreciation between her big brown eyes before flying to the house and blessed warmth. My strange experience had lasted almost two hours and needless to say that lock was replaced by one that no loving cow could nuzzle into place.

—Lottie Manning

Cows and the Green Bay & Western Railroad

We have been "about cows" in this small community of Northport for many years. We are the last farmers to farm "in Town." We own land all around the area; in fact, I don't know where all of it is located. I find it hard to answer the question, "where is your farm?"

Years ago my husband drove the cows up the road to pasture across the railroad tracks, a few blocks up the hill. This is a letter he wrote back then, probably in the 1950's, to the Green Bay and Western Railroad:

Dear Sir,

I got 22 cows what I chase every morning and every night over your railroad tracks here in Northport. Up until two weeks ago everything is fine, no trains is coming in the morning at 8 A.M. when we drive our cows over the crossing.

Then last Thursday comes a little pip squeak of a train with maybe six empty box cars going like a bat out of hell he comes at just 8 A.M.

I think maybe this is a special so I hold my cows from crossing. Now day before yesterday comes the same darn train with those six empty box cars and I just get my 22 cows over the tracks when he comes barreling through.

What I want to know is who is this

To make one pound of Butter requires 21.2 pounds whole milk
Whole milk cheese " 10.0 lbs. whole milk
Evaporated milk " 2.1 lbs. whole milk
Condensed milk " 2.3 lbs. whole milk
Whole milk powder "7.4 lbs. whole milk
Powdered cream" 13.5 lbs. whole milk
Ice cream (1 gal.)" 12.0 lbs. whole milk
Cottage cheese" 6.25 lbs. skim milk
Nonfat dry milk" 11.00 lbs. skim milk

Spray-can artistry made a homemade Holstein out of this cattle crossing sign in rural Madison, Wisconsin. Photo by Don Davenport.

guy the railroad presidents son, so they give him his own little train to play with or some stupid conductor what forgets to take these box cars along on the regular run.

I would appreciate very much if you would tell this hot shot engineer to kindly take another cup of coffee in the morning so he should get here later than 8 A.M. and not maybe make hamburger out of my holsteins. Either that or he should stop at the Northport crossing and look both ways to see if any thing is coming what looks like cows. You can tell the people from the cows because the cows got a smarter look.

You got a pretty nice little railroad and I don't want to make you no trouble, so you tell these guys they should send this little train through at maybe noon huh?

Okay and thank you very much, I am

Yours truly,
John Kraske
R.3
New London, Wis.

Fairtime

In the cattle barns, empty and quiet all these months, there is the warmth of the animals now, the sweet smell of hay and the hopeful chatter of the youngsters as they prepare for the shows.

The pick-up trucks and cars rattle into the parking lots and the dust rises on the hot summer morning. The doors of the wooden exhibition barns are slid back and the morning light streams into the dim, cool interiors and falls upon the boxes of neatly arranged vegetables—fat heads of lettuce, tender onion sprouts and plump green beans. Nestled in among some of the boxes are ribbons, red and blue, sometimes pink. Through the open doors in the opposite end of the barn you can see trees, dark and drowsy, and insects in the dusty beams of sunlight, as if in a painting, and a girl trotting a tethered horse in a bright field.

Then it is noon, and the sun has grown hotter. Behind the screen windows of the long, white food stand, cooks work over the splattering griddles frying hamburgers and hot dogs, dashing salt over piles of glistening french fries. Hundreds of cans of soda, green, red and orange cans, bob and clink in long steel water troughs filled with ice that has already begun to melt.

Families with dusty tots in tow come wandering from the show and cattle barns and fathers line up to order lunch. They carry the tissue-wrapped sandwiches, steaming cups of coffee, cold cans of soda, to freshly-painted green picnic tables beneath arching shade trees.

Soon after lunch, the carnival opens. Up and down the midway, the barkers begin their chants and children clamber aboard clanking rides to be whirled and tossed and spun and thrown in dizzying loops. And there is more food—lemonade shake-ups and taffy apples, cotton candy and caramel corn.

Now the cows are being led into the show barn—the heart of any summer fair. Outside in the bright sun, boys and girls in spanking white uniforms hold the halters of their spotlessly groomed animals, waiting. Inside the judge is at work and the youths in the sandy ring watch him closely as he inspects their cows.

There will be winners and losers.

For the losers, it is early yet. There will be other shows this summer, many more hot afternoons of waiting outside the show barn with the great and comfortable hum of the fair all around and the warm flank of an animal under your hand.

—Ron Seely
Wisconsin State Journal
Madison, Wisconsin

Who is it that said
something about a cow
resembling its owner?
Minnesota State Fair photo.

The members of the Jefferson County Calf Club display Holstein and Guernsey calves. Photo courtesy Hoard Historical Museum.

Robin's Cow

I wrote this for my daughter Robin, and it was published in *Wisconsin Agriculturist*, in January, 1971:

We Sold Your Cow Today

Dear Robin,

This was one of the hardest days your dad and I will ever have. Many pictures and memories went through our minds this morning when we shipped your cow.

We saw you wanting a calf of your own, you were nine and ready to show cattle just like the rest of the kids. Finally the big day came when you would take your junior calf outside. "Do you want some help? No! Okay, you can do it yourself."

The morning must have been long for that poor little calf. She made endless trips up and down the lane with you proudly pulling her every step.

Finally the fair came. You showed her proudly and got your ribbon, it was a red one but looked very good to you.

The next year when you showed her she came home with the Grand Champion ribbon. And you came home with smashed toes. There is nothing like a purple ribbon to heal feet.

When she was getting ready for her first calf you would have thought royalty was being born. A heifer! We had to view her every few minutes. It just had to be the prettiest calf ever. Why doesn't your cow milk better?

Another year, more ribbons and shows, another calf, still a poor milker.

"Dad, keep her until after the fair anyway. She has got to go to the fair, Dad, or she would feel bad. Okay, Dad, just this last year, then we will sell her."

Your last year with her came just a little too soon for all of us. "I'm going to take her into showmanship, Dad. I know she's hard to handle, but I want to."

I thought placings at the fair would never be over. Kid after kid was pulled from the ring. I held my breath each time the judge went over you, but you were right. She was doing just beautifully. Finally just you and three others were left.

The trophy is placed in your hands. I can see tears close to the surface. I turn my back so you don't see my eyes are full, too.

Today for the last time we led your cow to the truck. She thought she was going to another show.

We all lost a little today, but it is a part of growing up. She will never be forgotten in our memories and our hearts.

Your Mother
—*Jeannine Schreck*

Bibliography

Apps, Jerry and Strang, Allen. *Barns of Wisconsin*. Madison, WI: Tamarack Press, 1977.

Adamson, Joe. *The Walter Lantz Story*. New York: G. P. Putnam's Sons, 1985.

Addy, S.O. *Folk Tales and Superstitions* (Originally published as *Household Tales with Other Traditional Remains*, London & Sheffield, 1895). England: E.P. Publishing, Ltd. 1973 (reprint).

Adventures in American Literature. New York: Harcourt, Brace and Company, 1947.

American Breeders Service A. I. Management Manual. American Breeders Service, DeForest, WI., 1983.

Baker, Dr. E. T. *The Cow Owner's Handbook*. New York: Prentice Hall, Inc., 1951.

Baldwin's Readers. First Year. New York, Cincinnati, Chicago: American Book Company, 1897.

Barbour, Frances M., ed. *Proverbs and Proverbial Phrases of Illinois*. Southern Illinois Press, 1965.

Barchilon, Jacques and Pettit, Henry. *The Authentic Mother Goose*. Denver: Alan Swallow, 1960.

Baring-Gould, William S. and Ceil. *The Annotated Mother Goose*, Nursery Rhymes Old and New, Arranged and Explained. New York: Clarkson N. Potter, Inc., 1962.

Bell, Martin C. *A Portrait of Progress*. St. Louis, Mo: Pet Milk Company, 1962.

Bettelheim, Bruno. *The Uses of Enchantment*, The Meaning and Importance of Fairy Tales. New York: Vintage Books, 1977.

Blair and Ketchum's Country Journal. "The Search For the Perfect Cow," February, 1980; "What's Black and White and Bred All Over," July, 1985; "What Pulls the Plow," June, 1986.

Blesh, Rudi. *Keaton*. New York: Collier Books, 1966.

Brand, Oscar. *Songs of '76, A Folksinger's History of the Revolution*. New York: M. Evans & Co., 1972.

Bringsvaerd, Tor Age. Translated by Iversen, Pat Shaw. *Phantoms and Fairies from Norwegian Folklore*. Oslo: Johan Grundt Tanum Forlag.

Bryant, Mark. *Riddles, Ancient and Modern*. New York: P. Bedrick Books, 1984.

Cassidy, Frederick. *Dictionary of Ameri-*

COW—The mature female of a bovine animal, genus *Bos*.

COW—to frighten with threats, to intimidate.

COWARD—in heraldry, an animal borne in the escutcheon with its tail between its legs.

COWARDLY CALF—a contemptibly timid or easily frightened person.

COWBANE—any of several umbelliferous plants supposed to be poisonous to cattle, and which augmented the supply of rattlesnake venom as a poison on Indians' arrows.

COWBELLY—a name for soft river mud, sometimes used for play by children.

COWBIRD—a kind of American blackbird that accompanies herds of cattle and deposits its eggs in other birds' nests.

COWBOY—a man who herds and tends cattle on a ranch. Or, according to truck drivers, a reckless or inexperienced driver, usually young.

COWBOY BIBLE—the little books of cigarette paper used for roll-your-own cigarettes.

COWCAKE—another name for a cow pie. Or cow pancake.

COWCATCHER—a triangular frame at the front of a locomotive designed for clearing the track of obstructions.— Also, a brief commercial on radio or television advertising a subordinate product or a service of the program's sponsor, and preceding the main part of the show. COW COCKIE—New Zealand or Australian dairy farmer. COW COLLEGE—an agricultural college. COW CREAMER—an 18th century silver or ceramic cream pitcher in the shape of a cow. COW DAB—a lump of cow dung; in the past burned to repel insects. If this was burned as fuel it was called COW WOOD. COW DUNG COOTER—a box turtle or striped mud turtle, so named because they eat cow dung. COWFISH—marine fishes that have hornlike projections over the eyes. COWEYE—a very round, sometimes protruding eye; hence, being "coweyed." COW FOOTED—clumsy. COW GREASE—another name for butter. COW HANDED—clumsy, awkward. And of a baseball batter, having the

can Regional English, Vol. 1. Cambridge, Mass: Harvard University Press, 1985.

Cohen, Daniel. The Great Airship Mystery. New York: Dodd, Mead and Company, 1981.

Cheviot, Andrew. Proverbs, Provincial Expressions and Popular Rhymes of Scotland. (1896) reprint, Detroit: Gale Research Co., 1969.

Coffin, William F. Esq. 1812; The War and Its Moral: A Canadian Chronicle. John Lovell, 1864.

Derleth, August. Collected Poems. New York: Candlelight Press, 1967.

Dunning, Stephen; Lueders, Edward; and Smith, Hugh. Some Haystacks Don't Even Have Any Needle. New York: Lothrop, Lee & Shepar Co., 1969.

Ensminger, M. E. Diary Cattle Science. Second Edition. Danville, Illinois: Interstate Printers & Publishers, Inc., 1980.

Evans, Igor H. Brewer's Dictionary of Phrase and Fable. Harper & Row, 1981.

English Proverbs and Proverbial Phrases. Hazlitt (1906); reprinted Detroit: Gale Research Co., 1969.

Farm Journal. "Artificial Breeding Won't Work," March, 1950. "We'll Never Keep Another Bull," April, 1950.

Farmer, John S., ed. The Proverbs—etc—

of John Heywood. Early English Drama Society, 1906.

Fergusson, Rosalind. Facts On File Dictionary of Proverbs. New York: F. on F. Publications, 1983.

Fowke, Edith. Ring Around the Moon. Prentice-Hall, 1977.

Fowke, Edith Fulton, and Johnston, Richard. More Folk Songs of Canada. Ontario: Waterloo Music Co. Ltd., 1967.

Frantz, Joe B. Gail Borden—Dairyman to a Nation. University of Oklahoma Press, 1951.

Fraser, Allan. The Bull. Berkshire, UK: Osprey Publishing Ltd. 1972.

Funk, Charles Earle. A Hog on Ice and Other Curious Expressions. Harper & Row, 1948.

Funk, Charles Earle. Heavens to Betsey! New York: Harpers, 1955.

Funk, Charles Earle. Horsefeathers And Other Curious Words. New York: Harpers, 1958.

Funk, Charles Earle. Thereby Hangs a Tale. New York: Harpers, 1950.

Gaffney, Sean; and Cashman, Seamus, ed. Proverbs and Sayings of Ireland. Dublin: Wolfhound Press, 1978.

Gallant, Mark. The Cow Book. New York: Alfred A. Knopf, 1983.

Grohman, Joann Sills. Keeping a Family Cow. New York: Ballantine Books, 1981.

Handy, W. C. *Blues—an Anthology*. New York: Macmillan Co, 1972.

Henderson, Andrew., ed. *Scottish Proverbs*. Glasgow: Thomas D. Morison, 1831. reprint Detroit: Gale Research Co., 1969.

Herbert's Remains. George Herbert: London, 1652.

Hill Top Decision. pamphlet, Hoard's Dairyman

History of Rock County and Transactions of the Rock County Agricultural Society and Mechanic's Institute. Janesville, WI: Wm. M. Doty and Brother, 1856.

Hoard's Dairyman, 1945.

Jensen, Dean. *The Biggest, The Smallest, The Longest, The Shortest*. Madison, WI: Wisconsin House, 1975.

Kane, Joseph Nathan. *Famous First Facts*. New York: H. W. Wilson Co., 1964.

Ketchum, Richard M. *Will Rogers—The Man and His Times*. New York: American Heritage Publishing Company / Simon & Schuster, 1973.

Kriss, Eric. *Barrelhouse and Boogie Piano*. New York: Oak Publications, 1974.

Kriss, Eric. *Six Blues-Roots Pianists*. New York: Oak Publications, 1973.

Lamb, G. F. *Animal Quotations*. Burnt Mill, Harlow, Essex, England: Longman House, 1985.

Lampard, Eric E. *The Rise of the Dairy Industry in Wisconsin—A Study in Agricultural Change 1820-1920*. Madison, WI: State Historical Society of Wisconsin, 1963.

Lampert, Lincoln M. *Modern Dairy Products*. New York: Chemical Publishing Co., 1975.

Leaf, Munro. *The Story of Ferdinand*. New York: The Viking Press, 1936.

Lincoln, Bruce. *Priests, Warriors and Cattle*. Berkeley: University of California Press, 1981.

Mace, Jean. *Home Fairy Tales —Contes du Petit-Chateau*. translated by Mary L. Booth. New York and London: Harper and Brothers, Publishers, 1867.

May, John. *Curious Facts*. New York: Holt, Rinehart & Winston.

Mourant, A. E., and Zeuner, F. E. *Man and Cattle*. Royal Anthropological Institute of Great Britain and Ireland, 1963.

Neil, Miss E. *The Everyday Cookbook And Encyclopedia of Practical Recipes*. Chicago: Regan Printing House, 1892.

One Hundred Years of Research—Wisconsin's Agricultural Experiment Station. Madison, WI: College of Agricultural and Life Sciences, 1983.

Outside. Vol VIII, No.7. Mariah Publishing Corporation, October, 1983.

Oxford Dictionary of English Proverbs. F.

hands in reversed position.

COWLICK—a tuft of hair, usually over the forehead and looks as though a cow licked it. Also, a piece of cotton left in the field after picking. Or illegible handwriting.

COWPOKE—a cowboy.

COWPUNCHER—another word for a cowboy.

COWQUAKES—quaking grass.

COWSENSE—practical knowledge of cattle-handling; common sense.

COWSHED—a shed serving as shelter for cows.

COWSKIN—the skin of a cow. Also another name for an ancient kind of prophylactic: "A good Cowskin, Crabtree or Bulls pizzle may be plentifully bestow'd on your outward Man." 1738.

COWSLIP—an English primrose, having yellow flowers—or, the marsh marigold. It grows in cow pastures and the name pertains to the *slip*, (ancient *slyppe*,) or cow dung among which the plant flourishes.

COWSUCKER—the cow snake that is supposed to visit cows and clandestinely relieve them of their milk.

COW'S TAIL—a nautical expression, an unwhipped rope end, any strand or rope end left hanging untidily. Also said of the person that is last to arrive, "You are always the old cow's tail." COW WITH AN IRON TAIL—a pump, from its use in dishonestly watering down milk. COWTONGUE—a perennial herb with greenish yellow flowers and blue berries. Or a two-faced person, from the rough and smooth sides of a cow's tongue. COWTOPPER—a bull. TO MILK THE COW WITH A SPANNER—said in England; to open a tin of evaporated milk with a can opener. At one time a well known condensed milk company conducted a contest for a slogan that would indicate how easily their product might be utilized. Someone jokingly suggested:

No tits to pull, no tail to twitch,
Just punch a hole in the son of a bitch.

THE LAND OF MILK AND HONEY—denotes the blessings of Heaven. MILK TEETH—a child's first, temporary teeth.

P. Wilson, Editor. New York: Oxford University Press, 1982.

Palmer, Roy. *The Folklore of Warwickshire*. Totowa, New Jersey: Rowman and Littlefield, 1976.

Paul, Barbara; and Paul, Justus. *The Badger State; A Documentary History of Wisconsin*. Michigan: Wm. B. Eerdmans, 1979.

Peck, Ann. *The Pageant of Canadian History*. New York: Green and Co., 1944.

Prose and Poetry of the Live Stock Industry of the United States. Denver: National Live Stock Association, 1904. (Facsimile ed. New York: Antiquarian Press, 1959)

Randolph, Vance. *Pissing in the Snow and Other Ozark Folktales*. New York: Avon Books, 1976.

Rawlinson, Fred. *Make Mine Milk—The Story of the Milk Bottle*. Newport News, VA: Far Publications, 1970.

Ray, Reverand J. *Compleat Collection of English Proverbs*. London: 1737.

Roy Rogers Comics. Vol. 1., No. 74. Racine, WI: Western Printing and Litho. Co. February, 1954.

Roy Rogers and Trigger. Vol. 1., No. 135. New York: Dell Publishing Co., January—February, 1960.

Savage, E. S.; and Maynard, L. A. *Better Dairy Farming*. Ithica, NY; The Savage-Maynard Co., 1923.

Select Rhymes for the Nursery. London: Darton and Harvey, 1808.

Sharma, B. V. V. S. R. *The Study of Cow in Sanskrit Literature*. Delhi: GDK Publications, 1980.

Simon, George T., ed. *The Big Bands Songbook*. Barnes and Noble, 1975.

Smith, Laura Rountree. *Children's Favorite Stories*. Chicago: A. Flanagan Company, 1918.

Spreckley, Val. *Keeping A Cow*. Devon, G.B.: David & Charles, Ltd., 1979.

Street, Len; and Singer, Andrew. *Butter, Milk and Cheese From Your Back Yard*. New York: Sterling Publishing Co., 1976.

Stevenson, Burton. ed. *The Macmillan Book of Proverbs, Maxims and Famous Phrases*. New York: Macmillan Co., 1966.

Stevenson, Robert Louis. *A Child's Garden of Verses*. Racine, Wi: Whitman Publishing, 1931.

Sturlson, Snorri. *The Prose Edda*. London: American-Scandinavian Foundation, 1929.

Tallman, Marjorie. *Dictionary of American Folklore*. New York: Philosophical Library, 1959.

Tichenor, Trebor Jay. *Ragtime Rediscoveries*. New York: Dover Publications, 1979.

Vigfusson and Powell. *Icelandic Prose Reader*. Oxford: Clarendon Press, 1879.

Vizetelly, Frank H. *Desk-Book of Idioms and Idiomatic Phrases*. New York, Funk and Wagnalls, 1923.

Wallace, W. S. *The Story of Laura Secord*. Toronto: Macmillan Co., 1932.

Withers, Carl; and Benet, Dr. Sula. *The American Riddle Book*. New York: Abelard-Schuman, 1954.

The Wisconsin Farmer. 1849, 1850, 1854.

Wisconsin Agriculturalist and Farmer. 1933.

Wisconsin Sampler. Madison, WI: Northword, 1983.

THE COW BARN IS OPEN—said to warn a man that his fly needs to be zipped.

I'LL BE COW-KICKED—meaning, "Well, I'll be damned."

COW-PEN TEA—a medicinal drink made from cow manure.

SACRED COW—any personal possession cherished by its owner, or a person held in such esteem or of such high office as to be above criticism. It could have been derived from the legendary hero of India, *Prithu*, who assumed the form of a cow in order to encourage his subjects to raise edible vegetables. Or it could have come from the Egyptian *Hathor*, goddess of love, who, in the form of a cow, was served by princesses. Perhaps it is even connected with the expression, "Holy Cow," used by Corliss Archer's boyfriend, Oogie, in the 1940 radio program.

This youthful milker first appeared in *The Only True Mother Goose*, published in 1833 by Munroe and Francise.

Don't miss these additional books from Voyageur Press

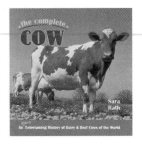 

The Complete Cow, by Sara Rath
The Complete Pig, by Sara Rath
This Old Farm, edited by Michael Dregni
This Old Tractor, edited by Michael Dregni
Toy Farm Tractors, by Bill Vossler
Vintage Farm Tractors, by Ralph W. Sanders

Available nationwide or order directly from Voyageur Press at 1-800-888-9653.